THE LONG WAY

STILL GETS YOU THERE

A 7-PART PATH TO RISE UP FROM WHERE YOU
ARE TO WHERE YOU'RE DESIGNED TO BE

ROB & SHANNON MALCOM

WITH ANDREW EDWIN JENKINS

For more information about content placed throughout the book, visit RiseUpOnline.info.

Published by ELAN Company, LLC, DBA Amplify. For more info go to AmplifyOnline.info.

For our family—

Lyn

Barb

Lisa

Jeremy

Blake

Kimberly

Matt, Abbey, Ando, Ello, Wilby

Greg

Countless prayer warriors

WALK WITH US!
FREE BONUS ACCESS!

7 MIND-SHIFT LESSONS

RiseUpOnline.info/7

Contents

Foreword, Tami Bonnell

Tami Bonnell, Co-Chair of Exit Realty Corp International

I have been in the Real Estate space for over 30 years and with EXIT for 25. It is where I met Shannon and Rob.

What connected us was not just them owning an EXIT Franchise, but that EXIT Realty is an organization which was built on human potential. The biggest part of my job is showing people who they can become. That is the common thread which truly connected us.

I bet that Shannon and Rob have been told multiple times for many years that they should write a book. I for one am so glad they did.

These leaders own their story. They have had experiences most people cannot imagine. They have hit rock bottom more than once, estranged from everyone including family, and found themselves addicted with no hope for their future.

Yet here they are leading a Real Estate Company, impacting lives for the better through leading agents and revitalizing a city

one home at a time, one person at a time. The fact that they were willing to bare their souls and share the good, bad, and brutal parts of their life— and own their story — to help others is a gift. This book is meant to be raw and to raise emotions, because that is what will make us take action.

One of the best ways to grow as a person is to be brutally honest with yourself and ask effective questions. Shannon and Rob have put together a 7-part path for you to do just that. This book is meant to be used, written in, and read more than once. When someone goes through what they have and they are willing to share and own their story, their transparency, regardless of where you are in your story can only be admired and appreciated, because it will truly help more people and deliver hope regardless of what you are personally going through.

The top award at EXIT is a beautiful sculpture of a man or woman carving themselves. It is to show that we are all a human *becoming* and hopefully we continue to grow our entire lives.

Rob and Shannon aren't finished with their story or their growth, but this book is a testament to their faith and their desire to help others. You owe to yourself to not just read this book, but use it as a tool to grow, and to share with others.

This story was written from a position of love. They had a goal and carried it through— not because it was easy— because it was important to lead by example. My hope for you is that *The Long Way Still Gets You There* helps you to dream bigger, set goals and achieve them, and pay it forward along the way.

With love,

Tam

Co-Chair of EXIT Realty Corp International

Foreword

Foreword, Setema Gali

Setema Gali, Owner & Coach, Game-Changer

I first met Rob Malcom when he signed up for one of my Flagship Titan Immersion events—part physical challenge, 100% mental marathon.

The multi-day program was designed to push participants beyond their limits. Most people have no idea what they're truly capable of. We often hit a ceiling—shaped by past experiences, others' opinions, or the achievements of those around us—and we quit too easily when things get tough.

Most people make excuses.

Most people quit.

That's why most never reach their potential.

Through my events, I've seen it time and again—people give up well before they realize how much more they could achieve if they just kept going.

You can always do more than you think. Always.

When I think of Rob Malcom, two things stand out:

1. He doesn't make excuses.

Rob's story isn't without excuses, but he chose to overcome them. You can always start over and rewrite your story. You can't redo the past, but you can create a new path, starting where you are.

For example, my Immersion program required participants to wear all black, including their shoes. Rob only had black sneakers with a white stripe, and buying a new pair wasn't an option after investing heavily in the event.

So, he grabbed a black Sharpie and covered the white parts of his shoes. Each night, as the ocean washed away the marker, he recolored them. Instead of making excuses, he made it work.

2. He is persistent.

On the final day, we challenged the group to march across the beach carrying bags filled with sand.

"If you can get through this," I told them, "you can overcome any challenge from your past or future. There is no finish line."

Rob was the smallest guy on the beach that day. With no end-time announced, we decided to stop the challenge when

Rob broke. But two things surprised us.

First, Rob accidentally grabbed the heaviest bag which was meant for the largest man in the group— the bag was between 80 to 90 pounds.

Second, he didn't quit. As others dropped out, Rob kept going.

"He's not going to stop," one of my coaches said.

And they were right. Hours passed, and Rob kept walking until we finally called the challenge to an end.

You, too, can have what you want— if you're willing to pay the price and understand that you can't do it alone. You need people around you— like Rob and Shannon— who push you to hope, believe, and endure more than you ever thought possible.

This book isn't just about one couple's journey. It's a guide to your roadmap —moving from where you are to where you're destined to be.

As you read Rob's story, see yourself in his shoes and apply the lessons he lives by. Your transformation is waiting.

See you at the top,

Setema Gali

Owner & Coach, Game-Changer

Foreword

Introduction

Ancient rabbis believed that each time a story of redemption was told, the retelling of the story carried the exact same power and imparted the same possibilities to those who heard it as the person who lived the story actually experienced.

In other words, you find yourself wrapped in that same power of the past *again* in the present.

Perhaps you've experienced it—

- You hear of a miraculous healing and sense faith rising.

- You hear of a restarted relationship and sense yours can be mended.

- You hear of a financial breakthrough and sense hope for your situation.

There's something powerful about stories. Especially the "overcoming" version that's transparent about the obstacles and failures encountered along the way.

Revelation 12 says that we *overcome* by two things— the blood of Jesus AND the power of your story (see Revelation 12:11).

That is, we overcome by—

1. That past work that Jesus has already done 2,000 years ago, *and*

2.   The ongoing work of declaring what He's doing in our lives right now.

When we share the stories— *when you share your story of overcoming—* people in the midst of their valley sense there might be a way forward.

This is one of the reasons we find so many instructions throughout the Bible to talk about the stories of God's past provision. For instance,

- God told the Children of Israel to continually talk about how they were redeemed from slavery and walked through the Red Sea (see Exodus 12).

- He reminded each generation to tell the next generation the stories of breakthrough and blessing, including all of those which happened during their lifetime as well as those leading up to it (see Psalm 145:4).

- The Children of Israel even created monuments to elicit questions and conversations, so they could retell the stories (i.e., Joshua 4:21-22).

Each time a story was told— and retold— of how God interrupted a catastrophe and ignited hope, the same power was unleashed again.

Our prayer is that this story is one of those moments for you. May you encounter God's presence, His power, and His provision for whatever wisdom, breakthrough, or miraculous intervention you need.

Here are three things to help you navigate the story you are about to read.

First, we shift back and forth, recounting our personal history (as best we can). If you look back at the table of contents, you'll notice that each chapter title is followed by a (R) or a (S). As you can likely guess, this denotes the primary speaker, Rob (R) or Shannon (S).

Second, although we've done our best to recount the stories as accurately as possible, understand that creating a rigid timeline is almost impossible. There's so much that overlaps and refers backwards and forwards and even to the other person's version of things.

Third, this book is designed to be applied— not just read. To that end:

- We wrote the story and then divided it into 7 natural sections. After drafting the manuscript, we looked back to see if there were major themes we could pull out from each part.

- Each of these sections contains a main idea (in the form of a summary statement), as well as questions to help you work through the material on your own, applying it to your unique circumstances.

To gain the most from this resource, we encourage you to—

1. Read the story.

There are incredible moments of celebration and major losses shared throughout the book. You're about to go on an emotional roller coaster ride.

2. Recognize the common patterns.

Though the details of your story and ours are different, there are common threads between us. In fact, dare we say... we have more in common than not.

3. **Reflect on how this applies to you.**

    Find the common theme, extract the principles, and see how they apply to your unique situation.

Use the "application" sections to do this. Just write directly into the book.

We would love to hear from you and continue the conversation this book births. Our sincere prayer is that our story becomes the roadmap— and empowerment— for some of your upcoming breakthroughs. And, in turn, that your breakthroughs become the boost someone else needs.

With that in mind, visit our website and register for the free bonus content at RiseUpOnline.info/7.

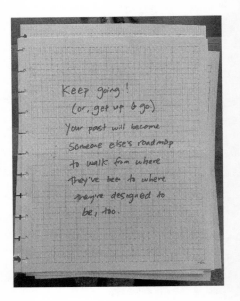

Keep going!
(or, get up & go)
Your past will become
Someone else's roadmap
to walk from where
they've been to where
they're designed to
be, too.

Part 1 | Excuses ≠ Explanations

Your past doesn't excuse your present decisions, but it does explain some things about you which can empower you to move forward in healing and wholeness.

1. If I Could Start My Story Over (R)

Rob's life flashes before him. An inmate shares an interesting perspective on the apostle Paul. Little conversations make big differences.

They say that just before you die, your life flashes before the eyes of your soul within a matter of milliseconds. Your mind slows down, the thought goes, such that what happens in an instant of "real time" seems to take minutes…

Whoever first said that— whoever the mysterious "they" actually is— got it right. I know, because it happened to me.

"There are so many other things that should have taken me out *years* ago," I thought. "Of everything that could have possibly done it, it comes down to smoking a cigarette around the corner of a church building?"

The driver was the shooter.

The warehouse where we officed The Program and hosted our recovery meetings sat at the corner of a busy intersection of Birmingham's Southside. The tall building on the opposite side of the street hid the one-way that approached our building from the north-south cross-street in front of of us, such that collisions occurred at least 2-3 times a week.

The quick screech of tires, followed by an abrupt crash of metal, were familiar sounds to everyone on staff at The Program.

"Call 9-1-1," someone in the office always repeated. "I'll go check on the people…"

I can't count the number of times we walked accident victims into our building— or even just sat them outside on the concrete bench and tables— and offered them something to drink while they waited for tow trucks or a friendly ride home. Most of them had no idea a bunch of prisoners and addicts helped assist them.

The drivers who frequented that intersection knew to stop at all red lights *and pause* before assuming "green means go." The blind corner at the cross-streets proved too risky.

When the white Mitsubishi 3000 GT slowed at the intersection it seemed *different* than just avoiding a possible collision at a place known for t-bones and spin outs, though.

"I knew it," Pee Wee said after the fact. "I should've yelled out. I second-guessed myself."

Standing at *almost* 5-feet tall, this slightly pudgy friend of everyone never had a hope of any nickname except Pee Wee. He was the visual representation of what a *Pee Wee*, a *Shorty*, or a *Smalls* looks like. His pants and shorts were always too long, even though he bought the shortest lengths, and his shirts never stayed tucked in. He wobbled rather than walked, and his head always bobbed from side to side.

He was one of the men on early release at The Program— through the Alabama Department of Corrections. Though technically still an inmate on paper, men like him were given the opportunity to finish the final 12 months of their sentence at a highly-structured halfway house like ours— a place that provided employment assistance, soft skills training, and help overcoming addictions and the other past behaviors that landed them in the penitentiary in the first place. They wore normal clothes and went by first names— or, in his case, nick names— rather than titles like "inmate" or even more inhumane monikers like their 6-digit inmate number.

"I could see it coming," another man in The Program observed. "I thought I had it wrong, but the way he leaned up while reaching under the seat and looking around... and the way the front seat was leaned way back... that's how all the guys in my hood used to do it."

Just to steer clear of the supposed stereotypes, this man was white— not black like Pee Wee.

He said most shooters keep their guns under the front seat. At the same time, they lean the car seats way back, so the metal piece between the front seat window and the back seat window can protect their head from a drive by shooting.

Men like this live in a parallel universe that, as different as it might seem from where you are right this second as you read this, exists right down the street from your school, your church, and the shopping strip where you buy your groceries...

As I pulled a drag from my Newport— that's the brand I always smoked, unless I was bumming them, but by now I was working and was always the one providing them rather than begging— I noticed the white car charge forward AFTER crossing through the intersection and then drop into super-slow speed as the driver veered over towards me where I was smoking beside the dumpster...

POW!

A sharp sting. I raised my left hand to my neck and felt blood running down my arm. Then I could see it...

POP!

Something hit my waist, just above my belt...

It was hot— my waistline and my left butt check felt on fire!

POOK!

A miss...

POONK!

Something hit the metal siding, a wavy corrugated metal on the building behind me that was hung in a vertical position.

PLOONK!

That hit my chest— my left ribcage.

"Holy shit!" I thought, now putting the pieces together. "This guy just shot me!"

I scurried over and crouched behind the metal dumpster. It was the one place on the side of the street I thought I would be safe.

"That was five shots!" one of the residents of The Program near me yelled. Then, the warning: "He has more!"

The vehicle stopped. The shooter pulled off the road at the entrance to an empty parking lot merely 15-20 feet away.

This was the scariest moment so far.

"I'm alive right now. But he's still got another round. This is bad— this is really bad! He's gonna get out and finish this."

I thought I should write his license plate # on my hand in case I didn't make it. Someone could figure it out afterwards. (It's weird what you think about when thoughts start scrolling rapid-fire through your mind.)

I tried, but there was so much blood...

Then I saw him eye-to-eye. He gazed back at me from the left hand side mirror of his car. He just stared.

I froze. He didn't move. I *couldn't* move.

Time.

Stopped.

Moments.

Moved.

Incredibly.

Slow.

That's when everything began flashing at the forefront of my mind, rolling in a scene-by-scene format, as if in real time. Some of the moments I saw were memories of things done in the past; others were possibilities, memories to create in the future if I made it through whatever was coming next.

- *Marry Shannon.*

   The guys on staff that have been telling you to marry her are right. She's the one. She's God's gift to you. Stop delaying...

- *Make a home of your own.*

   You've worked here almost three years and lived here while doing so. This has been a great run. It's time to step into the next chapter.

- *Move to your next goal.*

Start the business, build wealth, and make an impact.

- *Make it right with Dad.*

Things are good, but they can be so much better— tighten it up.

- *Specific faces...*

People I still needed to talk to— some to set things right with, others just to say how much I appreciated them.

- *Things I always said I would do but didn't get to...*

More dreams— places I wanted to go, things I never got a chance to experience.

There were so many things that flowed...

Slow.

As.

If.

Watching.

Them.

In.

Real.

Time.

The blood shot from my neck pretty fast. My hip and chest burned.

"I need to get some help!" I thought.

The shooter shifted his eyes from me back to the road ahead and sped off. I left the refuge of the backside of the dumpster and made my way around the building, back to the front, back to the office.

"I've gotta get help before he circles the block and finishes this," I reasoned.

Men from The Program gathered around and ushered me to the door. They helped me lay on the office floor.

"I've been shot a few times," one of them said. "Here's what you're about to feel…"

That man described the sting and the pain and then the mindlessness perfectly…

"Don't go to sleep," Dr. Jimmy said. Then, slower— "Do *not* go to sleep."

I got aggravated with Dr. Jimmy as he kept instructing me to "keep your eyes open for us, Rob. Keep looking at us. Don't close your eyes."

Doc, as many of The Program participants called him, was the licensed counselor on staff. He had worked in rehabilitation programs for years and was well-versed in what it was like to get shot— even though I don't think he was ever on the receiving end.

Another resident coached me through the breathing and every other detail: "Take long, deep breaths. Try to keep your heart rate normal."

I remember thinking, "Dang, these men have been shot enough to know how it feels and what to do?"

Then, in what seemed like a matter of insta-seconds, I was in the back of the ambulance.

It's important to note that so much of the timeline just blurred. As much as I would love to make it sound like I was tough, I feared I was going to die that afternoon. I might have— if it wasn't for those EMTs.

I don't remember anything they did in the back of their ambulance.

"We've got you, man. Hang in there," one of them said.

They could tell I was scared.

"You're going to be alright," the other added.

I felt secure.

Neither of them knew anything about me, but they jumped in at full speed and began serving a complete stranger...

"Has my past *finally* caught up with me?" I thought.

Until recently, I lived super-fast and extremely hard. I changed— so much so that very little in my present indicated the kind of past I had. At the same time, nothing in my past would have indicated I could ever make it to the life I was now living. Things were that dramatically different...

Moments later, the two paramedics rolled me into the emergency room just a few blocks away. As slow and protracted as the live shooting was, the time from the office to the operating room felt warp speed the exact opposite.

....

After I (finally— yes, it took a long time) got clean, I decided I wanted to give back. I wanted to help others— men in particular— who were walking the same rut I hiked. I felt like I had something I could, in turn, share with them to empower them to move forward. I not only knew the terrain, I had a map out of the mess.

I started working in a residential re-entry / rehabilitation program. On the re-entry side, we helped men make the transition from life in prison back to life in society. On the rehabilitation side, we helped addicts find freedom from their own private prison of drugs and alcohol.

The two facets of The Program were highly related.

- Most inmates find themselves behind bars because of an addiction. That is, at some point in the past they've shackled themselves to something no one else quite sees.

- Most addicts, if they're not careful, find themselves living in a physical prison.

I observed this during my stint(s) in jails and rehabs (as both a participant and as a staff member): There are a lot of jailhouse conversions and rehab redemptions that don't stand up to real life. A lot of guys just "pray a prayer" or go along with whatever Bible study or sermon is being taught. When they get out of prison, the conversion "gets out" of them.

I'm not saying they go into it intending for their faith to work that way, but it often does. It's flimsy. It lacks foundation.

For those who truly accept it, you see a depth that's unseen virtually anywhere else. They're bold. They exude grace. They imperfectly endure the trials which inevitably come.

While working in that program I hosted a completely voluntary Bible study for any of the guys who wanted to attend. I lived in a staff apartment smack dab in the middle of a large apartment complex that housed 75% of our participants.

Whereas some of the clients used to break in and steal my DVDs (so they could pawn them for drugs, just as I had done to others before) and whereas others always plotted the next opportunity to "sneak out" and get tangled into the shit-of-the-moment (something which only set them and their own recovery back— not anyone else's), there were a few who used to gather in my living room to take a raw look at the Bible.

By *raw*, I mean honest and "non-churchy" and "let's-just-be-candid about what it seems to say."

"The Apostle Paul was one beast of a mother-fuckin' gansta," Pee Wee observed.

He *really* said that. Guys just said what they thought in this group.

We were studying 2 Corinthians 11. In the middle of that chapter, Paul lists specific traumas he endured.

- Too many imprisonments to count— by comparison, the "worst" of our guys knew *exactly* how many times they had been in and out

- Beaten and left for dead *a handful of times*— one of which he responded to by returning to preach again the following day to the same people who tried to execute him

- Whipped by the Jews *on 5 different occasions*— the way they publicly reprimanded people with 39 lashes, because 40 was considered too brutal for any man to bare

- Stoned

- Shipwrecked three times

- Left without food, without a place to stay, and without anything to wear

Apparently, that's just the highlight reel.

Paul also talks about sneaking out of a walled city by being let down through windows in baskets, as well as getting robbed while traveling, and being swept away in raging rivers.

Yes, Paul must have been part-gangster.

The thing that hits me hardest, though, is that Paul's greatest concern isn't the trials he endured. He confessed that his greatest concern— even beyond all of these worries— was for the people he loved (see 2 Corinthians 11:28-29). In fact, his pursuit of people often placed him in the middle of these tribulations.

The people…

....

I saw Pee Wee soon after I got shot.

I had been out of the hospital a few days and was recovering at Matt & Abbey's (my brother-in-law & sister— we'll come back to them much later in the story).

Amidst the questions about what happened and what the doctor said and what I needed to do next, he started asking deeper questions.

"Do you believe all that shit you read in the Bible?" he asked.

"I do," I told him. "It took me a really long time to get there. But I believe it."

"It ain't for me," he admitted. "God don't care for people like me."

"Why?"

"Because I know what I've done." After a short pause, he added, "Matter of fact, I know the guy who rolled up on you, and I plan on takin' that piece of shit out!"

I didn't even acknowledge what he said about retaliating and exacting street justice. I skipped right over it.

"You're not worthy of God because of your behaviors," I replied. "I'm not, either. You're worthy of it because God claimed you as His son— and loves you regardless of anything else."

"What do you mean?" Pee Wee asked.

"OK," I said. "You *do* actually believe God loves *me*, right?"

"Yeah, man. No doubt. I see what you do around here…"

"Well, you also believe me when I tell you that my past is not much different than yours, don't you?"

"For sure— you're a crazy white boy!"

"Well, check it out… God loved me even in my wildest days, and He loves you, too."

I paused and watched him absorb the words.

I suggested, "Matter of fact, God loves that dude who shot me, too. He doesn't love his actions, but he loves him as much as he loves me and you."

"Nah, man…"

It wasn't an emphatic declaration of fact this time— like when he said I used to be a crazy caucasian. It was a whisper, as if he was processing new data — something he'd never heard before.

I continued, "You see, there's nothing you can do to make God love you less and there's nothing you can do to make Him love you more. He perfectly loves you, completely, at all times."

Pee Wee wept.

He *seemed* to change the subject after that: "I heard you told Tajuan's daughter that you forgave her dad for shooting you," he said.

"Well, yes and no... I didn't forgive him to his face. I would, but they picked him up. He's in jail, now. Tajuan came by to check on me and brought her. We all talked. Tajuan believed it was her fault, because she thought he was going after Kelly that day..."

Kelly was Tajuan's fiancée. For a season, he was an inmate on early release in The Program. Then he became a case manager. Then he became the operations manager.

They eventually got married in front of their friends, their family, and a bunch of homeless people in the park on a Sunday morning. While I worked on staff at The Program, the guys created a food truck out of a utility trailer. They loaded a sound system on it, outfitted it with a generator, and began hosting early morning worship services at the big park in downtown Birmingham around 8:00 am.

Hundreds of homeless men and women— and sometimes even homeless kids— gathered every Sunday to sing, listen to a short sermon, and eat breakfast from that trailer. They did it rain or shine. When it rained, everyone knew to find the trailer underneath the Interstate bridge, just a few blocks away.

Kelly helped organize the services, so he and Tajuan married there in front of the people they worshiped with each week— black suit, white dress, wedding cake, flowers, everything...

Tajuan met Kelly years after her baby's daddy went to prison. They were done and had been for a long while.

Having found Jesus and freedom from drugs and prostitution, Tajuan began a program for women who were victims of human trafficking.

It's a much longer story we'll refer to later in our own story (because she eventually helped Shannon at a pivotal moment), but the short version is that Tajuan ran her new program from the offices of the same program where I worked. In fact, our team gave her organization, named The Wellhouse, the platform to get started. Most people don't know that now, because we never advertised it, but that's how it officially began.

The baby's daddy came looking for Kelly, after a family court hearing didn't go his way.

(As you'll see, abusers often *don't* retaliate against their primary victims only. They often go after the abused's loved ones as another way of keeping them in line and under their control.)

That fated day, one of two things happened—

- Either the man thought I was Kelly.

Or,

- The man knew I wasn't Kelly. He was just pissed and, loaded gun in hand, drove to our building hell-bent on killing someone— anyone.

We'll never know.

Anyway, Tajuan blamed herself for me getting shot.

I affirmed, "This isn't your fault, Tajuan. You're not responsible for what he does…"

"Please forgive me, Rob."

"You don't need to be forgiven," I said. "It's not your—"

"But, really forgive me," she begged. "Will you *please* forgive me?"

"You're forgiven. I don't hold anything against you at all," I said. I looked at her young teenage daughter and added, "I even forgive your Dad. Sometimes, we get hurt by others. God knows I've done enough bad things to hurt other people in my life. Everything is going to be alright."

Somehow, Pee Wee heard about all of that. I didn't tell him. I frankly don't know who told him.

Pee Wee asked, "How do you forgive someone for doing something like that...?"

"Your favorite gangster," I told him. "He says to remember how much we've been forgiven— and to treat others the way God has treated us..."

"Really?"

"For sure. In Ephesians 4:32 he says to forgive others in the same way that God has forgiven you..."

"I've got a pretty big, bad list of stuff I've done," Pee Wee confessed.

"Me, too. At first glance you want to look at the offense the other person has inflicted on you. Then, after a bit, you step back and realize, wow, God has written off so much more that I've done."

I could see the cogs cranking in Pee Wee's mind...

"I heard that God *won't* forgive you if you *don't* forgive others," he said.

"Well, that's one interpretation of a verse in the Sermon on the Mount," I replied.

"The Sermon on the *what* or *where*?"

"The Sermon on the Mount. In Matthew 6:14-15, Jesus talks about forgiveness in a long speech He made to a group of people. Some scholars think this is the sermon He taught before feeding the 5,000. Others think it was just one of *many* of His talks. Many pastors agree that Jesus says our ability to forgive doesn't earn God's forgiveness, but it *demonstrates we've truly encountered forgiveness*. Once we see ourselves as we were— and recognize God's *acceptance of us in that condition*— it's easy to accept where others are and absolve them of the ways they hurt us."

After a moment, I added, "God loves me, and that makes it easier for me to love others. Even when it's hard."

I could see the invisible lightbulb illuminate in Pee Wee's mind...

He began to cry.

"So God actually loves me, too," he said— half-asking, half-declaring.

"Yeah, no doubt."

"I believe that. I accept that." Looking to Heaven, he stated, "I receive it..."

It was the most concise profession of faith I've ever heard: *I receive it.*

....

A few months later, Pee Wee's EOS (read: *End of Sentence*, the day an inmate officially becomes free and can go home, having served their prison term) date came. He moved back to his hometown, so he could live closer to his family and help look after them.

I always wondered what might happen. They often tell you that to truly start over you sometimes need to change the scenery— that you need a different location.

Pee Wee settled in. He began working a job. He reconnected with all the important people in his life. He started dating a young woman.

One day, Pee Wee sat in the car waiting for her to get off work. A jealous man walked straight to the driver's side, loaded pistol in hand, and pulled the trigger.

His story played out much like my own.

The shooter didn't miss.

Yet there was one major difference: unlike me, Pee Wee didn't make it.

"What if I didn't get shot, and what if Pee Wee didn't come visit me?" I thought. "Did Pee Wee's eternal destiny change because of me and my decisions and the fact that someone else did a bad thing and pulled the trigger on me?"

I don't know, but maybe…

1. If I Could Start My Story Over (R)

2. There's ~~Almost~~ Always A Reason Behind It (S)

Shannon recounts her earliest memories and begins putting the pieces together. Young Shannon sleeps in an abandoned house. Young Shannon clarifies who looks out for her

Looking back on my story, a lot of things make sense— how I ended up the way I did. More than that, after you hear the story, you'll wonder why I didn't end up in a radically different place than I am now— why things aren't worse than they could be.

For sure. That sounds like I'm talking out of both sides, but bear with me. It will all come together, I promise.

Let me start right here...

Almost none of the women in my family raised their own kids. This goes way back, as far as I can trace, to my great-great grandmother.

Don't get me wrong. We're family. And we all take care of family. You might have seen us together on social media or heard our podcast and just assumed things have always been like they are right now.

Let me explain...

Someone once said, "Your past doesn't *excuse* you, but it does *explain* you."

I don't think I receive a free pass on some important things just because that's how I saw them play out in the previous chapters of my life, but just as any subsequent chapter depends on the content in the previous chapters of the book... the past explains how I got to where I am and it demonstrates why I needed to (eventually) make better, different decisions going forward.

Mom was living in Los Angeles when she met a young Hispanic guy. His family owned a lot of property in California and Mexico, and they had money. She got pregnant, quit high school, and got married.

She settled in, but the new rhythm abruptly stopped when my older sister, Lisa, was just 18 months old. Mom's husband stood in the kitchen one evening, playing Russian Roulette while cooking a late night breakfast.

In case you don't know, that's a game in which you load one chamber in a 6-shot revolver with a bullet. Each player spins the cylinder until it stops. Then, they take the pistol and place it against their head. In one version of the "game" you touch the muzzle to your temple; in another you stick the gun in your mouth. With a 5/6 chance of surviving— just 83.3%— you pull the trigger. Some people live; inevitably, others die.

With a 16.7% chance of meeting certain death, Mom's first husband spun, fired, and fell over.

Mom awoke to the sound of the gunshot and ran to the kitchen. She experienced the sights and sounds and smell of the entire thing.

She drove Lisa, just a toddler, back to Alabama. That's where she met my Dad.

Dad was as interesting as Mom— even though I don't know him well. He was a Vietnam War veteran who got out before the war was over. I was born in 1973, and the war didn't end until 1975, so I did some math.

I learned he enlisted right after high school to get away from his environment. He was a Marine.

He made it back and then returned to fight again. Whereas many young men tried to dodge the draft, Dad did a second tour. I wondered why.

Turns out, he got in trouble with the Law upon returning from deployment. It was probably alcohol-related, based on the other parts of his story. After all, during that era they actually gave American soldiers cheap beer in their daily rations.

"Do jail time or go back to Vietnam," the judge offered.

My father chose the latter.

Two weeks before his discharge on that second deployment, Dad ran point on a recon mission. He was out front, leading the other men.

That day was notable for two reasons.

1. This was the *only* day he wasn't stoned on marijuana.

2. You hear all these stories about men who get shot the day before their deployment ends— and even some who die. Dad was one of those men.

- 43 -

As he led his troops through the jungle, he stepped close enough to a land mine to shift the debris hiding it and triggered the blast. The explosion blew him back several feet, slinging him through the air. In the process, shrapnel from the mine and whatever-else-the-Viet-Cong-slung-together-with-the-mini-bomb found its way into his body.

He survived, but was never the same.

The addictions he had before the war were amplified by the fact the U.S. military nurtured it— and even encouraged it— during the war. Then, rather than getting the help he needed (jail probably would have been good for him at that point— I know it eventually was for me), he went back overseas to the one place where American soldiers fought bravely while riding a wave of daily alcohol consumption along with— yes— heroine.

So much heroine flowed through the front lines that the early version of Homeland Security checked incoming coffins of our troops and strip-searched surviving warriors to make sure they weren't smuggling drugs back with them. That's all stuff for another time and place.

Dad met mom right after he returned. In fact, when the two of them found each other, he had just gotten discharged from the hospital, still walked with crutches, and had a shaved head.

Back in the U.S., he just kept the addictions going. In a way, you can't blame him. Addiction is a hard thing to overcome when you're at full strength, and he wasn't. His body, already battered by two back-to-back tours in the Vietnamese jungle, shuddered under the shreds of metal spiked throughout him.

He carried a lot of emotional and

physical pain. Again, the past doesn't excuse it but it certainly *explains* things.

Another thing about the women in my family is that they don't always live with their husbands and they don't expect them to necessarily be a "one woman man," either. Later, I'll talk more about that as it pertains to my personal choices.

I remember that Dad regularly hosted parties— lots of them.

He spent a lot of time at beer joints, honky-tonks, and pool halls.

And he always had a new woman at his side.

Mom and Dad eventually divorced— she had enough of the straying. At the same time, he was certain he wanted to be with someone else.

I bounced from house-to-house. Sometimes, I stayed with my Mom. Other times I stayed with my Dad. I spent the rest of the time at my great grandmother's, on friends' couches, and even an abandoned house some evenings— even as a kid.

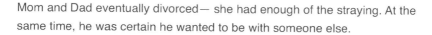

In the early morning hours, Dad's newest girlfriend drove the two of them down the Bessemer Super Highway. That's the kind of multi-lane road they built through all of the suburbs in our city back in the mid-1900s. These four-lane arteries originally connected various parts of the city together until the

Interstates moved in and shopping and restaurants and just about everything else moved in those directions, leaving impoverished areas in their wake.

Predictably, Dad and the driver were both drunk. The two of them were probably headed home for the day after binge-drinking all night.

She lost control, crossed the median, and collided head-on with another car. Even though he survived two combat tours and a land mine explosion, Dad couldn't pull through that crash.

I was nine.

I was at my great grandmother's when the call came— mid-morning.

"I don't believe you," I replied upon hearing the news he was dead.

Dad had been so "in and out" of my life at that point I couldn't actually mentally connect the dots to realize he was now *permanently* gone. Not only did I not know much about grief, I couldn't assess if I felt any grief at that point— *or if I even should.*

The oddest thing I remember about Dad's death was that whereas I felt very little emotion about any of it, my sister hysterically wailed. He had adopted my sister, Lisa, who was— is— seven years older than me, just before I was born.

We— my Mom, my sister, my brother, and I— were all living at Grandma's when Daddy died.

My great grandmother— I called her Grandma— helped make sure we got to school and took me and Lisa to church every Sunday morning, each Sunday night, and all the Wednesday evenings the church was open. Whenever we were at her house, we had to go.

I learned how to play the piano. I sang in the children's choir. I listened to a lot of long sermons that seemed to last far longer than the minutes it took to deliver them. But this really gave me a foundation for later in life, something I eventually came back to.

Since I was bouncing from house to house anyway, I decided to go back to my Mom's after Dad died.

"I need a full-time parent," I rationalized.

I was 9. At the age in which most kids learn to master their times tables and plod their way through long division, I made decisions about parenting.

....

Mom soon remarried and had a son. This was husband number 3– if you're counting.

- The first was the Hispanic man whose family owned land, the guy who got her pregnant and caused her to drop out of school. He accidentally committed suicide with the revolver in the kitchen.

- The second was my Dad— the double-duty Vietnam Vet who survived the land mine but not the drunk driving accident.

- The third was yet *another* alcoholic and addict.

Oh, and the third was also an abuser and child molester who came from a long line of men who not only cheated on their wives, *they chose to do so with children*.

I began playing the hokey-pokey with Mom's house. I would go for a while. Then, something would happen, so I would go back to my great grandmother's— to get away from it. Grandma's was my safe place.

But then I would feel the desire to be near a parent, particularly my Mom, so I would return. As you probably imagine, "it" would happen again so I would leave.

It became an ongoing struggle for me, deciding how to balance the anticipated molestation with my need for my mother. Further, my confusion compounded when she found out about it and responded *by making excuses for him.*

"He was probably drinking and didn't know it was you?" she reasoned, half-stating and half-asking.

Even if he didn't know it was me— a pre-teen— I thought, he had to know it was a kid and that it wasn't my mom!

I've talked openly about the sexual abuse, so people have asked me the obvious questions…

"Why didn't you tell anyone?" is the most common.

He made sure I didn't.

"Tell your Mom, and I'll hurt *her*," he always said.

Or— perhaps even worse— "I'll hurt your *little brother*."

Looking back I see this same pattern happened with the men who abused me. They knew they were hurting me as much as they possibly could, so they never threatened to hurt me further. No, they always promised to do something to a family member, often a child.

That man— my Mom's husband— also molested other females in the family. People began talking about it.

It continued for about 18 more months until Mom had to make a decision. It was time to take ownership of it and confront it. But, rather than dealing with the problem, she just left him.

It's easy to read the story and judge her for her actions. I know I did for years. However, until you walk in the shoes of the abused woman, there's no way— as I eventually learned firsthand— you can possibly understand. You *think* you can (and likely even just shuddered at that sentence), but you can't.

"I'm not with him anymore," she could then honestly say.

It was her sincere way of wanting to close the chapter and move on. Most victims— I know, because I'm one of them— just want to move forward.

. . . .

I hated everyone after that— especially God. I was so angry at "God," whoever He was…

I remember singing all those songs at Grandma's church about Jesus loving the little children, knowing His eye was on me because it was presumably on the sparrow, and the suggestion that He has the whole world in His hands. I didn't buy it.

As a kid you hear about Santa Claus, never considering the reality that not all houses have chimneys and not even all kids in the world even live in houses— some stay in huts and teepees and even, as I did, on friends' couches and abandoned buildings. Then someone pulls back the curtain: there is no Santa Claus. He wasn't the one lavishing great presents on some kids and just a few trinkets on others; it was the parents the entire time.

And then there's all of this "God-stuff."

Was that just the parents and half-parents and step-parents, too?

And if it wasn't just the parents— if God is real and He truly is all-powerful and loves us and wants what's best for us— how does that fit in with the shit show we often live?

I decided it was all a lie. The Santa. God, Jesus, whatever.

Once Mom finally left him for good I went back to stay with her and my little brother. My sister was born to a guy I never knew nor was related to. My half-brother was born to a molester who was technically my step-dad (though I wouldn't claim it). My actual Dad died.

My sister is 7 years older than me.

My brother is 8 years younger than me.

(It sounds like an 5th-grade math problem just trying to sort it all out.)

Mom replaced the molester with another man of equal caliber. To be honest, I don't know that he ever sexually abused anyone (at least not me), but he liked to drink and occasionally did drugs.

He was the kind of angry drunk that hit women and even kids.

And he was as faithful to my Mom as his predecessors had been.

During this season, we were the kids whose Mom had them sleep with their clothes on at night— in case the boyfriend came home drunk and mean and we had to abruptly leave.

With all the chaos happening, I needed an outlet. I was hurt, I was already an introvert, and I was angry.

Grandma and Lisa— who was now 20– pulled together money to get me into sports. I began playing softball and volleyball.

My big sister— Lisa— always found a way to handle my needs. She even took care of my of my *wants*.

Clothes, school supplies, extracurricular activities... Lisa was always there.

She did the same for my little brother.

Then, later, she did the same for my kids, Blake and Kimberly.

She never married. She never had kids of her own. But she was a Mom to all of us.

No one attended my practices or games— I was the lone kid who came and left on their own. Many times, I opted to stay at a friend's. Weekday, weekend, whatever... I began to fend for myself.

When I wasn't playing sports, I spent a lot of time shooting pool and drinking — just like Daddy had (he taught me to shoot in the bars when I was just a little girl. He stacked milk crates, so I could reach the table).

There were two halls I frequented. Mom always knew where to find me, because I became such a regular.

When things got heated around her house she often drove and asked, "Can you find a place to stay tonight?"

There were no cell phones back then— and as people who struggled to pay rent and, remember, sometimes slept in clothes so we could leave in the middle of the night— she had to physically come look for me. It was always an easy "yes" when she asked about me finding somewhere to stay.

What kid wouldn't jump at the chance to spend the night with a friend yet again?

One day, I put myself in a stupid position and got raped by a man 9 years older than me. I was 14.

Most nights, I rotated through a series of homes— teammates and classmates. When I couldn't find accommodations for the evening I knew of an abandoned house near one of my pool halls. I often stayed there and had friends pick me up on the way to school.

Looking back, I recognize the absurdity of wearing the same clothes to school during the day, wearing them to a bar and shooting pool in them half the night, sleeping in them, and then returning to school in them the following day... sometimes for days at a time.

But no one ever noticed.

None of my teachers. None of my coaches. None of my classmates said anything about it if they did. None of the friends or even friends' parents who picked me up from an abandoned house ever even asked.

Every person who was supposed to look out for me failed. I figured that, best I could, I would need to look out for myself.

Application for Part 1 | Excuses ≠ Explanations

Main idea: Your past doesn't excuse your present decisions, but it does explain some things about you which can empower you to move forward in healing and wholeness.

What would you see if your life flashed before your eyes like Rob experienced (see chapter 1)?

You might want to consider:

- 3 things you're thankful for

- 3 things from your past you would change (even though you cannot change them, you can still learn from them as you move forward)

- 3 things left undone (people you need to connect or reconnect with, places to go, experiences you would like to have, etc.)

_____

_____

_____

_____

_____

_____

_____

_____

_____

_____

_____

What are some of the stories or limiting beliefs that keep you from moving forward (some may relate to income, education, past mistakes, etc.)? Beside each you list, write 1-2 action steps you can take now to overcome them.

_____

_____

_____

_____

_____

_____

_____

_____

_____

_____

In the same way Shannon's experience (see chapter 2) was affected by her parents' decisions, others are affected by yours. The bad decisions you make impact your family and friends— the good decisions enhance their situation, too.

Let's focus on the positive side of this.

List some of the people who will be directly touched by your progress. And, write how they are specifically changed *for the better.*

WALK WITH US!
FREE BONUS ACCESS!

RiseUpOnline.info/7

7 MIND SHIFT LESSONS

Part 2 | Learn from the Leaders

Look ahead— not behind— while searching for the wisdom you need for the next win. Yes, learn from your mistakes, but also seek instruction from people who are currently where you want to be.

3. That's Exactly What We Do (R)

Rob reveals where the "can do even if you don't yet know how to" attitude came from. Rob wins a strange bet that leads to Ben's bluff. The first investor comes onboard after an interesting meeting.

At one time, Dad ran the biggest painting and wallpaper business in Birmingham.

If you know the Birmigham area and have ever driven through Homewood— or did in the early 2000s, before they started leveling apartments and replacing them with higher-end real estate— you would have seen all these apartment complexes. A few still remain. Dad painted and wallpapered almost all of them.

Before he went into wallpaper, he was just a painter. A really good one, but only a painter.

This was right before I was born. He was 22, maybe 23.

Every morning he did what many other contractors do: he drove to the shop — in this case, BLP Paint Store— and purchased the paint, spackle, and tape for that day's jobs. He always arrived early enough to drink coffee, check the lead board, and shoot the bull with the guys.

One day, it was slow…

A man walked into the shop, approached the salesman, and said, "Hey, I'm a new builder in town. We're constructing a few hotels in the area, as well as several apartments. I need a reference from you for a good wallpaper hanger."

Dad was standing right there. There was no one else around— just Dad, the guy managing the paint shop, and the builder.

Realizing he had never even *touched* wallpaper, much less hung an actual roll of it, Dad asked, "How big is the job you've got?"

The builder described the project.

Dad immediately replied, "I've got a crew that can handle that!"

The man looked at him. "You serious? Really? Well, we'll need you to start fairly soon. Phase 1 is ready. Phase 2 is just a few months behind that…"

He described how many buildings it was, how many floors were in most of the buildings, and how long the job might last.

"I got you," Dad said. "Drop a set of plans off here this week, and I'll look it over."

The man penned an address on the back of his business card and handed it to Dad.

"Here's the project address," he said. Then, after handing him the card— "What are the chances you can start and finish this on time?"

"What would you say the chances are, Wes?"

Wes, the store manager, shouted, "100%!"

3. "That's Exactly What We Do" (R)

"Yeah, 100%," Dad agreed, flashing a smile to reveal his gold tooth.

"Wow. That was easier than I thought," the builder said, looking across the counter to Wes. "Thank you." Then, to Dad— "I'll see you soon!"

Dad watched the builder walk back out the door…

He turned back to Wes: "I need two things from you. First, I need a list of everything I'm gonna need to learn how to hang wallpaper. Second, I need someone to show me how to do it."

He bought the supplies and learned to hang the wallpaper at home. It was the early 70s, so YouTube was still 30+ years into the future. If you wanted to learn how to do something in those days, you had to read the tutorials, find someone who could show you in person, or stumble through it yourself.

Dad started with a handful of guys who knew *even less* about wallpaper than he did. Like him, they all showed up to work early and worked hard well past quitting time. Eventually, he ran the largest outfit in the Magic City, topping more than 90 painters and hangers at the peak.

(Of course, somewhere during the learning curve he managed to plaster an entire Shoney's restaurant with wallpaper he and his crew hung *upside down.* No one ever questioned it.)

It all began with a simple, "Hey, I can do that…" after seeing the opportunity.

. . . .

It's getting ahead of the story to go ahead and tell you about how Ben and I started selling bundles of houses to investors, but the way we did that is exactly what Dad did here. In fact, hearing Dad's story of building a wallpaper business is one of the factors that proved to me I could grow a house-flipping biz.

- 61 -

(In like manner, maybe our story of building a business will convince you to create something, too!)

You see, a lot of people continue looking for the "next thing." All the while, that next big thing might be staring them in the face.

Others wait for an "open door." The truth is that there are unlocked doors all around you. Sometimes, you just need to turn the handle and see what's on the other side.

I saw that in Dad.

Let me explain how this played-out for me...

....

You never forget your first big project. Mine was on Fulton Avenue. A 3-bedroom, 1-bath house with a massive radio tower bolted to the side, it smelled like the local dump when my business partner and I purchased it for a mere $2,500.

Vacant for years, every flea in a one-mile radius must have moved in the moment the last humans abandoned ship. Then, the bugs multiplied... exponentially.

My best guess is the fleas followed dogs we never saw. We found dog poop at every stage of decay in each room.

"We signed up for this," I thought, toting my third or fourth bag out of the front door before we could even begin making a renovation plan.

I wasn't complaining— I chose this. Moreover, I loved every second of it.

One day, just as we finished cleaning out the property, someone pulled up next door. I immediately sized him up. The man didn't seem to fit the profile of the neighborhood.

"He's not from around here," I told Ben— he was my business partner.

"Agreed," he said. "He looks out of place."

I looked at Ben.

"I bet you $20 that guy is from Utah," I told him.

He smirked. Then laughed.

Then he roared— "No way! How do you know?!"

"I'm just guessing by the way he's dressed." After a moment— "You taking the bet or not?" I asked him.

(We made small bets like this constantly. Sometimes, we flipped a quarter to bet on the color of a wall, other times we wagered who might run a red light or walk through a door...)

"I'll take it. Odds are at least 50-1— and probably more in my favor than that — since we're nowhere near Utah right now."

Ben approached the man's truck and waved. One of the things you gotta know about Ben is that he's been an addict and done hard time, but he's *totally approachable.* He has a natural way with people that just sets them at ease.

In fact, if I didn't tell you what I just told you about him, you would never guess he has a past. (Then again, we all do— some of us just feel the need to hide it rather than walking in the freedom that owning your story and moving forward in transparency brings.)

"Hey, man. How are you?"

"Good," he replied. "I guess that southern hospitality thing is true. You guys live around here?"

"No," Ben replied. "We're out doing some work. We both live on the other side of town."

That question was the set-up. And it lead right into the bet. Ben was sure he was about to take a Jackson from me...

"What about you?" Ben asked. "You moving this way?"

Ben knew the man wasn't— like I said, the man didn't fit in.

"No," the stranger replied. "I'm *from Utah...*" (Boom. Twenty for me; zero for Ben.) "... I'm out here checking some investments. I'm the acquisition manager for a pretty big investment fund."

Our new friend from Utah then posed the question every person you meet inevitably leads with, as if "what we do" to earn a paycheck is the most important part of us *and* the thing we should most be known by (hint: it's not — on either count).

"What do you guys do?" he asked.

Now, this could have gone about 17 different ways from here. For instance—

- Option 1 = *We could have told him the truth.*

"One of us just got out of an early release program from the Department of Corrections and the other one of us was freshly clean & sober & working at a rehab— the one where we got together and formed this business partnership."

- Option 2 = *We could have talked about our current dilemma.*

"We just bought this house for about $2,500– it was given to the non-profit where we were, and they decided to just cash out and roll the money into ministry. We scraped everything we had together to buy this dump and now we're trying to figure out how to fund the renovations— as soon as we get all the fleas and dog shit out of here, that is."

Of course this option would have needed to include something like, "Oh, and that van we're driving— Ben paid $1,500 to the non-profit for that, because even though someone gave them the vehicle they had no use for a barely-running cargo van."

Ben, the electric type of extrovert who doesn't necessarily lie but doesn't feel obligated to tell the absolute truth as long as it leads to a connection with others, chose Option 3.

"We're real estate investors. We find houses, we fix them, we fill them with tenants, and then we package them to sell to other investors."

"Really?" the Utahn replied— that's the official nickname for people from the Mormon state. "What's the volume? How many do you do?"

Ben, far off the reservation of truth at this point, said the first thing that came to mind: "We do eight a month. Sometimes, we do ten. Eight to ten. Usually ten."

I thought, "Eight to ten? But usually TEN?"

We hadn't even flipped the first. Sure, we had both worked in construction for years— and even worked on renovation crews. It's a whole different game, though, when it comes time to do it yourself. At that point, you don't get off at 5 o'clock and stop thinking about it until you arrive on the job the next day. And you don't get paid just because it's everyone else's pay day. You become more like a modern-day bear hunter, the kind of guy that doesn't eat unless he completes the kill.

"I'm interested," the man who made me $20 richer told us.

He handed us a card, headed to inspect his team's investment next door, and then drove off.

....

You never know when chance meetings might turn into big moments— those moments that create movements that shift the next complete chapter of your life. That's what this was. The fact Ben and I made that nonsense bet— something we'd done dozens of times before about other things— and the fact that Ben went and met the man and then mustered the audacity to assert we "do 8 or 10 houses every month— but usually 10" catapulted us forward.

We laughed for a few minutes about the entire conversation.

"I can't believe you told him…"

And, "Oh, yeah, and then you said…"

But then it hit us….

In less than 30 minutes, we shifted from worrying about fleas and poop and wondering about renovating this fixer-upper (a radical understatement) to an even bigger set of problems.

Aside from the "How are we going to fund the flip of the Fulton house?" concern, two more monkeys just jumped on our backs.

- Monkey 1 = the original monkey, the current project (just to clarify)

- Monkey 2 = we now need *9 more homes*— presumably houses that are in such poor condition that we're not only able to find them, we're also able to afford both the acquisition and purchase for each

- Monkey 3 = we need to fill all of these homes with tenants so they're each generating revenue, making them attractive for investors

Furthermore, we needed all of them this cheap, we needed them fast, and we needed a steady stream of them. Ten more houses every single month.

We started networking.

Every day we phoned other business leaders, offering them all the same line: "We're in the same space and we'd just like to meet other people who are doing the same thing."

Thankfully, most of the renovators and house flippers agreed to meet us for breakfast or lunch. Every time they did, we leaned in close and listened hard.

We took copious notes. Not during the meeting, mind you, because we never wanted anyone to realize that we had no idea what we were doing. It was on-the-job training, and this was our school.

To be clear, these were legitimate investment groups. Ben and I— at that moment— just pretended to be an investment group. Eventually, we were legit, but not yet. We picked up a few things we immediately put into practice.

3. "That's Exactly What We Do" (R)

"We never buy houses with bad roofs," one of the more successful owners told us. "The problem is that you not only have to spend money on a new roof— and new decking— but you never know how much water damage the inside of the house has."

He explained it thoroughly…

As he did, Ben articulated the full scope of the worst case scenario: "So if the water goes through the roof of a two story house, it might leak through the attic and ceiling of the second floor, then through the floor of the second floor, then through the ceiling of the first floor, through the first floor…"

"Exactly," the experienced flipper replied. "You could end up repairing or replacing 6 or more layers of surfaces *just because of one bad roof*. Plus, you can get into mold and other unseen issues once you have water to deal with. We don't even take a further look. We skip straight to the next house on our list of potentials…"

As soon as we stepped into the camo truck after that lunch meeting (yes, I painted the truck exactly like I painted airplanes back during my Marine Corps days), I told Ben I had a new strategy for us.

"Here's what we need to do. We can't outbid these guys, so we've got to make sure we never bid against them."

Ben was sure that wasn't possible. "Everyone sees the same MLS," he said. "As soon as the properties list, anyone can find them."

"True," I told him, "We've got to outsmart these guys!"

"How are we possibly going to do that?" he asked. "We're obviously going to them for advice, because they're smarter about this than us."

"No doubt," I replied. "But he just told us they don't bid on houses with bad roofs. They're afraid of the unseen damage and the hidden costs."

"We can't buy those houses with bad roofs, either," Ben replied. "If they can't afford those repairs, we definitely can't."

(Another lesson we learned from these pros is that while every amateur gets enamored with their selling price— "We'll make bank when we sell this house for $_____ [insert some pipe dream of a number that solves all of your financial woes]— the numbers to really be concerned with are the price you buy the house at, as well as the renovation and repair costs. Whereas the market often changes your selling price, the other costs are more fixed. If you don't manage them, you're done for...)

"We won't have to," I said. "Let's go to Home Depot and grab a bunch of tarps. As soon as a house goes live, we'll drive over— early in the morning— and throw a big, blue tarp over the roof."

"Oh, when the investor does their drive-by, they'll think it has a bad roof and they won't make an offer!"

"Bingo."

That became our play:

- Identify a house we wanted to purchase

- Toss a tarp somewhere conspicuous the moment the listing posted

- Make an offer we knew would likely be accepted

Another strategy we pulled from those "peer-to-peer" lunches and dinner meetings (they weren't really peer-to-peer; we were in no way professional equals with the men we met) was not to get into bidding wars.

"Don't artificially raise the price on a home that you don't want as your own personal residence— one that you're just going to fix and flip away. There are plenty out there. Go find another."

Our early morning tarp-tactic helped solve some of this issue, but not all. We supplemented this strategy by removing "for sale" signs from front yards. Since "the sign" is the key identifier that this property remains on the market, this likely caused some potential buyers to simply drive by, looking for the next lingering property.

In those days, there were *so many* vacant, foreclosed homes.

....

I'm ahead of myself. I told you about the houses, but I didn't explain the money. It didn't matter how many homes we could identify if we could not execute a purchase. Nor did it matter how many we could buy if we couldn't fund the renovation and then afford to carry them while we filled them with tenants and then sold them to hedge-funds and other higher-level investors.

I tried to "shop the money" to find a lender 69 times before number 70 finally hit.

(That's not a made-up number. I actually counted them and documented the entire journey.)

After 25 or 30 turned us down, I began asking for feedback.

"You've already turned us down," I communicated back to many after receiving their verbal or written denial. "I would love some feedback from you, if you don't mind…"

Most were happy— and even honored— to help.

"If there was one thing we could have said differently, or if there's a means we could have used to better present the opportunity, something that would have made you join us, what would it be?"

We received great coaching, just for asking.

(And, as an aside, one of these investors eventually— years later— began backing some of my projects.)

Number 27— let's just say that was his number— told me, "You seem too needy. Investors want to back business opportunities *more* when they feel like they'll miss out on something if they don't— like someone else beats them to it and they're left behind. They don't want to be the first in. Once you get a few people onboard, it will be easy to get others..."

This investor— who turned us down— even suggested, "Once you have funding in place, tell people you're now looking for *cheaper* money. And don't make it outlandish. For instance, if you have someone willing to invest at 12%, tell them that you're looking for someone to lend you money at 10% instead..."

Number 64 suggested we were *selling* far more than just *sharing*. That sounds counter-intuitive, for sure, because people are never going to get behind your project unless they know what you're asking for. But the "this is what we do..." approach seems to work better than the "if you do this then we'll be able to..." attitude.

....

One afternoon— well beyond lunch hour— Ben and I drove to a nearby sandwich shop. They weren't super-busy, but after waiting at the table for a while it dawned on Ben...

"I think they forgot about us," he said.

I hadn't noticed. We had been crunching numbers, trying to figure out how to make everything— or anything— we had learned over the past 69 meetings apply to our situation.

We both walked to the counter.

"Man, I'm so sorry," the guy in the back said. "What did you have? We missed it. I'll get it right now."

"No problem," we replied. "Take your time…"

We repeated the order.

A few minutes later the guy rushed-walked to the table, tray of sandwiches and chips in hand.

"I'm really sorry, guys. This is my place. This isn't how I try to run my business…"

"Hah. I get it," I told him. "We have those days in our business, too."

I'm not sure how it happened, but within the next few seconds, we invited John— that was the owner's name— to sit down. We began dialoguing about the struggle that operating something you own can truly be.

He was exhausted.

We were tired, too.

Obviously things weren't rolling his way that day. Moreover, they weren't really churning in our direction, either.

"What do you guys do?" he asked.

We went to the standard line— the spiel I refined over the past 69 iterations.

3. "That's Exactly What We Do" (R)

"We find houses we can fix. We find tenants to occupy them, so they become income generating. Then we flip them to investors— usually in packs of 8-10. We try to do that every month."

This is what I learned from Number 64. Don't act like you would do it if someone got behind you; just step into the pitch and swing— do it. Whether or not they get onboard with you is a completely different concern altogether.

To my surprise, John looked interested the entire time those lines rolled from my lips.

"How do you fund it?"

I continued my non-salesy sales pitch: "That's a great question. Right now we have some investors who earn a 12% return on their money in 90 days. That's how long it takes us to buy the houses, build them out, and then batch them into a sale. We obviously have more than 10 going at a time, because they're all in different stages."

I added the bit I learned from Number 27: "We're looking for cheaper money right now. I'd love to find an 8% investor. But, I would be thrilled to find a few to back us at 10%."

"I want to know more," he replied. "Show me how it works."

"What do you mean? You want to go see a house?"

Turns out, he did.

So, right then and there, we finished the southwest chicken rolled sandwiches, loaded up, and led him to Fulton Avenue. It was somewhat in the works, but still had no electricity or running water.

"This will give you an idea of how they all begin," I said.

"All?" Ben whispered. "This is how the *only one* has begun..."

We walked through the house, making a few comments as we toured it.

"We've learned that knocking out a few walls creates a more open floor plan that makes some of these smaller homes look much bigger," one of us said. "So we took this one out…"

Another added, "And back here… we're adding the laundry room here. Section 8 pays more if the property has a laundry room."

"That makes sense," John replied. "Great idea." Then— almost like clockwork— "I really need to go. Where is the bathroom?"

"The water isn't on…" Ben confessed.

"That's because we're still deciding how to best situate that extra bathroom," I interjected.

"I really need to go," John said. "I've kinda been holding it."

"Just go outside," Ben suggested. "The trees around the yard are overgrown and haven't been cut back yet. The neighbor's won't see."

"Can't," John replied. "It's number 2."

As I thought about what to do— not wanting potential investor 70 to leave the site after getting him to the property— Ben, always fast on his feet, grabbed a five gallon bucket.

"Let me show you what we do," he said, pulling a leaf bag from a box in the corner of the room.

"What's that?"

"This," he continued, "is a construction toilet."

"A construction toilet? I thought they used porta-potties."

"Not always. Come with me," he commanded, as he began striding back through the house, placing the bag in the bucket and folding the top of the Hefty Cinch Sack over the rim as he walked.

He led John to a random closet, opened the door, and set the bucket inside.

"The only condition for using this toilet," Ben continued, "is that you do your own walk of shame."

"Walk of shame?"

"Yeah. You pull the bag, tie it up, and carry it away from the site yourself. You take it with you." Then— "Wait a second. One more thing. I'll be right back."

Ben walked back out the front door to his rehab van, grabbed a roll of toilet paper, and carried it to the closet.

He tossed the roll to John: "I always have one of these in the vehicle with me — because you never know."

John smiled and disappeared into the makeshift bathroom for a few moments.

"I can't believe you said that," I smirked.

"Didn't want him to leave. I mean, we finally got an investor out here, and we've got to get rolling."

John emerged and laughed pretty hard. He stepped outside and tossed the bag into the back of his pickup.

"I'll do it," John said. "I want to help. Let's sit down and write-up the terms."

Looking back, I think the construction toilet is one of the main reasons John invested in our new business. Whereas we basically *begged* others to lend us money— "Awww... this is going to make us money and help you make bank!"— and *reeked of desperation*, the bit with the construction toilet diffused every bit of solicitation. We didn't seem moochy; we looked legit. Even though it was the first house.

John remains one of my primary investors to date, by the way. The houses have gotten bigger, the sales prices have increased, and the margins have grown.

It's exactly what we do.

And it has a lot to do with the construction toilet.

4. Why Good Girls Go Back to Bad Men (S)

Shannon drops out of high school after discovering she's pregnant, lives in interesting accommodations throughout the pregnancy, and explores the age-old dilemma of leaving an abuser

---

I continued playing sports throughout high school. Running stadiums, pounding volleyballs, and smashing softballs provided me with an outlet to unleash my aggression.

I also wanted to get out of Mom's house permanently. I wanted a different life.

I suppose this is why I was attracted to a man in his twenties. As unhealthy as he was, it was an upgrade from the life I had at home.

The first week of my high school senior year, I took a pregnancy test. It immediately hit.

My mother was consumed with the latest man and keeping him more on the "appeased side" and less on the "punching side," so I decided not to tell her.

Grandma and Lisa seemed more solid. I thought they would be the safe place to land.

"Get an abortion," my Grandma suggested.

My sister considered the dilemma a few moments before chiming in. "I'm *hugely* disappointed in you."

She emphasized *hugely*, as if there's a degree of disappointment we might find acceptable.

Outside, I held myself together. Inside, I deflated.

Grandma— who, mind you, was the churchgoer and should have been the most gracious (especially with their pro-life stance and all)— added another layer to the tension: "If you don't have that abortion you're not in our family anymore."

To be honest, I didn't really feel like I was in the family— and whether or not I chose to have an abortion had nothing to do with it. I mean, my sister and brother both had a consistent place to stay. Each had a parent— or parental figure. Neither, to my knowledge, had been abused and then disregarded. I felt like an "outsider" the whole time.

I chose to go tell my Mom about the pregnancy.

"You can do whatever you decide to do," she offered. "This is your choice."

That was it.

No advice. No veiled threats. No encouragement. *Nothing*.

4. Why Good Girls Go Back to Bad Men (S)

"Do whatever you want to do."

I had been doing "whatever I want to do" (read: *whatever I had to do to survive*) my entire life, it seemed.

So, with Lisa disappointed in me, with a Grandma who'd give me the abort-or-leave-the-family declaration, and with a Mom who clearly didn't have a dog in the fight, I decided to go with the guy. His name was Kenny.

....

Kenny's Dad found work in Kissimmee, Florida— near Disney. This was in the early 90s, back when the area began to boom.

He towed a travel trailer to a KOA campground near the worksite. Kenny's parents slept in the camper, and the two of us stayed in a small tent we pitched next to it.

A tent in a campground was one notch below couch-surfing and one notch above an abandoned house. I slept on the ground in a low-grade tent the majority of my pregnancy.

About eight months in, work slowed. I learned the little house next to my Grandma's was available for rent, so we moved back to Birmingham. Fairly quickly, we learned that wasn't going to work.

It's hard to secure steady employment when you refuse to show up (like Kenny), and no one wants to hire you when you're about to pop any moment (like me). With no money and no place to go, we married and moved in with Kenny's parents.

A few months later, when baby Blake was just a few months old, I went back to high school. I graduated that year, newly married, with a one-year old on my hip. Though I didn't carry him across the stage to receive my diploma, I did hold him up with one hand and shoot the bird to a camera with another— just to let the naysayers know.

About two years later— when I found out I was pregnant *yet again* — the family never spoke with a consistent voice as to how I should move forward. At the time I needed encouragement and help the most, they only agreed on one thing…

"See, we told you. You've ruined your life."

Turns out, they were right…

… and they were wrong.

. . . .

Kenny was a bum.

There's a verse tucked in the back of the Bible that says, "A man who won't provide for his family is worse than an infidel" (1 Timothy 5:8).

I always tell the beautiful ladies I meet in rehabs (and in other desperate, non-rehab situations alike) that if a man won't rise up, stand with them, and support them *now*, they need to move on. Rather than holding out hope that he'll change— that *you* can perhaps change him— know your worth. Move on.

I should have seen the flags. There were so many red flags waving in my face.

1.   My first red flag with Kenny should have been when, at the age of 23, he was interested in a 16-year old girl. I mean, to put everything in context, sleeping with me was legally statutory rape— and mandatory jail time— in any other context.

2.   The second flag should have been when his parents went to Florida for work, and he moved me and *in utero* Blake into the Walmart camping tent.

3.   The third flag (since they apparently didn't tabulate quick enough in my mind in real time) should have been when I had to secure that rental next to Grandma's— just before Blake was born.

4.   The fourth (I know, so much *always* makes sense in hindsight) should have been when I bought our new family our first home…

Yeah, our first home.

It was a single-wide trailer with a living room on one end and a "big" "master" on the other. In between, down the line, sat a kitchen, a postage-sized bathroom, and two shoebox-sized bedrooms.

It was nothing fancy. Kenny's parents let us park it on their land next to their place. Most of the time, the living room featured a non-working motorcycle that Kenny promised to get running. Sometimes, a non-working engine sat on the kitchen table.

Kenny didn't help much— not with the money nor with baby Blake. In fact, it's almost as if he forgot that when he got married he was supposed to actually take care of his wife and kid AND stop having sex with other women.

I think there's an entire subculture of people who simply act that way. Maybe they just do what they've watched their parents do:

- That's how my Dad treated my Mom.

- That's how all the other men in Mom's life treated her.

- That's how Kenny treated me.

It just seemed "acceptable."

In fact, Kenny's friends acted the same way. Some of them were married; others were dating (even though no one really used language and labels like that). Yet most of them had one thing in common— they all thought they could sleep with me while Kenny was out doing his thing.

Whereas Kenny was always away— not working, mind you— his parents were around and helped a lot. I would not have made it during some of those hard months, I don't think, without them.

In time, with my husband never around, I decided I wanted out.

That was hard for me to reconcile. As irreligious as I acted in that season, and as poor and unsupportive as my great grandmother's "Christian" advice had been about my out-of-wedlock pregnancy, I still had that Biblical foundation. All those supposed "lies" I believed about God loving me, about Him having plans for a hope-filled future, and about Him taking the worst of situations and transforming them into good took hold.

The same book that spouted all of that advice *also* assured me that "God hates divorce" (Malachi 2:16).

And— "The wayward wife doesn't stay at home" (see Proverbs 7:5-27).

Was God going to hate me if I chose to leave a husband who had already left me and only shared a physical mailing address at a home that I purchased with work I did while he did pretty much nothing except work on engines, cheat on me, and make me feel like I was "not enough"?

And would I be the wayward one if I moved on?

I didn't want to repeat the patterns I saw play out in Mom's life. She was three husbands in— and numerous boyfriends— by the time I could legally drive.

Just when I got over the religious clutter about it all, I found out I was pregnant.

"Now I'm really stuck," I told myself. "Two kids. I'm here forever."

The tension with Kenny gradually escalated throughout the pregnancy. It peaked around the time Kimberly was born.

Like the proverbial frog in the kettle— the one you toss in with room temperature water, gradually notching it up a few degrees at a time until, unbeknownst to the amphibian, he begins to bubble up and steam off— I hit my boiling point.

When I went into labor with Kimberly, Kenny was so drunk that his father drove him to the hospital. Finally, he passed out.

I was happy he was there. I was even happier he was "out of it" while he was.

I delivered Kimberly completely naturally— no epidural and no painkillers through 16 hours of hellacious labor— because her heart rate dropped every time they tried to induce. For sure, it's easier to feel your body and know where and when and how to push when the bottom half of you body isn't blocked up by spinal taps, but you also feel *everything*.

I kept silent as a church mouse in Grandma's Baptist meeting hall through each contraction, because I didn't want to awaken Kenny and unleash the Kraken within.

"Scream your way through these contractions," the charge nurse coached. "It will help you find your way through them."

I couldn't make myself do it.

As tears rolled down my cheeks from the pain, I remained quiet. "Please don't wake him up," I cried. "Not even when the baby is born. Just leave him there."

Shortly after they held Kimberly up and laid her on my chest, he woke up. He picked up the hospital phone off the end table and phoned a friend.

"It's a girl this time," he said. "I got one of each, now."

Then, he bolted— back out for a few hours or few days of frivolity. I couldn't decide if I was relieved to have him gone or pissed that he didn't say anything— at all— to me.

No—

- "Congratulations!"

- "I'm proud of you."

- "Wow, I know that was a really long labor."

- "Do you need anything? What can I do for you?"

Nothing.

At that point, I hadn't yet resolved in my mind that I was leaving him. But, it didn't take long until the breaking point came.

One day he walked through the front door of my trailer, tossed his car keys on the counter, and grabbed a tall boy. Somehow I knew he had been out with another woman.

"Do you not realize we're married and you have *two* kids?" I told Kenny.

The mental, emotional, and physical abuse from years of trauma, shame, and abandonment caused me to want to fight. I'm sure we screamed, cussed back and forth, and maybe even put hands on each other.

I'd been punched before. Heck, I had been raped, I had spent the night in abandoned houses, and I had fended for myself and been making major life decisions since I was an elementary aged school girl.

"I've had enough of this," I told myself.

When he left, I packed some of my things, loaded the kids, and I vacated the trailer-home that I had purchased. I went to my Mom's place to stay for the night.

It took Kenny half a week to figure out his wife and kids abandoned ship, because he always left for days at a time. Since I vacated within an hour or so of his latest escapade, it was 72 hours or so before he returned from his latest bender.

· ·

Kenny went looking for me.

This was long before the days of Life 360, smartphone location-sharing, and apps like SnapChat that reveal exactly where you are to trusted friends and family. Flip phones hadn't even made it to the market yet. The few people who owned cell phones carried them like "bricks" they kept in a backpack or gym bag — or they had the actual "briefcase phone" that had to be plugged into the car's cigarette lighter to charge-up. I share that just to let you know that it actually required a little bit of effort to find someone in those days.

Back then, you might call someone and leave a voice mail on an answering machine while they were out. They might not get it until later that evening or sometime the next morning. Then, when they called you back, you might be away...

They might leave another message— or "Star 69" the last caller (you).

This could continue for days until you finally connected. And that was normal.

As you might imagine, the kind of poor people who have money for cheap booze and sell enough drugs to get theirs for free didn't usually have any of those kinds of phones. No brick phone. No landline. No message machine.

Kenny found me in person.

"We need to talk about what's going on," he said.

He ployed as if he wanted closure...

And, whereas he *had been* aggressive before, this time he whined and pined. He knew exactly what to say— and how to say it— in such a way that I would agree.

"Maybe he's changed," I reasoned. "Maybe this was the wake-up call he needed."

Abusers have a way of knowing precisely what to say— and how to reel you in. It's as if they all read the same, sick playbook and then just pass it on to others.

His final pull was something like "You're the best thing that's ever happened to me. I don't want you to leave."

Don't.

Fall.

For.

It.

Like.

I.

Did.

I consented to take the kids to his Mom and Dad's house while Kenny and I went to the Cahaba River. That was a place we often went to party around a campfire with plenty of beer.

Rather than having an intimate conversation that brought us together or moved us towards closure, though, all of Kenny's friends ended-up being there. With the kids taken care of for the night, we partied all evening.

Alcohol flowed.

At some point, the mood shifted. We physically fought. I tried to run down the dirt road, but he caught up to me.

He tossed me into his truck. It wasn't hard to do, because I weighed less than 100 pounds. He drove off before anyone could intervene.

(And it's not like they would have stepped in anyway. Most people didn't stop domestic things like that. They just told people not to do it or said to get them some medical attention. They never really addressed the problem. Everyone felt more obligated to "mind their own business" than they did to help someone in danger.)

Kenny mashed my face into the middle of the front seat and kept my head plastered there by grabbing the hair on the back of my head with his right hand. I was the kind of gal who would jump out of a moving car if I didn't want to be there— as I'll reference again later. With his left, he drove.

And remember, he was lit.

When we got home, I went back into my trailer. I hibernated inside for a few days, so no one would know I was beaten and bruised.

Kenny had his mom watch the kids for a few days— remember, their house was next door to our trailer.

"Watch the kids?" he asked them. "Shannon and I are trying to patch things up, work it out. We need to focus on us for a few days."

They didn't question it, and they never knew to come check on me.

When I was well enough to be seen in public, I decided to revisit my failed escape plan. One afternoon, he said he was going out for a few hours. Knowing "a few hours" might be a literal few hours or a few days, I decided to take immediate action and leave.

I gathered my things. I loaded the kids. We made another exit.

They say the average victim of domestic abuse takes 7-8 tries before leaving for good. And that's actual "leaves"— that's not times she attempts to go and gets caught or gets talked into staying, so she remains. That's actual *exits*.

Something non-victims don't understand is that some sick pull keeps yanking you back. It works a lot like gravity.

- Sometimes, they say the "right thing" that makes you believe this is *the magical time* everything falls in line and they change.

- Other times you're so *desperate to keep your family together*, to not break up your people— married or not— that you push through.

- Then there are those *layers of religion* and the negativity you've heard in the past...

- The *fear of starting all over* on your own.

- The embarrassment and *shame*.

- The *sunk cost* of the time and energy you wasted when you could have been doing something else (including all the other times you left and went back)— and now that you've invested so much time and energy it feels like a bigger loss to throw all of that way.

- And a list of other thoughts that cluster in your mind, captivating you just enough to *second-guess the decision* to stay gone once you are gone.

- Plus, *there's the reality that people do actually change*. You hold out hope that maybe— just maybe— your person is one of the people who do.

I filed for divorce this time, and that was the end of it.

4. Why Good Girls Go Back to Bad Men (S)

5. The Malcom Luck (R)

Rob's mom and the hobos, Rob's brother thinks they're rich (and they almost were), luck is often hard work in disguise

---

I was 7 years old— first grade— when I saw my first homeless person. Actually, it was a group of homeless people, and they were at my house.

Our home in Shreveport, Louisiana backed-up to a train track. I don't know where the tracks came from, and I have no idea where they went. All I knew was *not* to cross the fence that separated our yard from them— because trains can hurt.

Oh, and trains carry hobos.

Though originally a slang term for migrant workers, people who criss-crossed the country to look for work (generally by jumping on a cargo train without paying), the word *hobo* eventually denoted anyone who looked homeless. Shreveport had a lot of them.

Hobos gathered *en masse* on our front porch, and my mother— everyone called her PK (her real name was Patsy Karen, but PK seemed to fit her personality better and it was faster and easier to say)— *invited* it. I remember stepping over them as I walked into the house from school.

Some sipped Mom's lemonade— she poured it from one of the plastic Tupperware pitchers like everyone had in the late 70s and early 80s. Others ate her tuna sandwiches.

Every single one of them stunk, but we didn't care. Mom certainly didn't. She just loved people— all people— and interpreted every encounter she had as a divine invitation to tell someone about Jesus.

So, yes, they ate the food and drank the lemonade, but they talked with her while they ate...

Now, she didn't force feed Jesus on them before letting them eat or drink like some church and religious groups did. She made certain while they visited, though, they heard about God's grace.

I'm not sure when the hobos started showing up. There were a lot of commercial buildings, supply houses, and stores near our house. The strip of trees and bushes behind us, between the fence and the tracks, provided them with a great place to camp and find cover.

It wasn't odd to see a few tents sprung up one day and then gone a day or two later... or to see a sleeping bag (or what might look like a make-shift sleeping bag) hanging over our fence. As far back as I remember, they were there.

Mom's friends often asked, "PK, are you sure you're OK with all those homeless people hanging around? You don't know where they're from or what they're up to..."

"Sure, I do," she might reply. "The woman you saw me talking to earlier"— because many of them were women; it's a mistake to think all homeless people are men— "is Susan. She came from St. Louis, and she's headed to Texas. She's got a son named..."

"That's not what I'm talking about, PK. You don't know what they've been into, what kind of people they are."

Mom honestly didn't care what "kind of people." She just saw *people*— God's people. And as soon as she met them and knew their stories, they were no longer strangers.

By the time I graduated high school, Mom worked at the Bible College in Birmingham. The Malcom Luck had run its course, so Dad moved us back just before I started 9th grade.

On the weekends and during the holidays, it was common for 5 or more college students who couldn't make it to their house to join us for a meal or even crash at our place.

Hobos and college students are a lot alike. They don't have much money, they rotate the same 2 or 3 outfits, and they're always agreeable to eating your food...

Mom might have 3 different kinds of homemade pies— and warm cookies— spread across the kitchen table for just a handful of college co-eds. Or, rather than walking across hobos on the front porch it might be a smattering of sleeping bags and assorted blankets and pillows stretched across the living room floor.

No one ever spent a holiday— or even a weekend— alone by choice.

Anyway, that's getting ahead of the story...

Before Shreveport we lived in Kinder, a tiny single traffic light town in South Louisiana. Work had dried up in Birmingham, and Dad had a friend who owned a farm.

"Come on down. I'll show you how to drive the combines through the rice fields. You can work for me."

Always one to do whatever it takes, Dad did that for a few years until an even better opportunity opened. He learned about an oil & gas company that needed men to go knock on doors...

That meant a move to Shreveport.

One night over dinner, my Mom asked, "What are you going to be doing?"

"I told you, PK, I'll be a land man. The geologists figure out where the oil and gas is located, I go meet the people who own the land, and I see if they'll sign a contract with us to place a pump on their property."

Technically, Dad's statement was half-true. I mean, he thought it was *completely true* at the time, but the geologists couldn't necessarily guarantee there was oil or gas underneath that dirt. After running all of their tests, it was simply a best guess— "There's *probably a good chance that oil might be here*" would have been a more accurate statement. That meant, at the same time, "There's probably a good chance that there's not any oil anywhere near here at all."

Dad was great with people. Like PK (everyone called Mom), he had no problem talking to a complete stranger about anything, and he always set people at ease.

He took the job and began criss-crossing the State of Louisiana, knocking on doors.

To be fair, Dad didn't know the first thing about geology and oil contracts. The owner hired him because he liked him.

Always a grinder, Dad got promoted by paying attention to the unnecessary details and by serving others. He arrived at the tan and brown office early every morning. The suite was located in a "high-rise" building in downtown Shreveport, on the 5th floor.

I'm not sure how tall the building actually was. When you're a kid, the 5th floor might as well be the top of the world. Especially when it's decorated in pure hunting lodge decor— elk heads, mounted fish, even a full standing bear. If there's an animal people hunt, it was stuffed and mounted in that office.

Due to the predominance of Bambi, we referred to the space as "the deer head office."

"We must be rich!" my little brother observed, taking it all one day as we rode the escalator up.

It's all a matter of perspective, I suppose...

Anyway, *every morning* Dad arrived early and made the Maxwell House or Folgers before anyone else showed up, turned on all the lights, and had the deer head office ready to rock for the day. As others pulled up, they filled the under-sized styrofoam cups and topped off their over-sized thermoses and got to work.

One morning, the owner arrived early. He had no idea all of this happened in the background. Dad— Lyn— was already there working through his normal routine.

"Shit!" the owner exclaimed, as he meandered his way around the half-metal-half-Formica desks. "We already have coffee!"

"Yeah, pour yourself some," Dad said.

"There's no one else here," the man observed. Then, he connected all the dots— "Lyn, are you the one who makes the coffee every morning and gets all this stuff ready?"

Dad almost didn't tell him, but the owner persisted...

"You've been doing it haven't you? I wondered how all of this happened."

"Yes, sir. I get here early and make it."

The man forgot about whatever work caused him to get to the deer head office early that morning. He sat down and talked with my Dad for a while— for a solid hour or so— before anyone else arrived.

He liked Dad's work ethic, as well as his humility.

A few weeks later he approached Dad with something like "I'd like to send you to a training event over in Atlanta. And I'll start giving you some more responsibilities around here. When you get back, it'll be more money, of course."

He never really had to set an appointment with Dad, because he always knew when and where to find him— in the deer head office, before anyone else even thought about showing up. By the time most of the employees had finished taking their morning shower, Dad had been working for at least 30 minutes to an hour.

Mom (PK) was a lover; Dad (Lyn) was a grinder. That doesn't mean PK didn't work hard, and it doesn't mean Lyn didn't love. It's just that, well, those are two of the strengths I remember about each of them.

Within three years Dad was the vice president of the company and reported only to the boss. Moreover, the owner presented him a special profit-sharing offer.

"How would you like to receive a portion of every hole that hits oil or gas?" he asked.

"What do you mean?"

The owner clarified, "Well, the geologists speculate about where the oil and gas is— and where all these underground reservoirs and arteries might be. Then, we contract with the land owner to place a pump there. They don't pay for that— the company does. If we hit, they get some of the proceeds and we get some of the proceeds. I'm offering you a chance to invest on the front end, so you can receive some of the profits off the back. What do you think?"

"That sounds very gracious," Lyn replied. "I think I will."

Dad invested in every single hole from that point forward.

I remember traveling with him as a preteen during the summer. As Mom fed and watered the hobos, we zoomed across the area— sometimes going as far away as Laurel, Mississippi. We slept in roadside motels, chomped on pepperoni pizza, and knocked on doors.

One hundred percent of the holes Dad invested in…

… were dry.

No oil.

No gas.

Nothing.

Nothing but dirt, that is.

And then this happened…

In the early 80s, consumers grew anxious about their carbon footprint. They didn't use that term back then, but that's what it was. All this environmental stuff… is nothing new.

Major auto manufacturers even began creating electric vehicles— which oil companies promptly paid lobbyists to manipulate congressmen to squash. In the wake of the hydrocarbon hysteria, oil prices began dropping.

Around 1986, right as Dad and I were bouncing around Louisiana and Mississippi, OPEC (the Organization of Petroleum Exporting Countries) dropped their prices AND increased their production. They made Middle-Eastern oil plentiful, AND they made it cheap.

The fore-runners of today's environmentalists continued driving their gas guzzling cars, and American oil took a hit.

With all the wells coming up dry in Dad's territory, and with the extreme availability of cheap gas rolling in from overseas, the deer head business model no longer made sense.

Dad told his boss, "I've got to find something else to do and take care of my family. I've got three kids."

"Can you hold on just a little bit longer, Lyn? I really think something is gonna hit. There's GOT to be oil or gas in this area *somewhere*. The speculators and geologists cannot be wrong 100% of the time."

"They have been so far," Dad replied. "I don't blame you at all. This was a great opportunity. I'm grateful that you gave me a shot." Then, after a moment— "If I was a single man, I'd stay here and keep trying. But I've got to consider PK and the kids."

"How about one more? I've got a lead on a possibility over in Mississippi. Can you just check that one? Just one more…"

Lyn considered it for about half a minute. It was a long half-minute.

"I can't," he finally answered. "I have a chance to pick back up in Birmingham…"

Dad told me the boss *begged* him to do it.

True to his conviction, Dad told him, "This just isn't providing for the family. So I'm going to have to pass."

The owner hugged my Dad, and they parted ways. Then, a few weeks later, the owner himself traveled to visit the land owner where the geologist thought a well *might* hit.

Turns out…

It did.

It does.

That well still pumps today.

The boss at the deer head office was right. The scouts weren't wrong 100% of the time. Eventually, they hit. And when they do, they hit big.

If Dad took just one more job, his entire financial outlook would have changed, and we probably never would have made it back to Birmingham. That means you wouldn't be reading this story right now. Or, at least, it would be very different.

"It's just the Malcom Luck!" Dad called it.

Anytime anything didn't roll our way— getting passed over for a promotion, getting hit in a fender bender by someone driving without insurance, or even getting a seat you saved taken by someone while you stepped away to go to the restroom— we referred to it (and still do) as the Malcom Luck.

We don't voice it with regret and trepidation. We laugh about it.

5. The Malcom Luck (R)

We talk about it as we linger around the dining table after Christmas. We laugh, even now, when something off-the-wall and unexpected happens.

Sometimes, life is just the Malcom Luck.

Application for Part 2 | Learn from the Leaders

Main idea: Look ahead— not behind— while searching for the wisdom you need for the next win. Yes, learn from your mistakes, but also seek instruction from people who are currently where you want to be.

When they first started renovating homes, Rob and Ben recognized they didn't need to learn everything from scratch. Others had already figured out many of the lessons (see chapter 3).

Yes, experience is a great teacher.

But experience also costs you one of your most valuable resources, *time*.

So, learn from the experiences of others who are ahead of you when possible.

Below, write a few things:

- Define the skills you need to know.

- Who do you know that already has proven expertise in these areas?

- Who do they know they might introduce you to?

_____

_____

_____

_____

_____

_____

_____

_____

_____

Are there books, courses, conventions, or workshops you should plan to attend?

If you cannot yet afford to pay for coaching, begin budgeting money to save for it while accessing free content (podcasts, videos, etc.), and cheap content (books, mini-courses).

Where are some of the resources you should access right now?

_____

_____

_____

_____

_____

_____

_____

_____

_____

_____

_____

_____

_____

_____

Your past is not a predictor of your future as long as you turn the page and create subsequent chapters (see Shannon's story in chapter 4).

Which parts of your past— no matter how big or small— do you need to "turn the page" on?

List them here.

_____

_____

_____

_____

_____

_____

_____

_____

To access leaders, do what leaders do. So far, we've learned that Lyn created a large wallpaper company by showing up to the supply store early every morning and having a "happenstance" meeting (see chapter 3). We also saw him arrive at the deer head office early (chapter 5), which created unplanned and unhurried space to connect with the boss.

What are some unique ways you can "go where leaders go" and "do what leaders do" by getting in the same room as them?

_____

_____

_____

_____

_____

_____

_____

_____

_____

_____

_____

_____

_____

_____

_____

Part 3 | You are the Common Factor

Wherever you go, there you are. Whereas we want to blame circumstances or others for many of our shortcomings, without denying that outside factors do affect us, we must remember that we are the common denominator in all of our past, present, and future experiences. Rather than focusing on what we can't control, we must look at what we can— ourselves.

6. I Can (Almost) Do Good All by Myself (S)

Shannon becomes a functional alcoholic, she realizes you can be a victim and the victimizer, the top producer flames out

---

Newly single mom, two tiny kids in tow, I resolved not to go back to my trailer. And, I never did.

I was working at a big medical insurance company at that time, making solid money. I was in medical billing/coding, working in the office all the days I wasn't hiding the hurt.

And I was productive.

I was so productive, in fact, that my bonus checks were more than my actual salary checks. I worked super-fast and super-hard, and the insurance company paid me well to make sure that they didn't payout one more cent for your medical bills than they were contractually obligated to pay.

You read that right.

Think about what they did— what they still do. They pay people like me (people who drink so much alcohol that they get the shakes by 9:00am and need to sneak to the restroom to grab a drink) to make health decisions. Moreover, these companies find it more financially lucrative to dole incentive payments than to just pay your bills.

Sick. It's just more crud from people you are supposed to trust to take care of you who, end of the day, consistently look out for themselves.

I stopped drinking and smoking and everything else during my pregnancies. Well, I did as soon as I knew. I didn't know I was pregnant with Kimberly for a few months, but then I cut it off immediately.

After the kids were born, I always boomeranged back to my old ways of numbing the pain.

While I worked at the insurance company, I met a guy named Poe. That was technically his last name, but it's the one he went by.

When he and I hooked up, I was already drinking, smoking, and using pot. He introduced me to cocaine... and, eventually, crack. (In case you don't know, crack— often called crack cocaine or "rock" is the version of cocaine you smoke. It creates a shorter but more intense boost.)

Poe and I mostly partied on the weekends. That's when I used the drugs. During the week I became an "everyday drinker," sipping alcohol in the same way the average person drinks water, soda, or sweet tea.

We were together a few years before we split. In hindsight, it truly had more to do with me than him because I pivoted and began treating the men in my life in the same way the men I knew had been treating me and other women.

"If it's good for the goose, it's good for the gander," the saying goes.

Why do men get a pass to sleep around and women get shamed for the same?

Why does a guy get a trophy for sleeping with someone's wife or girlfriend, but a woman gets labeled a *home-wrecker* or *whore?*

I started dating other guys *while* I dated Poe. When I did, I removed all the restraints.

(Shortly after having Kimberly, I had my tubes tied. I worked at the medical insurance company and had great coverage. Rationalizing that a tube-tie is far cheaper than a pregnancy, a delivery, and years of insurance for another human, most insurance companies gladly pay 100% for that procedure. I chose to do it, because I didn't think I would ever escape Kenny. Once I made my way out, though, it became my license to sleep with whoever I wanted, whenever I desired, without worrying about another pregnancy. Plus, back then no one worried about STDs and emotional baggage— they just slept around.)

For instance—

- One night I brought another, older man to the house that I shared with Poe— with no regard as to whether or not Poe might be home or walk in on us.

- Other nights I left him at home and went to the pool hall, leaving my kids with him while I went to numb the pain.

It wasn't uncommon for me to walk up to a strange man, swap names, and then state "I'm taking you home with me tonight."

Or— "Wanna hook up after this game?"

I was a mess.

I started picking fights, and I continued the promiscuity. It was all an attempt to feel something— *anything.* Of course, all of it demonstrates more about the condition of my soul than anything else. Poe was a genuinely nice man

— even if hooked on cocaine— who sincerely cared for me and my young kids.

....

Shortly after Poe and I broke up, I became a blackout drunk.

"I'm concerned about you," he confessed. "There are nights you're not even sure how you're getting home— people just carry you to the car and take you home. Something could happen..."

He didn't get it, I don't suppose.

Something already *had happened* to me. My life was one big episode of "this happened to me" and "so, what, because no one gives a crap about it."

Remember, there were seasons in my life in which I was clearly the victim.

- Mom's third husband molested me when I was 11-13.

- The guy raped me at 14.

- Kenny abused me, and many of his friends forced me into non-consensual sex (perhaps some was consensual if you consider drunk-sex consensual).

Aside from all that, there were other forms of abuse, too. The abandonment and being forced to fend for yourself and "can you stay at a friend's house or just find your way to an abandoned building?" moments that became more the norm than the exception...

But— and this is super-important for you to see (because you might relate, if you're honest with yourself about your past situations)— *I also victimized others*. Not only was I hurt, but I also hurt others.

Life is more complex than just "black and white." Most of life exists in lots of shades of grey— even shades we don't know yet.

So, yes, I was a victim. People did things to me they never should have done.

I was also the victimizer. I did a lot of bad things that hurt a lot of people— even people I didn't know and won't ever see.

And the anger I directed at my sister and my mother.

And my kids— who embraced me with open arms.

Part of moving forward is realizing that you are the consistent factor in every chapter of your past, good and bad. You can't move forward— and step into the full potential of your story— until you admit that, yes, this is YOUR story. You remain the constant.

You are the good and the bad, the victim and the victimizer alike.

Once you own *all of that*, you can find healing. And when you find healing, you not only help yourself move forward, you also serve so many others who find themselves stuck in the same tricks and traps that snagged and ensnared you in your own past.

One day, Poe proposed a wager...

"I bet you can't make it through one whole day without drinking."

"Sure, I can."

I knew I was lying to myself. There's no possible way I could get through. I drank beer while the kids ate their cartoon-character cereals.

Poe knew it was a lie, too.

"I call *bullshit* on your answer," he replied. Then— "Take a day off work. You've got some vacation time and PTO [paid time off] built up. Let's spend the entire day together— me, you, and the kids. We'll just hang out."

Now, some people might look at this and contend it was a ploy to get me back— that I was falling for the abuser trap again, letting a guy lure me back in after leaving him in the rearview mirror. This clearly wasn't that, though. First, Poe never dishonored me in anyway. And, he genuinely cared for me and the kids.

The biggest problem— and the reason it couldn't ever work out between us — was because I didn't love myself. I didn't even know I *should* love myself.

(Even Jesus presumed we would love ourselves. "The greatest commandment," He said in Mark 12:30-31, "is to love the Lord your God with all your heart, with all your soul, with all your mind, and with all your strength… and *to love your neighbor as yourself.*" Christians know it as the Great Commandment— and there it is, in red letters. *Love yourself.*)

I kept the kids home from school and daycare the next day.

I called-in. Took the day off work.

Poe drove over and got us. We went to the park, walked around, did some other stuff that all became a blur…

I got nauseous. I got the shakes. I became spiteful and angry and vented against him from mid-morning until late afternoon when he dropped us back home.

"Shit," I said. "I have a problem."

That was the first time I admitted it.

I hallucinated. I broke into a cold sweat. I developed a migraine.

I gave up, and put the kids into the bathtub and had them in bed at 6:00pm.

"It's still light outside," they said.

It didn't matter. I was too far gone.

The oddity here is that Poe is the one who got me started using cocaine. Even a drug addict— that's what he was— saw that I had crossed a line, though. If he hadn't called it out, I likely wouldn't be here today.

....

The following day I took the kids to their daycare / school. I drove to work, still reeling from the quick detox— that's what my body was doing.

I didn't feel right, so I walked to the on-site nurse's office as soon as I arrived at the medical insurance company where I worked.

She got bug-eyed when she saw me.

"Sit down, honey. Here…"

I sincerely don't remember anything that happened after that— until I woke up in a hospital.

"You had a seizure," the nurse said.

Another added, "It was an alcohol withdrawal induced response, it seems."

The insurance company said I couldn't return to work until I completed a 30-day inpatient rehab program. They even offered to cover it. It was included in my employee insurance program, of course— because it's more cost-effective to cover that than to pay for all the medical bills and lawsuits and everything else that could flair up from something like my Dad's drunk-driving collision a decade and a half earlier.

That said, I countered with the company.

6. I Can (Almost) Do Good All by Myself (S)

"I can't take off 30 days," I told them. "I'm a single mom. I don't have anywhere to leave my kids at night. I can't do in-patient."

It was half-honest, half-weaseling. My Mom and my sister probably would have kept the kids. In fact, in the near future, Blake lived with my Mom and Kimberly bunked with my sister.

"We'll let you do out-patient," they agreed.

At that point, I saw that *what they really wanted* was for me to tap out— to quit. But, like any insurance company they simply ran the risk ratios and realized the numbers suggested the percentages stacked better for them if they didn't fire me but let me either "fire myself" or just stop showing up.

I completed my 30-day stint, and they stopped giving me those fat bonus checks.

They also denied me every time I came up for promotion.

And, even though it was probably more "in my head" than reality, I consistently felt like everyone watched me— that everyone judged every single move I made. A lot of single mothers probably *already* feel that, but add a 30-day rehab run in there…

"Where's Shannon?" I envisioned…

And what were they gonna say?

"Oh, she's at the beach."

Or— "She's _____."

There's no good way to explain an enforced month-long vacation from a place of employment— especially when you've been one of the top producers. I stayed sober for about ten months, but I resigned in the process.

7. Tricked Into Christmas (R)

Rob illustrates why gas stations make you pay in advance, he discovers you can't outrun your problems, and he "enjoys" a strange birthday celebration

---

I sold drugs when I was in high school, but I wasn't a very good dealer. The best dealers know not to touch the stash, because you might get hooked. Plus, even if you don't, you still cut into the profits AND you don't keep a clear mind. It's hard to run a business— and bad things happen— when you can't keep it clean and clear.

I always bought enough ecstasy to fill a freezer bag. They called it MDMA in those days and sold it in powder-like form.

One day, I loaded the clear gel capsules from GNC and sold them at the beach to make enough money to fund my drinking while my buddy Chris and I were there.

In case you don't know, MDMA is often called ecstasy. In addition to the powder, MDMA can be found in tablet form, and can even be stamped with logos or created in various colors to look like candy. It's considered a "club drug" and is often mixed with alcohol or other substances like marijuana.

MDMA affects the brain cells which release serotonin— a chemical which counteracts depression (among other things). MDMA can causes feelings of euphoria, sexual arousal (think: party drug, group sex), and cause a person to release their inhibitions...

That said, I kept a little ecstasy for me, moved the rest, and funded the trip. It was fairly easy to do when you don't mind staying in cheap motels and you don't eat much.

I jumped into a 3-day party with perfect strangers. I woke up one morning on the beach, having apparently gotten jumped and beat up the night before.

My money was gone.

My MDMA disappeared.

The only thing remaining were the clothes I wore and my car keys. Whoever jumped me probably would have taken those if they knew where I parked. Or maybe they realized most stolen cars are eventually tracked down...

"How in the hell am I going to get back to Birmingham?" I wondered.

I walked towards my 1981 Cutlass Supreme. It was a silver four-door with a blue ragtop, double-tinted black windows, and a diesel engine. Even though I had no idea where I was, that car was always easy to locate.

"What happened to you?" Chris yelled, as I approached the vehicle.

He was stretched across the hood and the front windshield, laying back on a towel.

"I don't know. I just woke up, and this is all I had left," I said, holding up my keys.

I got into the car and cranked it. It always blew a puff of black smoke when it started.

POOF!

Engine running, I rolled down the window. They were so dark you really needed to roll them down to see where you were going if the space was tight. If you didn't, you were just kinda guessing as to whether or not you were gonna bump anything. That car was a land yacht.

"We don't have any gas left," I sighed.

Chris leaned over and eyed the gauge.

"Nada. Down to vapors," he observed.

"No shit, Sherlock."

I wasn't happy about the gas, I wasn't pleased with the black eye, and I was pissed about my stash.

"I'll figure it out," Chris said.

After a few seconds of thought, I told him, "Already have."

Since the mid-90s, gas stations all over the country have insisted you pay at the pump (a prospect that became easier once debit cards got more popular) or pay in advance. I'm one of the reasons why you can no longer fill the tank up, see how much it takes, and then walk in and pay your bill like everyone did in the 80s. I helped eliminate the honor system.

"I'm going to keep the car running," I told Chris. Then, as I turned into the nearby Exxon, "You get out and pump the gas. Keep your door open. I'm gonna watch the guy behind the counter. Put the nozzle back when it's full, but don't get back in until I tell you. Just act like you're still pumping gas…"

Chris topped the tank and then gave me the signal.

I looked into the little station-store and waited until a new customer approached the counter, someone with a load of drinks and snacks.

"OK, now," I shouted. "They're looking at other things and they've got too many people lined up to leave the booth…"

We rolled off at normal speed. Go too slow, and you get caught. Leave too fast, and you just draw everyone's attention your way.

A few miles down the road, we finally looked to each other about the same time. I checked the rearview mirror again— for good measure.

"Easy peasy, Mr. Greasy," I laughed. "A successful heist."

....

Chris and I talked about the Marine Corp on the way back. We'd discussed it before. Back in those days, recruiters had a free pass to basically show up at high schools throughout the week, set up their tables, and actively push the military on juniors and seniors who hadn't already made up their minds where they were headed next. Outfitted in their dress blues, the uniformed men always looked impressive.

Moreover, they were just a few years older than the kids in high school. It wasn't uncommon to bump into the recruiters at weekend parties, some of them funneling as much as a case of beer at a time.

"Maybe we should join," I surmised. "Getting beat up and left on the beach isn't working too well."

"It would be a steady paycheck. And they obviously have free time to do what they want. Plus," —and this was the understatement of the year— "it doesn't look that hard."

"Yeah, how difficult can it actually be to be a Marine like Rambo?" I said, mumbling something in my best Stallone voice.

The main problem with the Cutlass was the gas mileage. It sucked gas like I consumed alcohol. In other words, it ran its course quick. By the time we hit Montgomery, roughly halfway back to Birmingham, the needle pegged the "E" again.

"Marine Corps or not, we gotta get more gas," I whined. "Next exit I'll pull over."

I rolled off the Interstate, took a strong right into the first gas station I saw, and located the diesel pump. We repeated the same drill. Chris pumped, I watched, and then we rolled off.

This time, we didn't leave the station and pull onto a two-lane road, we merged back onto I-65, a super-wide four-lane freeway that moves ultra-fast. We succeeded in stealing fuel *a second time.*

I dropped Chris off and went straight to our house. I navigated my way to my upstairs bedroom and collapsed on the twin. Remember, I had been partying a few days in Panama City and passed out the final evening— at some point that was likely closer to sunup than sunset. I'd been running hard for almost three straight days.

Mid- afternoon, Dad creaked open the bedroom door, knocking in tandem with the opening motion.

"Rob, wake up."

I didn't budge.

He walked over and tapped me.

"Rob, there's someone here to see you."

Nothing. No movement.

This time he gently shook and talked louder: "Wake up. There's a detective here to see you."

"A detective? What?"

He motioned for me to follow him downstairs. Whereas I was surprised a detective showed up at my house, Dad wasn't alarmed in the least. He was accustomed to the shenanigans and mishaps by then.

It was normal back then for a police officer to knock on our door. Whether they were looking for my brother or for me, police visits followed by crazy stories about the previous 24 hours' escapades were common at the Malcom residence. Chalk it up to more Malcom Luck.

As I walked down the stairs, a plain-clothes policeman asked, "You're Rob Malcom?"

"Yes, sir."

"You were outside of Montgomery earlier today?"

It was a statement of fact posed as a querry, not a fact-finding question.

"Yes, sir."

"That silver Cutlass Supreme outside your car? It's registered to you…"

"Yes, sir."

"A gas station attendant wrote down the tag today. Says you pulled off with a full tank without paying. Did you forget to pay, or do you think you're above other people and don't have to pay?"

"Yes, sir."

"Which one, son?"

By now, I was waking up. I couldn't believe they traveled 90+ miles from Montgomery to Birmingham over a tank of 90 cents a gallon gas. That's what fuel sold for back then.

"I forgot the question, sir. I'm a little confused…"

I confessed to the heist. This was the first theft I ever got caught for. Approximately 17 gallons of diesel fuel— about $15.30 at the retail price.

The officer asked, "You want to explain yourself?"

Recognizing "no" wasn't an acceptable answer at this point, I rushed to find my words.

Dad chimed in: "I'd like to hear…"

"I got jumped the night before…"

I didn't say anything about waking up on the beach after partying for three days straight, my drugs being lifted, and everything except my car keys and the clothes on my back being swiped. I was still in those clothes, by the way, the same ones I wore on the beach. I just skipped all those most relevant parts.

I continued, "I wasn't sure how I was going to get back, so that's when I made the decision."

I didn't even tell them about Chris doing the pumping or the fact he was even there at all.

"Well, the owner said he wouldn't press charges and pursue it legally if you paid up."

"How much?"

It really didn't matter if it was a million dollars or just $15.30. I didn't have any money at all.

"Let's see...."

The detective looked at his notes and gave me a number. I don't even remember what the actual total was— because, again, I didn't have any money. It didn't matter.

After a moment, the officer asked, "So are you paying up or are we taking a ride?"

"I don't have it. I didn't have it then. I don't have it now."

I looked at Dad and shrugged my shoulders. He pulled out his wallet and started counting out the money.

"Just keep the change," he said. "Give it to the owner for the trouble."

I suppose that was back in the days when they didn't worry about chain of custody, paperwork, and all the legalese. For the most part, people— other than people like me, who might drive off with your gas— said what they meant, they followed through on what they said, and everything flowed smoother because of it.

That was in the days when kids played outside all day, Nintendo was an afterthought, reserved mostly for days it rained, and teachers at school spanked kids for infractions as mild as chewing gum, disrespect, and cussing.

It was also a time when parents took the teacher's side against the child and never led with, "My child would never do things like that. He— or she— is a perfect angel. You just have them confused, or— if they did it— you must have provoked it."

Dad had no misconceptions of the kind of teenager I was. The proof was in the number of times he answered the front door for a knocking police officer and how many times he had to pick me up from the local jail.

Dad showed the detective to the door and then told me to go sleep it off. We would talk about it later...

....

The following day (or whenever I woke up— it could have been a few days), I told Chris what happened.

"I'm thinking about enlisting. I mean, MDMA and all of this stuff is so easy to get, and it's great for quick cash, but I just don't think that's the life."

Chris talked about a few of the older Marines we knew. Those guys, only 3-4 years our senior (which, in teenage years, seems like a decade), always looked impressive (there's the word again— *impressive*). They looked strong, they stood tall, and they didn't take shit. They didn't have to— no one ever offered them any.

The next week after school, I headed to the recruiter's office.

"I want to signup," I told him.

"Really? Well let's get your paperwork going..."

I hesitated a second and then offered, "I gotta come clean before I do. I've got a few issues..."

I explained the gas heist to him.

"There's nothing legal going on with it. That's done. It's in the past. But it happened because of a bender at the beach…"

I outlined the details of my addiction, confessing my constant use of cocaine, the fact that I might as well have had alcohol on an IV drip into my aorta, and all the other bull I was into.

"I also take a daily dose of LSD or mushrooms," I confessed.

"Shit," he said, holding the word out and repeating it super-slow. "H-o-l-y-s-h-i-t."

The words sounded cooler coming from a Marine. I knew even *more* that I wanted to be one. They even cuss better.

"When did you get hooked on all of this stuff?" he asked.

I wasn't sure if I should tell him or not. But, knowing they make you take a drug test, that they give you a physical exam, and that they're going to find out all of this stuff anyway, I figured I might as well pull back the curtain.

"Cops are different down here. They're starting to change a little, but you don't get in trouble for all the things. There's almost an acceptable line you can go up to. As long as you don't cross that…"

"What do you mean?" he asked.

I told the recruiter that we quickly learned if we got caught smoking weed or even drinking, the cops definitely pull us over, but they never do the paperwork and take us to jail.

I reminisced about a few specific encounters: "They make you dump the beer out while they watch and then send you on your way. They've done that to us a bunch."

"Really?" he asked. "That's it?"

"Yeah," I continued, "Or, they catch you smoking and then follow you home, knock on the door, and tell your parents. That means you're done for the night."

"No consequence?"

"We discovered that the worst that would happen is that we would lose our weed," I explained. "But, the upside is we can always get more and start over the next night out."

....

Either the recruiter really believed in me, or he was short on his numbers. He allowed me to enlist.

"I'm putting you on waivers," he said.

"Waivers? What is that?"

"Well," he explained, "you told me you had epilepsy as a child. And you're a self-declared alcoholic and drug addict, right?"

"True. I told you I *definitely cannot* pass a piss test right now."

He told me, "You've got to stop using..."

"Forever?"

"Ideally," he continued. "For now, let's set a short term goal of three days or so. Hydrate a lot, and that should give you enough time to piss clean."

Notably, after that short speech, we did a couple of shots of vodka from his desk drawer.

"You ready for that, Hard Charger?" he asked.

(Recruiters referred to recruits as "hard chargers" back then— think of a Marine "hard charging" up a hill.)

I stopped everything except weed. It takes way longer to flush out of your system and— even back then, before they had legal versions of marijuana— it was often accepted and overlooked in some circles.

The day of the test, predictably, the panel for THC popped.

"I'll let you in, anyway," the recruiter said. "Good job on the rest of it."

He signed a few papers, I autographed some things, and then we continued the process. They must have *really* needed guys back then.

I thought joining the Marines might help me outrun my problems.

"Wherever you go, there you are," the saying goes.

I learned the truth of that statement.

....

Our son, Blake, serves in the military today— the Navy. He says they have financial counselors and mental health providers. We had none of that.

In fact, they routinely shamed guys in our platoon at boot camp. The "fat bodies" became the easiest target.

They were the guys who snuck food back from the chow hall or got caught with snacks in their footlockers. The oddest thing about these "fat bodies" is that if you look at the pictures of people today— over thirty years from when I was in the military— the fat bodies just look average or even underweight for today. Culture has gotten so much... unhealthier.

Our sergeants painted two red stripes on the fat bodies' shirts. Spray paint. That way, the people serving in the cafeteria knew to give them less food.

"Here, have some extra mashed potatoes," the guy working the food line might say to someone like me.

It was nothing to see them double-up on the smaller guys. Then, to the fat body, he might offer just a half scoop. Or even take some off his plate and put it on mine or some other smaller guy's tray right there where everyone could see exactly what they were doing.

One day a fat body snuck food back to the barracks. The drill instructor either heard about it or saw it— I don't remember which.

"Oh, you guys want to act like fuckin' dogs in here!" he yelled.

He continued rambling for a few minutes— like they always do in the movies — and added a bunch of words I wouldn't even know how to repeat. He kicked guys' shit around, slammed a few doors, tossed some crap on the floor.

"Tell you what," another instructor added. "Since you guys want to act like dawgs in here, " (he said it different from the first guy), "I'll just let you be dawgs..."

They made us strip down to our underwear and face each other in two straight lines. Again, you've probably seen soldiers line up like this in a movie scene— in *Platoon* or a film like that.

The first commanded, "On the ground. Cracks to concrete."

They made us crab crawl around like animals. Half of us were trying not to laugh, which added to the intensity of the entire situation. If the drill instructors saw anyone laugh they always trained us twice as hard.

But how are you supposed to react to grown men rambling around in their underwear?

They did strange shit like this all the time at Paris Island— where I went for boot camp. You're considered a recruit until you graduate boot camp. Make it through, and you become "one of the few, the proud, the Marines." At this point, I was still a recruit.

....

On Christmas Eve one of the sergeants walked through the barracks acting *extremely* nice— *way too nice* for their normal demeanor. Something seemed off.

"Merry Christmas," he said. "Ho, ho, ho!"

Somebody replied, "Merry Christmas, sir."

"Would you girls like a Christmas tree?" the Heavy asked.

(The Heavy was the enforcer in the group. Think good-cop-bad-cop.)

"Sir, yes, sir" a few of the Marines yelled.

"What about the rest of you? Would YOU like a Christmas tree?"

Every man in the barracks chimed in this time: "Sir, yes, sir!"

"Grab your moon beams and follow me outside."

(A moon beam is just a flashlight.)

I thought he might lead us to find a boxed tree we could assemble and set up— or that they might have even placed one in the mess hall.

As we continued marching beyond all the buildings I considered that *maybe* we were going to find and cut down a tree. My suspicions seemed more likely when he stopped us in front of a group of pines, some of them rising 50 feet or more.

"You recruits like this one in the middle?"

"Sir, yes, sir!

I started looking around for an ax or a saw of some sort. Nada.

Sergeant Carter— that was his real name, just like the Sarge on Gomer Pyle — pulled a few of us out of the group. Rather than chopping *down* that tree, he insisted we climb *up* it.

"Spread out and turn this way so all the recruits who want to see a Christmas tree can see!" he shouted.

Yes, he put us IN the tree to be the ornaments and the lights on that 50+ foot pine.

"Turn on those moon beams!"

I thought that was the end of it, that the Drill Instructor had his fill of fun. He was only beginning.

We could all smell the alcohol on the DI's breath— that was nothing new. We weren't going to say anything about it, of course. This was a different level altogether, though— all of them were lit!

Around Thanksgiving, mothers and wives and girlfriends started mailing holiday cards and sending care packages to the base. Rather than sharing those items with the Marines as they arrived, Sarge saved them until Christmas Eve— after the Christmas tree incident. They had been holding them for such a time as this.

He ordered us to sit on the floor— like the Last Supper painting by DaVinci.

We looked at each other as if to silently say "What the fuck is this?"

He invited the Drill Instructor to bring *all* the bags and boxes into the barracks and then dumped piles of cookies and candy on the floor in front of us. He had the "house mouse" help.

(The mouse is a helper, hand-picked by the staff. He inspects barracks, gets everyone prepared, and works as somewhat of a liaison between the DI team and the recruits. He's half-hated and half-adored, because he exists in an odd "no man's land" status.)

"Eat up, recruits. All of it. Eat every single bit of it!"

"Sir, yes, sir!"

We began reaching and munching, fast at first and then... as time wore on and we realized how much food was actually there— and how difficult it is to continue chomping on sugary snacks— slow. Very slow.

"Grab some water!" he ordered. "Go fill those canteens to wash it down."

We ran straight to the head— the bathroom— and filled our matte green water bottles from the bathroom sinks.

"You gotta finish all of this food!" The DI screamed.

Amidst shouts of "sir, yes, sir" recruits continued chowing and drinking, stuffing cookies and cake down their "pie hole."

About five minutes into this, the Heavy ordered, "Line up!"

We arranged ourselves in two rows, facing each other, just like we always did when receiving this order.

"Silence!" he yelled. "It's a silent night tonight," he added, making a reference to the most famous Christmas carol of them all. "It's baby Jesus' birthday and all."

As we stood there trying to swallow the giblets of food in our mouths, continued, "Ready… drink!"

He demanded we finish *all the water* in our bottles. We had to hold them upside down to prove they were empty.

"Better not be a drop left!"

Then he ordered us to fill them— and drink all of the water— a second time. Again, we had to prove it, and if anything dripped, we had to start over.

At some point, the Heavy suggested— no, he ordered— us to sing *Silent Night*.

We began, "Silent Night, Holy Night, All is calm, all is bright. Round yon vir-r-gin, mother and child, holy infant…"

None of us knew more than two lines, so we just sang those on repeat. We were an over-fed, out-of-tune, broken record.

The order came again, "Fill 'em up!"

We ran, returned to the lines, and waited.

"Now drink up!"

Then, another added, "Don't forget to sing *Happy Birthday* to Jesus!"

Amidst demands to sing louder, orders to hold up our canteens to prove they were empty, and suggestions about the lyrics to *Silent Night*, we found ourselves running back to the head.

The third time, recruits began vomiting. Plus, there's nothing like the sight of barf to make other people barf. Men everywhere began blowing the groceries they'd just eaten.

Happy birthday, Jesus…

Indeed, happy birthday.

··

I graduated bootcamp.

I went to several places, bumping my way through various training programs…

I was originally slated to go into Air Traffic Control. But, the stakes in that job are incredibly high. I was one of the few they didn't quite know what to do with, because we couldn't get our addictions under control.

I got assigned to El Toro— a now closed Marine Corps Air Station just outside of Los Angeles.

The change of scenery— a different side of the country (or even a completely different nation, at times), a new city, a new schedule— did nothing for my addiction. In fact, some of the places I lived (like California) probably amplified those addictions because of the quick availability to so much more.

The government paid us on the 1st and the 15th. By the 3rd and the 17th, we were all broke. We accumulated nothing (except memories and baggage) for the future.

8. Mayhem in Marshall, But I'm a Good Mom (S)

Shannon aspires to be a pool shark, she learns to stay awake for up to a week at a time, and she makes two tough career moves.

"Change the people and the places," they tell you in rehab.

That is, don't go where you used to go, and don't hang with the people you used to hang with.

"If you don't," they say, "it's only a matter of time until you relapse."

Turns out, they're right.

After I quit the medical insurance job, I had more time to hang at the pool hall. Gabriel's— that was the name. Just like the arch-angel that announced Jesus' birth. This place wasn't sent from Heaven, though. It came straight from hell.

I joined a pool league at the bar, even while trying to stay sober. I was good, so most people wanted me on their team. I had been playing since I was a little girl, well before I slept on friends' couches and in abandoned houses.

Back when Daddy taught me how to play (and helped me reach the table by standing on milk crates), he made bets with his drunk friends. I wanted to be as good as I remember him being.

When Daddy died, all the people he played against and the partiers from the honky-tonks attended the funeral. The line to the casket was long; the funeral parlor was packed.

"I want to be respected like that," I thought.

Anyway...

I jokingly tell people, "I won my second husband in a game of pool."

One evening, during play, he watched me closely.

"If I win," he said, "I get to buy you dinner." He added— "If you win, you can call whatever you want."

"Fair enough," I replied. "If I win you're coming home with me..."

"Deal."

Mark and I— that was his name— shook on the bet.

I won.

He fulfilled his obligation and came to my house afterwards.

He never left.

I white-knuckled my sobriety through this "new" relationship all the way until I earned my one year chip.

"Let's go celebrate!" Mark suggested.

He took me to a big party. After drinking enough to catch a buzz, he introduced me to methamphetamines as a prize for my progress. Yes, I celebrated clean time by partying.

The irony.

Mark and I had a strange connection. I could literally *feel* him when something happened. It truly felt like a soulmate connection.

Though the thought of that sounds inviting to some ladies, he became more and more paranoid— as if he was clinically paranoid schizophrenic. His addiction overtook him, such that everything I thought I wanted in a man morphed into the personification of Satan himself.

- His addiction overtook his capacity to trust me or be trustworthy himself.

- His addiction overpowered his ability to function throughout the day.

- His addiction overrode his certainty about what he actually saw in reality as opposed to what he thought happened.

And when you *feel* everything they feel, you feel *everything* they feel…

....

He took me and the kids to Waskom, Texas— where he's from. Waskom is a small city near Marshall, which is probably the largest of the small cities in the area you can actually find on a map. If you leave Birmingham (where we live) and head west on I-20, it's about 3.5 hours to Jackson, Mississippi and about 3.5 more hours to Shreveport, Louisiana (and the deer head office I would later hear about) and about 3.5 more hours to Dallas, Texas. Waskom is in that last third— and sits about an hour west of Shreveport, just as you cross over the line into the Lone Star State, slap-out in the middle of nowhere.

When we arrived to our new "home," I learned Mark used to be mixed up with a motorcycle gang. Much like Sons of Anarchy, this tightly knit group of insiders ran drugs, used women, and said "to hell" with just about everything else. I was living the— just a made up name— Mayhem of Marshall.

My dream man turned into the devil, and that became our life for the next few years. I *felt* it all.

I lost a lot of time to drugs.

I don't just mean I "lost time" in the sense that I spent the years doing something destructive rather than productive (and, besides, later I learned that God truly does redeem that lost time), I mean that many of those moments just seem to have disappeared.

Mark got paranoid— and unsafe.

I, in turn, became hyper-vigilant.

Due to my past, I already lived more "on alert" than most people. That's one of the signs of post traumatic stress. When trauma occurs somewhere in the past, your default mode of living forward becomes always looking for the next crisis— and making sure you protect yourself and your loved ones from every perceivable threat. Some of those threats are real; others are just imagined.

In the same way you get woozy when you watch someone climb a tall building on television or "jump" when you watch a scary movie and know that

Freddie is about to slaughter someone… even though you are completely OK in both scenarios, your brain doesn't differentiate the real from the unreal, the imminent from the impossible. It tosses you towards panic-mode.

You develop a hyper-alert, adrenaline-driven way of living. You can stay awake for days at a time— especially when you add speed and other "uppers" to the blend of your emotional overload.

At the height of his paranoia Mark screwed every window in the house closed. He placed Radio Shack security cameras everywhere he could think of— both inside and outside. He installed key-lock-only deadbolts on every door and locked us inside the house when he left.

"If the house ever catches fire," I thought, "we'd be dead. Me and the kids either burn alive or, perhaps even worse, suffocate from smoke inhalation."

Blake always took care of Kimberly. *Always*.

Most days, he woke himself up and then got her up for school. He fixed their cereal. He made sure they caught the bus.

On one occasion, upon discovering the door was dead-bolted from the inside and they couldn't get out, he crawled her out through a window to catch the bus.

"I guess Mark didn't get them all," I thought.

That doesn't mean the paranoia de-escalated. Not at all.

That Christmas, my Mom and Lisa— my sister— made the trek from Birmingham to Marshall. Fearful of what might happen (read: irrationally paranoid), Mark refused to let them visit.

"They *c-a-n-n-o-t* come here," he said.

"Why not? It's Christmas— Mom just wants to see the grandkids. And Lisa is my older sister! She's their aunt!"

He didn't have a good answer— just a lot of jumbled thoughts about absolutely nothing coherent at all.

"What if they don't come here to the house?" I finally asked.

He conceded: "They can come get them and take them to a hotel somewhere. They can't come inside or stay here, though."

So that's how we worked it out. To their credit, even though they didn't fully understand, they understood. I know that sounds like double-speak, but Mom and Lisa were there for me in oddly wonderful ways— despite some of the flaws and hard conversations I've already referenced.

It wasn't uncommon for Mark to wake us in the middle of the night.

"Someone is in the attic!"

There never was, of course, but he had to check it out, everyone had to move to a safe place in the house, and no one was able to go back to sleep.

On multiple occasions he demanded I help him move furniture around the house— at strange hours.

For instance, in the a.m. hours he woke me and the kids and had us move their twin beds, the dressers, and their toys into our room. In turn, we drug all of our furniture into theirs...

I upped my methamphetamine dosage just so I could stay awake— for sometimes a week at a stretch— just to make sure Mark didn't do something dumber than the dumb we were already doing that might injure the kids.

(Methamphetamines— sometimes called "meth" or just "amphetamines" or "speed"— are stimulants that accelerate your body's central nervous system. Known as "poor man's cocaine," it's highly addictive, creates feelings of anxiety and agitation, and makes people extremely paranoid.)

"I'm being the protective Mom," I rationalized.

I funded my addiction by selling enough drugs to get mine for free. If $100 of stock from a dealer could sell for $200 on the street, I covered my own needs with that gap. In real life the math worked out a bit different than that, but you get the idea...

I found employment at Marshall Medical Center, just a few miles down the road. With my background at the medical insurance company it was an easy transition.

Whereas Mark was legitimately paranoid and always thought he was being watched, followed, and about to be taken down, I actually did begin noticing the presence of ATF— the Bureau of Alcohol, Tobacco, Firearms, and Explosives— around the hospital.

They're a part of the Department of Justice that tracks the illegal use and trafficking of guns and ammo, drugs, and more. You probably heard about them during the David Koresh, Branch Davidian cult situation outside of Waco in the early 90s. ATF officed from one of the taller buildings that sits on I-35, the main north-south interstate that runs from Mexico, through Texas, and all the way up to Canada. That HQ is just a few hours from Marshall.

"Random employee-wide drug test," an office memo said.

"What in the world?"

The nice ladies I worked with— mostly suburban moms who were raising the kids the "typical way" and had worked at Marshall Medical for 20+ years— couldn't fathom it.

"We've never been drug tested— ever!"

It was in the employment agreement, that they *could* be tested. They just *never* had been.

My hunch, after seeing enough men walking around the building in jump-man gear, tactical vests, and ATF badges, was that they were looking for me or Mark. I often wondered if he flipped and became an informant.

"I can't be tested," I whispered. "I'll light that 14-panel up like a Christmas tree."

Here's some more information, just in case you don't know. When you take a drug test, you pee in a cup— just like you probably did at your regular checkup at the pediatrician when growing up. The test administrator *usually watches you pee*— to make sure you don't slip something in the urine to invalidate the test OR swap your urine for someone else's. (Addicts who know they're subject to get tested often carry a small vile of "clean" urine with them so they can pass a test at any moment's notice.)

The test administrator places a drop of urine from your pee-cup onto the test panel. Whereas a pregnancy test has a single panel that reveals a line to show you're pregnant (and omits it if not), the 14 windows on the drug test each denote the presence of a different illegal substance in your system.

Though alcohol passes from your blood within 10-12 hours, it remains traceable in your urine for up to 5 days. Most people assume it only affects you a few hours; its effects last much longer.

This is true for all drugs. Though some of the timing depends on your age, weight, and metabolism, most substances exhibit predictable patterns:

- LSD & MDMA (ecstasy) last for about 3 days.

- Heroine (and methadone, the synthetic form they dispense at "clinics" to "help" addicts) remains present for 4 days.

- Cocaine stays for up to 5.

- Methamphetamines— like I popped— don't pass for about a week.

- Pot, marijuana, or cannabis— whatever you want to call it— often lingers up to a month.

(This is what made it almost *impossible* that I would ever pass a test during this stint in Texas.)

Bottom line, when ATF visited the hospital and the call went out for a mandatory drug test, that was the end of the line for me.

"Am I just being paranoid here?" I asked myself. "Am I starting to act like my insane husband, because this behavior has just normalized with me?"

As I pondered it, I looked at my desk. I caught glance of my keys and my wallet, and my ID badge. Marshall Medical issued driver license-type IDs to every employee. We flashed those cards every time we walked through the special employee entrance.

No badge, no entry.

Supposedly.

Mine went missing a week or so earlier— right when I recognized the presence of law enforcement. Though I finagled my way in the past few days, I began putting the pieces together.

"I didn't just *lose it*," I reasoned.

People who don't have much and depend on the little they do have in order to survive don't lose things. They know exactly where all the things go, as well as when they're not placed where they're supposed to be.

"I found your badge," an unknown supervisor said, approaching my desk one day after lunch.

"Where was it?"

"In the parking lot," they stammered.

It took them longer than it should have taken to get the words out. The whole thing never sat right with me. It seemed shady— or like a shakedown.

Like I said, I was hyper-aware of everything around me. When you get molested at 11, raped at 14, stay in abandoned houses at 15, and get beaten up as often as I had, you have to be. The Mayhem of Marshall and the momma-bear mentality only intensified my predisposition to notice every person, each object, and all the things which seemed out of place. I *lived* in fight-or-flight mode.

There was only one thing to do. I knew how to do it, because I had done it before.

I knocked on my supervisor's door.

"Hi, Shannon. What can I do for you?"

"I quit," I said.

She didn't ask for the ID badge they made everyone return upon resigning. That sealed the deal for me. They probably already had it flagged. I was being tracked.

I left— and never looked back.

Before I go on, let me put this in perspective:

- *I had a great job at the medical insurance company.*

  I received rave reviews and stacked bonuses bigger than my paycheck by saving the insurance company money on hospital claims. But I quit, because I was a functional alcoholic who couldn't make it past the early morning game shows on TV without drinking and landed in rehab.

- *I had another great job at the hospital, working on the billing side.*

I performed my tasks at high octane speed, even though I stayed awake for days at a time, fueled in large part by what I thought was a necessary dependence on speed.

I walked away from both of these carrier-type jobs.

....

I took a job at a pawn shop. It was a downgrade from the insurance company and the hospital, for sure, and it played right into the addiction scenario.

Pawn shops are interesting animals. Though most middle class people assume they're just innocent stores— some sort of hybrid between retail and a garage sale— the truth is that they're quick cash for addicts.

Need a hit of your preferred drug?

Take some of your hard-earned stuff to the local pawn shop and swap it for money— with no intention of ever redeeming it (read: buying it back). The shop gives you 30-50% of what the item is actually worth, making it a win for them if you don't reclaim it in time (they can sell it and make the profit themselves).

Cash for you = cheap inventory for them.

Win-win.

I watched men turn in tools they needed for work in the middle of the week, rationalizing they could get a quick hit now, and then make it to the weekend when payday came. They rarely thought about the need to get those tools back, lest they lose the job. Such simple mental gymnastics are never part of the addict's cognitive computations.

Plus, if I had drugs to sell— in order to fund my own habit— I had a steady stream of cash-rich customers. They pawned the tools; they purchased the stash.

Win-win-win.

Except everyone was losing, self-included.

A few months into the saga, two things occurred. They're each obvious by now, if you've been paying attention.

First, the corporate headquarters of the shop decided it was time for *yet another* one of those seemingly "random" drug tests.

You know how that rolled...

"I quit. I'll be back later this week for my final paycheck."

Second, Mark continued orbiting further and further from reality and concluded I was against him. He began beating me, and— by now— I fought back.

We fist-fought so hard (even with the kids in the house) that we got to the point we were both black, blue, and bleeding. Gasping for air, unable to stand straight and swing— because neither of us could have even walked a sober line at any point during any of this— we warred with one another.

A school counselor, noticing out-of-character behavior in Blake, asked him about his home life.

"Anything unusual happening at the house?"

"No, Ma'am."

He was— is— totally honest. To a fault, even.

To him, nothing strange ever occurred. Everything he experienced *seemed normal to him.* He never knew anything different until he got older and discovered that the massive majority of people don't live like we lived.

When the counselor got involved, that triggered an alert with Marshall's equivalent of DHR (Department of Human Resources), Child Welfare, or whatever. They made a home visit, but I was able to pull myself together and "look normal"— just like I did at the medical insurance company and the hospital.

Plus, I actually "sold it" to the case-worker that I was a good mom. I bathed my kids every night, I cooked dinner each evening, and I always tucked them into bed. Those were my metrics.

Sure, I was addicted and numerous shenanigans occurred amidst the Mayhem of Marshall, but I didn't have to lie to the welfare people anymore than Blake lied to counselors. I told the truth according to my own standard as to what constitutes good parenting. We have strange ways of fooling ourselves into believing what we want to be true, no matter how untrue it is…

8. Mayhem in Marshall, but I'm a Good Mom (S)

9. We Put Hercules on the Ground (R)

Rob and the Marines make an odd decision while on a mission. The guys teach a man how to drive. Rob discovers he was living with a prison mentality.

One day the Gunny delivered the orders: "We've got a Westpac scheduled. We head out next month."

Westpac was verbal shorthand for Western Pacific. If you leave California and travel towards Asia, you cross the Pacific Ocean. I'm not sure what the official designation is, but— in our minds— anything beyond Hawaii was considered "western." A Westpac was a mission in those far-from-home areas, on the other side of those islands.

Gunny explained what was about to happen: "We're going to the motherland, men. We're going to Japan."

Some of us had no idea what was coming, but Gunny had been several times. We could tell by the excitement on his face and the pitch of his voice there were a lot of shenanigans about to unfold.

"For the next couple of days, we're going to pack some BFBs!" he shouted.

(A BFB is a big f'n box— just like you probably imagined.)

After providing a few instructions, he asked, "You got it?!"

Though we really didn't understand all of the details, we offered our customary answer: "Yes, Gunny!"

We spent the next few days packing the entire squadron. Literally, the entire squadron. Men. Clothes. Equipment. Tools. Vehicles. Everything.

Now, remember...

Most of the Marines with whom I served were just like me.

- *Young* (i.e., 18-24)

- *Addicted* (if we didn't have an addiction when we joined the Marines, we eventually acquired some sort of vice due to the availability of cheap alcohol, all the travel, and the ample free time with nothing else to do)

- *Creative* (and in desperate need of an outlet)

Let me explain that last one in a bit more detail. You might have a heard the statement that "an idle mind is the Devil's playground." You wouldn't, at first blush, consider a young, addicted Marine's mind to be idle.

But, when you're constantly told what to do, when to do it, and exactly how it must be done... well, you learn to perform at an extremely high level WHILE ALSO conserving your mental margin for other matters.

For example, the guys at El Toro celebrated my 21st birthday not with alcohol (that already flowed freely) but with a fighter plane wash. A fighter plane wash consists of capturing the birthday boy, duct-taping him to the missile rail of a jet, and towing him by tractor— attached to the plane— to the wash bay. One water hose is stuffed down the Marine's pants and the man receives a birthday bath with the plane.

Stuff like that happened constantly.

For example, in the same way construction workers often send newbies around the job site to find a brick stretcher or a left-handed hammer (tools that, just in case you didn't know, *do not* exist), we regularly sent new Marines on odd assignments.

"This is the wrong form. You need a different one," a seasoned Marine might say. "You know how much a stickler they are around here for paperwork. This won't work."

"Which one?" newly-assigned man replies.

"Go down the hall and ask the secretary for an ID-10-T."

Inevitably, the man follows through, at which point the the secretary hands him a blank sheet of paper and says, "Write your name across the top of this page— and then, in big letters, I-D-1-0-T."

Eventually, the man sees it clearly. In this Marine-version of snipe-hunting, he's labeled himself an *IDIOT*.

One day, a group of Marines learned that Gamache (a guy from Boston) never learned how to drive. He didn't need to where he was from.

"You wanna learn? We'll teach you…"

A few of us loaded a cooler of beer in the back of DJs faded maroon pickup. It was a bench-seat Ford Ranger with a sliding window in the back, overlooking the bed.

The only non-driver in the group, Gamache made his way to the driver seat and cranked the truck. That's as much as he knew about learning to drive.

"Now, open that window," DJ said.

Gamache reached back, unlocked the small latch, and pulled the glass panel over as far as it would stretch.

"Drop the truck *in reverse*... yeah, right there. Keep your foot on the brake and..." the guy in the passenger seat explained how to shift from the lever on the steering wheel column of the vehicle.

"Now let your foot of the brake," a man from the bed of the truck yelled through the window and into the cab, "and gently give it a little gas."

Gamache looked puzzled.

"I've never seen anyone drive backwards unless they're just backing into a parking spot."

"This is how you learn, though," one of the Marines said. Then— "Be sure to come to a complete stop at every stop sign."

Yes, we taught Gamache how to drive *backwards*.

Shit-faced drunk, it worked well until two Navy MPs pulled next to the truck. They rolled down their window and looked our way. The two vehicles sat side-by-side on the road, facing opposite directions.

"We've been watching you morons for about 10 minutes," the MP driver told Gamache.

His partner then asked, "What the fuck are you doing?"

Gamache, not comprehending why everyone in our vehicle— all 5 of us or so— were laughing so hard, innocently confessed, "They're teaching me to drive?"

"We were trying to figure out what the hell was happening here," the MP replied.

Then, his partner let Gamache in on the truth— "That's not how you do it."

They had jurisdiction over the security of the area, so they— through their own laughter— ordered Gamache to park the truck back where it goes.

"And don't drive in reverse to get there."

....

I was chosen as part of the lead crew of the Westpac. There were 12 of us total— from various fields of expertise on the base. One was an engine man. Another was the hydraulic mechanic. Another was a medic. One managed all of the equipment.

You get the idea...

I was in *corrosion control*. That's a fancy— read: government— way of saying that I painted the aircraft.

Basically, the metal gets rusty, so you coat it in order to protect it. The best way to protect metal... well, you "corrosion control" it with paint, and you— if you're the government— check the thickness of that paint as specific flight hours accumulate to make sure you don't need to sand it down and re-corrosion-control it again (read: repaint the aircraft).

I'm not sure how this group made the cut, but we were selected to board a C-130 and make the first jump to Wake Island before everyone else. It's a tiny piece of land, less than 3 square miles in size, about 2,300 miles from Honolulu (i.e., Wake Island is about 2/3 of the way across the Pacific from the continental U.S. to Asia).

The U.S. used the airstrip to refuel and bomb the Japanese after Pearl Harbor. The island still has concrete bunkers and reinforcements. When I was there, brass from the ammunition was still laying around.

Hercules is the nickname of the C-130, a massive 4-prop cargo plane that Lockheed began building for the military in the mid-1950s. The plane isn't fast, but it's big and it can take off & land on an unprepared (read: piece of shit) airstrip. Allegedly, the name C-130 refers to the 130-page proposal that was submitted for this cargo transport back when the U.S. put out a request for bids.

Oddly enough, some of the bigwigs at Lockheed originally thought making a massive, unarmed, low speed aircraft would be the "death of Lockheed." However, this machine has maneuvered its way through dozens of configurations and has the distinction for the longest-serving military plane.

My job— with the other 11— was to fly ahead of everyone else in the Westpac mission, land, and make sure the site was ready. Then, we would receive the planes and check them. In effect, our part was to seamlessly help everyone else leapfrog forward.

That's all I can tell you. It's not that the mission was top secret— that's just all I remember and probably all I ever cared to know about it.

We arrived at Wake Island, this tiny gem in the middle of the Pacific, and started chugging beer as a soon as we landed. Then, group-think entered the picture and a plan presented itself out of nowhere.

"This is really nice," one of the guys observed.

"There's nothing here except us, basically."

Another Marine made a few remarks about buying beers for less than a quarter— even in the mid-90s— and how everything else at the PX was super-cheap.

Someone affirmed, "This is fuckin' paradise." Then, he made an observation, "It will all change when the chase crew gets here in another day or two."

"When do they head this way?"

"After we call them and give Sarge the all clear."

"So we get to decide when they get here?"

One of the Marines put the pieces together. The entire squadron was coming, but they weren't leaving Cali until we told them to come. Whereas they anticipated we would land, check our plane and the island, and then immediately call them to head our way within just a few hours of arriving, *they were waiting on us...*

(I'm obviously skipping the technical details of the mission here, because they involve moving a lot of people and millions of dollars of equipment in a highly orchestrated sequence.)

"What if we found a reason for them to delay the trip by a few days?" one of the guys suggested.

There it was. Someone said it. Sure, it was just hypothetical at this point, but it was out there.

The idea met absolutely *zero* resistance.

A small group of us brainstormed possible reasons to keep them back on the mainland, but none of them stuck until one of the mechanics mentioned the "fuel probe." I know what you must be thinking— what is a fuel probe, and why can't you just fly without it?

The fuel probe is used in the process of aerial refueling (also known as in-flight refueling, air-to-air refueling, and tanking). To make the cross-globe, over-ocean jumps we were making, you gotta have it.

"Phone it in," one of the men suggested.

"I'll drink to that."

Then the rest of us in that huddle, "I'll drink to that, too."

We called back to the base and gained an extra two days of solitude while they sent another probe our way from Hawaii to replace the perfectly good fuel probe we already had. Yes, *we created our own problem*.

As a result, we lived it up in paradise— or what we thought was paradise— for two days.

....

About a decade after this incident I was working at that facility that helped men coming out of prison, off the streets, and from addiction— it's the place where I got shot. Among the clientele we had custody of dozens of men who were "plain clothes prisoners" and stayed with us while they completed their sentence.

We started a lawn crew and a renovation business to help some of the men who didn't have a government-issued ID (a requirement for employment) begin earning some money while we helped them "rebuild" or acquire their identification. Sometimes, that took months, as we had to find birth certificates, social security numbers, and more... and then clean up warrants before we took them to the courthouse or State Trooper's office to get the official license or non-drivers State ID.

A few weeks into that lawn care company the executive director made a remark about the wear and tear the guys were putting on the equipment...

"How in the world do you break two commercial lawn mowers a week?" he asked. "We're pouring every bit of profit back into replacing brand new equipment that's literally just a few weeks old."

The business manger chimed in, "It's also cutting into profits the other way, too. We can't keep them all working if they work an hour or two and then can't finish the day. We don't do all of the yards, we don't make the money..."

They sat there struggling to figure it out, jumping through the absurdity of it all.

Finally, it came to me.

"I'll tell you what's happening here," I said, putting the pieces of my past together. "They're breaking the equipment on purpose."

"What do you mean *breaking it on purpose*?"

"Yeah," I confirmed, "It's the fuel probe all over again..." Then, I acted it out there in the office. "Oh, here's a stump sticking up. Let me just run the new mower right over that. Whack. The whole engine frame bends. Whoops! I guess we can't work today. We get a day off. Because we don't have the equipment."

"Who in the right mind would do that?" the business manager asked.

"A Marine like me or a plain clothes prisoner that self-sabotages their own progress in the name of taking a break."

"What?"

"That's what we do!" Then, catching myself, I clarified, "Well, not anymore, but that's what I used to do, back in the day…"

I explained the story of the Westpac.

The executive director asked what I would do if I were him…

"Start charging them for broken equipment. Make them sign it out in the morning and initial the number of dents, the fact that it starts, the condition it's in… *everything*."

"Just like you do with a rental car?"

"*Exactly* like you do with a rental car."

The business manager added, "I'll have someone verify it when they return. We can go out there and check the truck. If it doesn't work, I'll deduct the full retail price of whatever they break from their paycheck."

That afternoon, the guys were presented with the updated plan. They were allowed to quit, no questions asked, and get replaced by someone else immediately. If they continued working, however, the new policy went into effect for them the following day.

We also explained, "If your equipment breaks, we're not coming to get you. You will still have to ride along with the truck all day— but, since you're not working, you won't get paid."

We didn't know if that was legal or not, but we slid it in there…

That first week, two more lawn mowers came back from the day damaged. True to our word, we charged the guys. Some walked away with just a few dollars for a week of work by the time the books settled.

None of them argued about it. Their expressions told the truth.

- They did the deed on purpose.

- They didn't think we would stick to our word and shift the burden back on them for the problem they created.

- They accepted the consequences when we did, because, as one of the men confessed, "I did this to myself."

After that, everything worked perfectly...

....

Think about what I just shared. And consider how it might affect you personally. You see, sometimes we are the biggest hindrance to our own progress.

If you think about it, those inmates— that's the technical, legal designation— received an opportunity of a lifetime. They were among less than 100 inmates in the State of Alabama who had the chance to work— and live— outside in the real world while they completed their sentence. And whereas other inmates earned a few cents (yes, cents) per hour, these men were paid extremely well. They were in a position to save thousands of dollars to effectively "start over" upon their EOS (end of sentence) date, effectively insuring they didn't have to go back to the old ways in order to just get by.

But they struggled to see it, because their mentality wasn't set to "forward." Rather, it was set to "who gives a flyin' fuck."

The strange reality about self-sabotage is that you most often have to do the work you avoid anyway.

- The men still had to cut the yards and edge the shrubs.

- The Marines still had to complete the Westpac mission.

The delay generally doesn't eliminate work, it adds to it and it raises the price you pay. Some of those men bought lawn mowers that didn't work and weren't able to send that cash home to their families. The Marines— at least the Westpac lead crew— chose an empty island (with cheap beer) over our ultimate destination which, turns out, was far better.

Application for Part 3 | You are the Common Factor

Main idea: Wherever you go, there you are. Whereas we want to blame circumstances or others for many of our shortcomings, without denying that outside factors do affect us, we must remember that we are the common denominator in all of our past, present, and future experiences. Rather than focusing on what we can't control, we must look at what we can— ourselves.

Shannon confronted the brutal facts about her drinking (chapter 6). She wrongly believed it was under control— even though anyone with all the facts would have clearly agreed it wasn't. She also convinced herself she was "a good mom" during the Marshall days (chapter 8).

In which areas of your life do you need to confront reality about what's actually happening and tell yourself the "most honest" story you can about your situation— so that you can move forward from where you are to where you truly want to be?

_____

_____

_____

_____

_____

_____

_____

_____

_____

_____

_____

_____

Rob joined the Marine Corps to run away from alcohol and drugs, in part (see chapter 7). Later in his story those become even bigger issues.

Starting over requires more than just a "change of scenery." In fact, you don't have to change your location in order to re-route your life to a different destination.

Share how this applies to you.

_____

_____

_____

_____

_____

_____

_____

_____

_____

The Marine Corps is a group. But, like all groups, it's comprised of individuals.

Sometimes, being a better "you" requires that you surround yourself with better people (as we'll explore in Part 4). There are over-performers and under-performers in every profession (in fact, in every place you go).

You need not dishonor or disrespect under-performers in order to "level-up" yourself, either. Just perform at your potential.

Who knows— perhaps you will inspire someone to step into their untapped prowess.

As we prepare for the next part of the book, who are some of the people you should surround yourself with?

_____

_____

_____

_____

_____

_____

_____

_____

_____

_____

WALK WITH US!
FREE BONUS ACCESS!
7 MIND-SHIFT LESSONS

RiseUpOnline.info/7

Part 4 | The Right Relationships Are a Superpower

Relationships either push you higher or pull you lower. We're designed for connection. When we don't unite in healthy ways, we align in unhealthy ways. The type of relationships you have is an incredibly accurate predictor of whether or not you reach your full potential.

10. Who Jumps Out of a Moving Vehicle? (S)

Shannon steals a truck, her Mom and Lisa make a heroic move, Shannon miscalculates a target

I grew more concerned for my capacity to not only fight Mark, but also to protect Blake and Kimberly. I also felt like it wouldn't be long until another school counselor got DHR involved again OR another opportunity for a "random" drug test presented itself OR law enforcement got closer.

"Birmingham," I thought. "I need to go back home."

In reality, home was *nowhere*.

I didn't have the trailer anymore. I gave it to Kenny since it was on his parents' property. I couldn't afford to rent anything.

Mom and my older sister now lived next door to each other in an apartment complex, so I headed there. I wasn't sure how they would respond. Mom was finally living on her own and wasn't with a man, and my sister was chronically disappointed in my life decisions. But, as the saying goes, "Any port in a storm."

I was in a typhoon, so off to Birmingham I drove. I bolted while Mark was passed out, and stole his truck when I left.

"I don't really want you staying here," Mom told me.

I knew it.

"Just a few days?"

She agreed— "But no more than that."

"That's all I need."

She also clarified that it was just me and the kids. She hated Mark. My entire family did.

"He's the devil," she said. "He cannot stay."

"He's not with me. It's just me, Blake, and Kimberly. Just for a few days."

10. Who Jumps Out of a Moving Vehicle? (S)

She welcomed us inside.

Before the end of the week, the proverbial shit hit the fan. And when it did, it slung and splattered everywhere...

Mark figured out where we were. He jumped in a Mazda Miata, drove straight through, and demanded we return to Marshall.

"Fuck," I said, seeing him get out of the strange vehicle. "How did he find us *here*?"

I'm still not sure how he did it. Mom and Lisa lived in a different place than when I first left and this was well before cell phones, "find my friends," and other tracking options.

"Get in the car," he commanded.

I didn't feel like I had an option:

- Would he unleash the same fury on my family— my Mom and sister — that he laid on me?

- What would I do now that I knew he could find me, presumably, at any time he wanted?

- Would he press charges about the truck, or report me about the drug use and drug-selling?

- Would he call DHR or child welfare and convince them I wasn't a good mom, that I somehow pulled a fast one on them?

Plus, there's the fact I mentioned earlier— that the victim of domestic violence typically takes 7-8 actual "leaves" to "not go back" to her abuser. No matter how difficult the current chapter of your life is, transitioning to the next is always hard.

"Let's go, kids..."

10. Who Jumps Out of a Moving Vehicle? (S)

Blake sat in my lap. Kimberly laid across the headrest of the two-seat Miata. That's how we made the entire 8-hour drive back to Marshall.

As soon as we left it was obvious he hadn't changed. I mean, it had only been a few days— a few dozen hours of nothing but a stolen truck, a multi-state escape, and a boomerang trip.

I walked into a different house when we returned. This time we were going to stay with his cousin and her family.

Blake phoned my Mom.

"We're back in Texas," he said.

She freaked.

I grabbed the phone.

"Come get the kids," I said. Then, I clarified, *"Now."*

"Right *now*, now?" she asked.

"Yes, if you don't come, I don't know what might happen. I'm stuck with him." After a moment, I continued, "The only way I'll get out of here is if I kill him or he kills me."

To their credit (once again), my mother and my sister hopped in the car *immediately*.

"You've got 30 days," she said, "to either get your shit together and be a Mom, or don't come back for these kids at all."

It sounded like a hypocritical order coming from a woman who had three kids with three different men who never spent any time with those men because one of them took himself out, another's girlfriend-of-the-moment took him out, the third molested the kids... and the man who followed them was so rambunctious that the kids had to find their way to couches and abandoned houses or Grandma's lest they rock the apple cart, tump the boat, or whatever real life cliche you want to drop in…

I shrugged.

I didn't care. Blake and Kimberly were safe, so I felt I could catch my breath for a moment and then decide what to do. A month is a *looonnng* time when you typically live moment-by-moment.

That said, Blake and Kimberly were back in Birmingham— 3 states and 8 hours away— in less than 24 hours.

I shifted my mental margin from trying to figure out how to protect the two kids to bringing closure to that relationship…

- How would I tell him I wanted to leave for good?
- How would I survive if I actually did tell him?
- How would I keep him from causing havoc and hurting people I care about?

Initially, the days seemed super-long. There wasn't much to do, and I didn't have a job or kids to guard.

But the remaining month kept getting shorter and shorter.

Finally, with less than a week remaining on my Mom's arbitrary demand to achieve something she hadn't done herself for me and "get my shit together within 30 days," Mark got picked up by the Law. It wasn't ATF or something major this time. It was an outstanding warrant for a DUI.

That was my cue to exit stage right.

I "got my shit together" because he didn't have his "legal shit" together. But, take the win. Good enough...

....

It didn't take but a few weeks for Mark to get out of jail. From the time he got out, it took him less than 24 hours to find his way back to Birmingham.

By then, I had my own place in the same apartment complex as my Mom and my sister. They lived next door to each other in small two bedroom units. The time blurs, still today, because I took so many drugs during this season.

- I do know Mark tried to get me to go back to Marshall.

- I also know I refused to go.

- I know, as well, I conceded to let him stay with me— at my place.

I didn't feel the kids were unsafe, because Blake stayed in Mom's spare bedroom and Kimberly bunked with my sister. Mark and I continued fighting with fists, and we kept banging away at the drugs.

We drove to the dope man's house one afternoon. I didn't want to go, but felt I didn't have any say...

Earlier I mentioned that I was known for jumping out of trucks and moving vehicles whenever I was taken somewhere I didn't want to go. I decided to run that play again.

As Mark cruised the winding roads near my apartment, I glanced at the odometer.

"38-40 miles per hour," I whispered.

I looked ahead around the curve and saw a ditch— with lots of thick grass.

"If I open the door and roll out there, I should— at this speed— land in the softest place possible."

It sounds odd. But, take it from a gal who's made enough moving vehicle jumps to know. Different surfaces feel different and you recover more readily based on when and where and how fast you're moving when you hit. Though it all seems like it might "land the same" and "equally hurt" to you, there's a major difference.

I quickly calculated the speed and surfaces in my head, shoved the door open, and leapt out.

Misfire.

I never got my legs under me— the mechanism that was supposed to carry me to a softer crash landing in the foliage. I landed on the concrete just behind the truck.

I tumbled...

Shoulder.

Head.

Tailbone.

Back to the head, splitting it open like a rubber mallet smashing a watermelon.

Mark slowed his roll, put the truck in reverse, and backed up. He walked around to the passenger side without saying a word.

Front passenger door still open from my exit, he scooped me off the pavement, kicked the door open wider with his right foot, and shoved me across the front seat.

He slammed the door, walked back around the front of the truck, and accelerated towards the dope man's.

He pushed my head into the seat— just as Kenny had done. Then, realizing his hand was getting covered with blood (it flowed from my skull steadily), he let go. It was obvious I wasn't going anywhere.

As we drove, I continued bleeding. My hair matted up and stuck to the seat, which continued soaking in the deep red liquid of life draining from me.

He didn't care. He was a man on a mission, and I'd thrown him an unexpected curve ball— one he'd never seen before.

Fading in an out of consciousness, I remember arriving at the dope house. He still hadn't said a thing to me.

- No "fuck you."

- No "you're a dumb ass."

- No "what the hell are you thinking, bitch?"

- None of the typical lines.

- *Nothing.*

He walked to the door, knocked, exchanged some money for a sack of meth, and made his way back to the pickup.

"Where's Shannon?" the dope man yelled. "She was with you when you called. You said you were both coming. I was gonna say hello."

Mark didn't answer, so the dealer followed him out the truck, trying to get his attention the whole time.

"Holy shit!" he exclaimed, as he approached the driver side and saw me balled up on the front seat in a fetal position. "What the fuck happened?"

"She jumped."

"Who the hell jumps?"

"She did."

"You gotta go to the hospital and get her some help."

"I'll get her some help," he promised the dope man.

But Mark wouldn't. Mark *couldn't*.

How would he explain to someone in triage at the ER that "she jumped" out of a moving vehicle?

And who in their right mind would actually believe that people exit— by choice— moving cars?

Then how would he explain the drugs, and what might happen if they did a pee-test?

And— oh, yeah— he went to that house in the first place because he wanted to get high right then and there, so he was already going to take a hit before he even pulled the car away...

Plus, were there any outstanding warrants that might land us in jail, because that's how I bailed on him the second time?

Mark took me back to the apartment. He laid me on a mattress in the middle of the bedroom floor. We didn't have any furniture at all. I laid there for three full days, moving in and out of consciousness while he sat in the other room getting high.

No food.

No water.

No medical attention or washing the wounds or bandaids or checking on me or anything at all. Just an empty room.

"You want some?" he occasionally said, offering a cut of the drugs whenever he saw me waking up.

Always in a liminal space— that kind of limbo in which you're not out of one place but you're not "in" another, either— I never answered. I couldn't. I floated in a "no man's land" of nothingness.

Finally, when I woke up and stayed awake for good, he wasn't there.

"Maybe I could leave again," I thought.

It was just a fleeting consideration. I didn't have a car, and I was in the one place I would go if I ever did leave.

Plus, each of the other times, he found me— and I took him back.

"I can't stand up," I whispered. "Shit."

I couldn't tell if something— maybe my tailbone—was broken or just bruised.

And I could barely move. I lost a lot of blood over the previous few days. Most of it was now dried deep in the mattress or caked in my hair.

I slowly stood to my feet, cleaned myself as best I could at the bathroom sink, crept to the front door, and hobbled to my mother's apartment. It was a small complex, and I leaned against and felt my way via the exterior brick wall the entire trek.

She opened on the first knock and just gazed at me.

I can't imagine what I looked like. It had been three days of bleeding. The bruises must've been awful.

10. Who Jumps Out of a Moving Vehicle? (S)

"I've got to do something," I said. "I'm just not sure what. Or even how."

Somehow, I think Mom related to that. Though she never did drugs or drank, she also made super-poor choices with men. She knew exactly what it meant that I had to take action but I wasn't even sure which way to move — or if it would even matter if I did.

10. Who Jumps Out of a Moving Vehicle? (S)

11. Sex Sells, But Comes With a Hidden Price (R)

Rob accidentally lands a job. He orders from the kind of menu that leaves a bad taste. He stays on the government payroll in a unique way

It didn't take more than a few hours in Okinawa to realize that the sex trade is just a normal thing. I'm not saying it should be, I'm just stating that it is.

Anytime we were in the area, a group of Marines visited Whisper Alley. It's an eerily quiet place, hauntingly hollow. If you've ever seen a Western and remember the stillness of the town before a gunfight duel and recognize the moments before the cowboys count off to ten and begin firing... there's sometimes a tumbleweed that's the only thing that moves. Imagine an Asian version of that place, and erase the two bandits. That's what Whisper Alley is like.

If you walk about a block down the covered sidewalk, you begin to notice little windows. Everything feels like you're in the middle of a black and white movie with the exception of those tiny windows— usually silver or gold— on the doors. Every other window is blacked-out or boarded.

11. Sex Sells, but Comes With a Hidden Price (R)

Knock on the door and someone inside, the *Mamasan*, slides the window open— just like you slide the back window on those pickup trucks.

"Hew-wo." She means to say "hello" but it doesn't quite come out right with the accent.

Just as you muster the bravery to respond, the voice calls again...

"What I do for you?"

(Yes, the words are spoken out of order.)

It's as if she asks because she has no idea that you're there for one thing, the only thing they do at what they would have called a "whore house" if you were were back in that Western.

They don't pitch it like this, of course. They just say "hello" and ask what you want...

Everyone knows you're there to meet a *geisha*. The Japanese word is a compound of two concepts, *gei* ("performing arts") and *sha* ("person"). Allegedly, these women provide great conversation, play instruments or sing, and converse with the male companions who hire them.

Like female escorts in the U.S., though, they really emphasize one thing. No one who hires them is uniformed about the main service they provide.

Mamasan always let me in.

- Not for the music
- Not to talk
- Not for mere "companionship"

Just quick sex.

Then she ordered me to drop my pants, so she could wash my balls with some sort of homemade concoction she kept in a wooden bowl. The water was always cold, which adds to the humiliation of standing there with merely your waist exposed.

(Think: Seinfeld episode where George claims "shrinkage.")

"Dat will be..."

She always holds out her hand to collect the rent. Without fail, you pay in advance.

Then, she leads you down a winding hall to whatever room...

It wasn't unusual to see dozens of dog tags hanging around the bed post— all trophies the *geisha* collected from G.I.s like me who were well-acquainted with illicit sex but completely ignorant about truly making love.

Today, people act like sex is one big nothing-burger. Teenage girls talk about their "body count" at rates that shame the numbers many of the most wayward Marines hit. It's as if, in just a generation or so, we've started praising promiscuity rather than hiding it in the back alley.

Certainly, people can make their own choices. For sure, I did.

What they don't realize, though, is that those choices always come with a price. Generally, that cost is higher than you want to pay, and the payment plan extends well beyond the momentary gratification you receive.

In 1 Corinthians, Paul talks about sex. The church members in the ancient city of Corinth were— literally— hanging around with prostitutes. Just like the G.I.s in Okinawa.

Notably, Paul doesn't shame the recipients of his letter. This book of the Bible is actually the written correspondence he sent them in response to some of their most pressing questions.

Rather, he tells them, "You have no idea what you're doing to yourself."

He then places this sin (everyone knows sex is an issue— that's why we defend it and get pissed when people talk against it) in a category all its own (see 1 Corinthians 6:18). This activity, he asserts, works different than pride, theft, lying, violence, and even drug or alcohol abuse.

"This is a sin against your own body and your own soul," he says.

It's confounding. Substance abuse is *not* a sin against the self, but promiscuous sex is?

He suggests that "the one who sleeps with a prostitute becomes one with her." That is, a new entity is created.

And since they're *already* one with whoever else they've already been with you become one with them *and* whoever they've been with *and* one with them *and* one with whatever spiderweb of dysfunction exists in their pasts. Your soul-shit transfers to them *and* all of their past baggage makes its way into you.

- You pick up habits and now have behaviors you never knew existed.

- You pick up mindsets and now think thoughts you've never entertained.

- You pick up demons and now carry companions with you that you thought only existed in B-rate movies.

I wasn't a virgin when I went into the Marine Corps, but I wasn't as messed-up going in as I was when I left. The stuff we did in Okinawa opened me up to things I never would have even considered before— things like going to the Bunny Ranch or the Mustang Ranch regularly.

I had a few days of down time before my run with the Marines ended. My squadron was slated for another Westpac— the same kind where we brought Hercules down. Even if no one sabotaged any part of this mission like we had before, they wouldn't make it back stateside before I was due to sign out, so I got to stay behind.

For the past few years, I had worked at MCAS Miramar in San Diego. I spent my final few days with the 3 other men who were left behind just hanging out in that hangar.

Now, behind Hangar One there was a small pink hangar. It probably didn't start off pink— it probably began as a painted tan, the kind of tan that has a little rose color in it and morphs into the color of bad makeup once it sits in the sun for a few decades.

To the right of the pink hangar, just next to the tarmac, I saw a small job trailer. It was the kind of temporary trailer you see parked at massive job sites where they build new shopping malls.

"What the hell is going on over there?" one of my fellow Marines who was also left behind with short-time asked.

Another Marine looked across the pavement. He squinted as if that might help him figure it out before finally admitting, "I don't know."

I started walking that way to investigate.

"There's a line out here," I muttered to myself— none of the other guys had followed me.

They were all talking about things like the Westpac where we grounded Hercules for a few days, the trips to Okinawa, and the things they thought about doing when they returned home. None of them had a plan— least of all me.

As I approached the trailer, I saw a sign. I leaned over a bit so I could read it.

"McDonell Fuckin' Douglass is here," I said to no one.

I knew who they were. They created a lot of the equipment we flew— a bunch of the planes I painted. They also hired former military personnel to fill open employment positions, since we were already familiar with the end users of their products.

I decided to jump in line.

I didn't ask any questions about what the line was for or what the job might be, I just slowly inched up as the line slowly got shorter. After all, I didn't have anything to do until I signed out in 3 days. Even after that, I didn't have anything to do…

"Next," someone called.

I peeked around the corner and saw a man sitting behind an architectural table.

"Come on in," he said, motioning me to take a seat in front of him. "What's your name?"

"Malcom. Rob Malcom," I said— just like James Bond might.

He flipped through a stack of papers, obviously looking for something.

"I don't see you here. The document from your first interview should be in here. Hmm…"

Apparently, I snookered my way in a line for the *callbacks*, for the guys who passed a supposed first round of interviews that happened at some point in the past.

"Might as well just fake my way through this," I thought…

As the interviewer grabbed a second stack of applications of people who qualified for the second round and began working his way through, he made small talk.

"Where you are from?"

"Birmigham, Alabama," I replied.

He returned a quick, "You for Alabama or Auburn?"

"Roll Tide!" I said.

That was enough. No first interview needed.

He set his stack of papers on the drawing table and asked me a few questions about my time in the service and then queried, "When do you get out?"

"In three days," I replied. "This Thursday."

"Can you start with McDonell Douglass on Monday?"

I didn't even know what the job actually entailed, but it didn't matter. I landed full time employment at McDonnell Fuckin' Douglass before signing out of the Marine Corps.

"I'd love to," I said, standing to shake his hand. "You tell me where to go and what time to be there."

With the long weekend ahead of me and a job to boot, I returned to Hangar One and told the guys the news.

As soon as I signed out, I looked for a place to rent. I split a house with 2 active-duty Marines, Ron & Fitz. I gave them cheap rent, which made my cost of living decrease to almost nothing.

Whereas you're supposed to walk through a background check, drug testing, and a series of interviews, I got hired on the spot. The first time I put in for vacation time, the issue surfaced.

"We were looking through your employee file to put a copy of this in there, and we noticed it's empty."

"What do you mean?"

"Well, we keep your original application and the notes from your interviews and a few other items in there. You don't have any of that."

"I didn't have it, because I skated past it all," I *wanted* to say. I couldn't throw the guy who gave me the job under the bus, though, and ruin it for other Marines, so I suggested the most obvious explanation: "Maybe it fell out or someone misplaced it."

With that, the issue disappeared as fast as it had come up.

One of the first things I noticed was the bump in pay. I jumped from $958.33 every two weeks to $23/hour— almost 2.5x what I earned while enlisted by the time you factor in the overtime. Plus, I had a lot more free time.

That put my addiction *into turbo.*

It's not that my addiction(s) needed any escalation. I went through three different rehabs during the four years I was in the Corps. Moreover, this wasn't isolated behavior to just me— our rowdy lifestyle was as accepted as our ability to do a 20-mile forced march at pace or fire a weapon and hit a target at will.

"A rifleman first," they say.

Might as well have added, "A rifleman *and an addict* first."

While at work, I painted jets for Top Gun school— for the best Navy pilots. We had to learn all the paint schemes and keep the planes corrosion free. This was easy for me. I worked *corrosion control* in the Corps.

While not at work, I used any substance I could find.

Eventually, McDonnell Douglass moved us to Fallon, Nevada— about an hour east of Reno. Easy access to the big city made things even worse.

That's when I started visiting the Mustang Ranch and the other, well… "Gentlemen's Clubs." Known around the world, each of these are high-end, legal houses of prostitution. You can find their websites online, where they advertise their services and fees like the local cineplex displays showtimes and offers tickets.

The internet wasn't as big of a deal back then, so we just showed up…

And then we kept showing up.

At the time, it worked like this…

1. *You ring a doorbell at the gate.*

    I initially thought this proved how upper-crust these establishments were. In hindsight, though this process certainly added to the mystique, it was simply nothing more than a ploy to provide the available women with a bit of time to get ready for new guests (read: paying customers).

2. *The gates open and you walk to the front door.*

    Someone opens the door, welcomes you in, and you notice that all of the girls stand in a row— lined up much like young boys line up when choosing teams to play a game of pickup basketball.

3.   *You're supposed to point at the girl you'd like to "hang out" with.*

Of course, a bunch of thoughts race through your mind. You think about what the rejected girls might think; you consider which gal the guys with you want; and you question what the hell you're doing paying for something that should be freely given in a totally different environment as an expression of intimacy instead of a business transaction much akin to buying gas or purchasing beer.

Now, at this point, you have options…

You can just "hang out" and shoot pool. Or talk. Or have a drink.

But you know you didn't go there to talk politics or play billiards— no more than you visit a *geisha* to listen to a lullaby or make small talk.

And you know what they say: "Sit in the barber chair long enough, and you'll get a haircut."

Or, "Walk in the rain… you'll get wet."

Yeah, you know where this goes. There's only one place it *can* go.

Sometimes, you just go back to the bedrooms. Other times, they give you a sheet of paper where you can place your order. It's a long page with boxes for check marks— like some sushi restaurants hand you.

They have weird names for everything— titles which have nothing to do with anything about sex whatsoever.

"What the hell is a *Space Cowboy*?" I once thought.

Or, "What about this *Pirate's Bounty* thing? What could that be…?"

You're always in over your head— not matter how many times you've been. THIS is definitely not how THAT was designed to be.

So, not wanting to look like you need one of those I-D-1-0-T forms in front of the ladies or your men friends, you look at the sheet of paper and act like you know *exactly* what you're doing...

... which probably reveals to the people running the brothel that *you're the only one who actually has no clue.*

"I'm the dumbass," you think. "The devil pulled one over on me yet again."

In truth, you're not that far off.

But you're not thinking with *that head*, as they say, so you pencil your preferences and let them know exactly what you'd like the girl to do to you. Or what you *think* you might like them to do— you really don't have much of a clue other than the "standard."

In dawns on you, "All of these orders are probably for the same exact service— they're just marked with different names and different prices."

To quote Pee Wee's favorite gangsta, "Professing to be wise, they broadcast their stupidity for everyone else to see" (Romans 1:22).

Like I said earlier, we were super-familiar with sex; we were grossly stupid about what it truly means to be intimate and share your body and soul with one other person as a celebration and enjoyment of oneness.

With a group of vets all working together at McDonell Douglass, there was always someone flying in and out to go see their family or friends. Weddings. Funerals. Other special occasions. No one drove, because Fallon sits in the middle of nowhere and everyone there had come from some far off place.

The unspoken standard in the office became, "You need a ride to the airport?"

That always meant you would leave an hour earlier than necessary so you could stop at the Ranch on the way. Loosen the guy before he leaves.

Since you're there, too...

The unspoken agreement was also, "Sure, I'll pick you up..."

That likewise meant a quick stop on the way back home.

....

I don't know another way to say it other than to just blatantly lay it out there: once those demons get inside you, the moral lines you once held keep moving and moving. In time, what once seemed to be etched in concrete seems to be sketched in sand.

It's not too long after that you sense the lines have disappeared altogether. At that point, you'll do *anything*. And, contrary to what most people believe, it affects *every* area of your life.

Every.

Single.

Area.

I started working for Boeing, because they were awarded the contract McDonnell Douglass had. The money was better, too.

A functional addict, I performed my work super-fast AND I did a great job at it. Plus, I made more cash for the same job.

That initially meant a lot of down time while I sat in the warehouse on the clock.

One day, I had an idea.

I called the guy who always relieved my shift: "Can you just clock me out when you arrive and clock yourself in?"

He agreed.

"No problem," he said. "I got you."

I even suggested we could find someone to do the same for him and keep the routine running for a full 24-hour period.

He didn't want someone to punch the clock for him. He agreed to punch it for me, though.

"You don't have to get it for me. I still got you…"

I don't think Boeing ever found out. If they did, it probably wouldn't have mattered, because the entire military-contractor, war-machine madness is a money-maker for the government and for some of the biggest business owners in the world.

The U.S. pulled your tax money and paid Boeing $76 an hour to pay me $26 hour, $3 more than McDonell Douglass paid me. That means that Boeing kept $50 of your tax money for every single hour I was on the clock.

Did Boeing care if I got my work done in just 2 hours a day?

They probably would have— and would have encouraged me to stretch it out— if they knew they would only get paid for those 2 hours. If they could bill for 6 more— plus some overtime— that's a $300 swing per day, assuming no overtime. Multiply that over an entire year and across numerous employees and piles of contracts and countless locations…

Yeah, it's a racket.

(Remember, these are the numbers from almost 3 decades ago. There's no telling what they are today.)

Boeing never checked on me, because it was too lucrative not to. "They," whoever it is that gets the fat bonuses the $50 per hour overage funds, just wanted us producing whatever work we were assigned to do AND punching the clock.

In turn, I earned about $1,700 a week, by the time the extra hours factored in. That doesn't sound like a pile of money now, but this was over 20 years ago. Plus, I didn't have a family or many other expenses.

If you have a hole in your heart, you'll fill it with something. If you fill it with *the wrong thing,* it eats away at whatever remains there and just makes the void to fill that much larger.

I decided to fill my ever-enlarging hole.

I built a house with a 3-car garage. My pickup should have been enough. But, with space to fill, I soon created my own mini-fleet. I acquired a Mazda Rx7 and a Ford Explorer for absolutely no good reason at all.

I lived in the desert.

I took co-workers to and from the airport.

I rotated vehicles.

I partied every night…

Every.

Single.

Night.

The demons who followed me felt right at home. With a surging hole inside my soul, they had more and more space to settle in and move around.

12. You'll Either Save Each Other— or at Least Won't Die Alone (S)

A friend introduces Rob and Shannon. Shannon ponders the toll a hard life should have extracted. Shannon gets preachy.

Mark left.

Just like that, he disappeared.

I told Mom, and her only response was "Well, you can't stay here. And you can't be around your kids…"

She didn't trust me with the kids. I didn't blame her. There's generally nothing a momma won't do for her babies, but I was so far gone that I wasn't even sure that anything I *would* do would actually be what I *should* do.

Alone, I gravitated to the only group of friends I knew, the group from one of the nearby pool halls. Well, really, they were acquaintances.

Whenever I was with those three men— Kenny, Poe, and Mark— my entire life encompassed whatever they were doing. I didn't really have any relationships— or any life at all— outside of those men.

12. You'll Either Save Each Other— or at Least Won't Die Alone (S)

I started going back to Gabriel's. That's the name of the pool hall closest to the medical insurance company where I no longer worked.

Within a few visits I bumped into a friend I knew post-Poe-pre-Mark.

"I've been worried about you," Patrice said.

He referenced the abuse and the trauma and the partial stories he heard about me playing the hokey-pokey with Texas and Birmingham and jumping out of a truck and all the other things...

When you read it (or even *hear* it), his name seems like it probably belongs to a girl. For sure, Patrice was a guy, and he happened to be the most responsible one— I think— of the entire group of friends. He worked in IT and was capable of holding a legit job for years at a time— not mere weeks or even months like the rest of us.

"I've got a roommate I want to introduce you to."

"Sure," I replied...

I always liked meeting new guys. At that point, I wasn't even a single mom anymore. The kids stayed with my mother and my sister during this season, so I would go pick up a new guy every night.

I'd sleep with them, and then kick them out. No cuddling. No talking. Just get my need of the moment met and move on to whatever else was next on my list. I was back to treating men like men treat women.

"Where's the guy? What's he like?" I asked.

Patrice continued, "He's in the same boat as you. You're both wasting away your lives, drinking yourselves to death. You're either going to end up saving each other and giving each other something worthwhile to live for, or— at least— neither one of my friends will die alone."

Fairly direct words. No beating around the bush.

"I'll get him to meet us here one night," Patrice promised.

A few days later, the mysterious roommate appeared at Gabriel's. Patrice made sure he was coming.

"That's the guy right there, my buddy Rob," Patrice told me. "Go introduce yourself."

He pointed to a short, loud guy who was sitting next to a blond girl.

I walked straight to him.

"I'm Shannon. Patrice said you and I should meet." Then, without hesitation I stated, "I'm taking you home with me tonight."

"Well, OK, Shannon. Great to meet you, too. Sounds fine with me."

The bleachy-blonde next to him interjected, "Hey, wait up. What if I'm his girlfriend?"

"You can come, too," I proposed.

She wasn't. And she didn't. She just happened to be a gal who was there that night. The two of them didn't even ride together. They just both ended up at the same place at the same time.

I thought about whether or not I should include details like that in this story. Rather than omitting certain parts, I decided to leave the places where I have to admit that it didn't matter who or where or when. I would hook up with anyone during those days.

White, black.

Single, married.

Men, women.

I simply wanted to feel something, *anything*. It didn't matter whether it was pain or pleasure.

Maybe you've felt— and even done— some of the same things. You see, we are created for connection. If we don't find it in healthy ways, beginning when we're young, we inevitably seek it in unhealthy ways. We're that desperate for it, and it's that ingrained into us that we need deep human connection.

The problem is that most of us don't get it, so we seek it in the worst possible ways. The results are always disastrous.

....

I don't share my past in order to glorify it. Sometimes, in my work in recovery, I meet people who almost approach their past from the perspective of "well, that was a run, but I had to give all of that up when I got a family" or something of the sort— some misaligned perception of years of pain and struggle that gets glamorized.

My past isn't that.

I only share it— Rob and I only share *all of it*— because it's our story AND it's the story so many others find themselves in some version of right now. If we can shortcut their off-ramp out of the struggle and into salvation, away from the rut and into redemption, we want to do that.

We are proof of grace, of God's rescue.

I sincerely don't know how I made it through my past traumas to where I am now without any STDs or lasting injuries. There are multiple times I statistically should have died.

I meet friends from that era who lost their teeth to crystal meth.

I bump into others who look 30 years older than their biological age, due to the weather-beating that drugs and alcohol and sexing around puts on the body.

Somehow, I can— when I dress right— look like a professional woman who knows her way around a bank or a boardroom or any kind of business meeting. Or, more relevant to *what we do right now*, a successful broker of a real estate company.

My best guess is that God knew all of this beforehand, and He understood where my journey would go, and who I would be. I don't mean to get preachy in a book as raw as what you're reading, but— at the risk of doing as much— there are a few verses buried throughout the New Testament which address this.

In Ephesians 2:8-10, Paul— I'll come back to him and his past later— talks about God's kind of grace. It's NOT the limited type that runs it course and then taps out when you repeat the same mistakes and addictions and make the same failed promises.

Paul clearly states that God's breed of grace saves you from sin AND it ordains a path of great works that you'll walk into and do. That is, God has a plan and purpose for you so good that no bad— not even your biggest bad— can disqualify you from it.

In Romans 8:28, Paul also says all things work together for the good for those who love God. He doesn't suggest all things ARE good. All the trauma I experienced and the hurt I caused are bad. Clearly.

Somehow, in God's math, He morphs all of that into good.

A converted womanizer himself, the ancient theologian Saint Augustine (ca. 400 AD) once surmised that "if all things work together for the good, that means God transforms even our worst moments and deepest pits into something extraordinary."

Or, to say it another way— the worst you've done cannot undo God's best for you. You're not bad enough to outdo His grip of grace.

....

That said, let's make an observation about labels and name-calling and all the other stuff that it's easy to get lost in when it comes to stories like ours. You might need to read and re-read these two points:

- Satan knows your name, but he consistently declares your shame.

- Jesus knows your shame, but He declares your true name.

(I didn't make up these statements— I've heard and read and seen several versions of them.)

This is how the enemy works.

Full time.

Over time.

In hyper-drive.

He does so to keep you down, to make you think you're not worthy of the life God has called you to— the life you actually desire. The life you might be afraid to talk about with anyone for fear they'll belittle it.

And when you run into a shame-er, a condemn-er, and a hate-spewer... someone who always plays the "devil's advocate," they've aligned on the wrong side.

Jump back 2,000 years...

There's a little known story in the back of the Book of Acts. Whereas the first four books of the New Testament (Matthew, Mark, Luke, and John) talk about what Jesus did while He walked on this planet, Acts (the fifth book) tells the stories of what His followers did after He ascended to His throne.

At the end of Acts, the Apostle Paul and Luke (the man who wrote the book of Luke and the book of Acts) find themselves in a shipwreck. They crashed on the island of Malta.

The 270+ travelers with them began warming themselves at a fire when a poisonous viper shot out from under the ground and fastened its fangs on Paul's arm.

The locals observed, "The shipwreck didn't get him, and now this snake has... the gods are trying to extract justice on him."

One even said, "This man is a murderer! He can't escape fate!" (Acts 28:4).

Contrary to the idea that God works it all for good, these men articulated what many of us automatically assume: bad things happen because that's what God judged I deserve.

The truth is, well, that second man *nailed* it. Paul WAS a murderer. He was the ring-leader at the death of the first known post-Resurrection martyr (Stephen, see Acts 8:1).

But that was who Paul was in the past. Not who he "is" now.

Paul yanked the snake from his arm and tossed it into the fire. The locals waited for him to die.

A few moments later, realizing he was fine, they changed their tune and took him to their chief— who lay on his death bed. Paul healed him, and then brought hope and healing to *everyone* on the island.

Later, Paul penned a like message on to others...

After listing a litany of pet issues that entrap most of us, he wrote, "And such *were* [past tense] some of you... *but you were washed, sanctified*" (1 Corinthians 6:11).

He observes that those things were true. We failed. All of us.

But, the shame of the past doesn't define your present. In fact, it may very well become a tool that empowers you to encourage others and set them free. They, too, often have one of those self-appointed "devil's advocates" (who often masquerade as "angels of light") pointing to their faults and flaws. Or, they have well-intended observers— like the locals around that bonfire— pointing to the obvious.

The failures of the past— of your past— can quickly become the soundtrack of your life. You can't change the previous chapters of story, but you can reframe the narrative. Yank the snake off and toss it into the fire. You can make the story go somewhere unexpected.

Remember, even Jesus knows your shame. That's part of the reason He came in the first place.

He knows it.

But He doesn't stir up your shame.

He declares your name...

Application for Part 4 | The Right Relationships Are a Superpower

Main idea: Relationships either push you higher or pull you lower. We're designed for connection. When we don't unite in healthy ways, we align in unhealthy ways. The type of relationships you have is an incredibly accurate predictor of whether or not you reach your full potential.

We focus a lot on WHAT we'll do when it comes to goal setting and dream-achieving. We also give HOW much attention (and get training on how to execute strategies and gain new skills).

Both of these facets of life planning are important— so much so that we talked about WHAT earlier and we'll discuss HOW in Part 5.

But we need to affirm that walking with the right people (WHO) is vital.

Who are the key people in your life?

_____

_____

_____

_____

_____

_____

_____

_____

_____

_____

We're created for connection. If you don't connect to healthy people in helpful ways, you'll connect to unhealthy people in harmful ways (i.e., see Shannon's story in chapter 10).

Where do you see both of these truths in your story?

_____

_____

_____

_____

_____

_____

_____

_____

_____

Look back at each key marker in your personal history — the highest points and the lowest. Each probably had as much to do with the people you were "doing life" with as anything else.

(This doesn't absolve you of responsibility for bad choices or remove credit for your accomplishments. It simply affirms the power of connection.)

Make some observations here about your story.

_____

_____

_____

_____

_____

_____

_____

We don't want to "use" people nor do we want commodify them. We want to honor everyone.

However, there is a difference between letting people in your "inner circle" and honoring them as fellow humans.

Who are the people who need to be in your inner circle who currently aren't?

Who are some of the people who don't need to be in your "inner circle" but you need to consistently honor and appreciate?

Who are some of the people you need to remove from your inner circle?

Application for Part 4 | The Right Relationships Are a Superpower

Part 5 | Implementation > Information

Many times we already know what to do; we just need to do it. Think progress, not perfection; think direction, not distance. We often overestimate what we can do in a moment but underestimate the power of significant moments strung together consistently.

13. We Met an Angel But I Kept Running With the Devil (R)

Rob discovers something about his Mom, Lyn travels to Vegas, and Rob tries to change a plan— all in the wake of 9-11

I lived out West for about 10 years, between my stint in the Marines and my time as a civilian contractor for the Navy afterwards.

I bounced through all the usual shenanigans out there for a few years before I finally thought about settling down. That transition happened when I met a gal named Liz, who had two kids.

I fell hard for her— but I'm not sure if I fell harder for her or her two boys. Within just a few years, I coached Little League baseball for the oldest and began spending a few afternoons a week instructing young boys how NOT to be afraid of a hard ball that was being flung at them, how to stay tight enough in the batter's box to swing a bat and smack that ball rather than giving into their natural instinct and jumping out of the box, and how to field grounders without the ball rolling between their legs.

We were together about four years. It was an awesome run until it wasn't.

Liz finally gave me an ultimatum: "I've got to look out for my boys. Your binge-drinking scares me, to be honest. You drink on the way to and from the game— and during the games."

"I've got it under control," I said.

"You don't. I don't even know about all the other times, and you probably don't either. You drink *constantly...*"

I chose the alcohol. It wasn't actually a conscientious decision like the kind you make at the ice cream shop— "I'll choose Rocky Road instead of Peanut Butter Fudge"— such that you deliberately pick up one and push away the other...

... like I did when Liz and I really started dating and I set down the Mustang Ranch and all the other bullshit behaviors that I never should have been clinging to in the first place...

This just kinda happened.

Consistent behaviors in a predictable direction create a pattern that, at some point, seems obvious.

"I decided this," you realize. "I chose this by my own actions. I'm responsible. It's me. I'm the problem."

We began to notice something wasn't quite right with Mom.

I was in San Diego (during my Marine Corps days) when we first noticed. I had to fly to New Orleans, so Mom and Dad decided to drive over from Birmingham and meet me. During that trip Mom couldn't quite figure out why we weren't going to see the ocean and why I "refused" to take her to my apartment.

We began putting the pieces together.

Over time, things got more serious— for me and for Mom. My drinking escalated even more, and Dad became more definitive about the state of Mom's health.

"Something is definitely wrong," he told me over the phone.

For a few months, I spoke regularly with Dad— more than I had done in the recent past. He knew I was drifting from Liz, that I was extremely heartbroken about it but wouldn't— *or couldn't*— figure out how to give up the one thing that would make the relationship with her actually work.

"You really like her, don't you, son?" Dad asked.

I told him that I do. "This has been different. I mean, I've had other girlfriends — someone on the side in each place the Marines went and a few girls here and there. I began actually building a life with her, though."

"Why don't you make it work, then?"

It was an honest question, but I didn't have an honest answer. Sometimes, it's only after you break something that you can figure out how you blew the whole thing apart.

"It's just not going to work," I told him.

One night Dad reported his latest news to me. "I'm not sure how to say this," he said. His voice quivered. Then— "Your Mom… she has early onset Alzheimer's."

"They can treat that, can't they?"

"No. Not really. It's a long road. She'll begin forgetting things…"

He explained it the best he could, describing the upcoming scenario as the doctor must have detailed it for him…

"It's going to be a long, painful road," he confessed.

As he spoke, I thought about what it would be like for Mom to listen to a man in a white coat tell you that some of the best memories you've been making and the people, places, and things most familiar to you will start to fade, gradually erasing themselves in reverse— from the most recent births, birthday celebrations, and holidays and then moving backwards, eating away everything else.

Dad told me that if you ask a person with Alzheimer's who the President of the United States is, they most likely won't tell you the name of the man currently in office. They'll tell you— with confidence— the name of the man leading the country 20 or 30 or more years ago. They'll be convinced he's the President now.

Or if you show them a current picture of their spouse, they might not recognize them. At the same time, show them a photograph from a few decades ago, and they'll know exactly who it is. They may even recount a touching story to you in great detail.

The disease is a neurodegenerative disorder. The brain processes slowly begin to deteriorate and progressively worsen, affecting language, disorientation, mood swings, and more.

Somewhere amidst our many convos— about Liz and about Mom— Dad offered, "You can move in with me if you want to come back."

"I've been on my own for a decade, Dad. I'm not sure how that will work."

"I've got my duplex. The other side is empty. You can have that complete unit to yourself. You'll have your own place— not just your own room. Then you can come back and forth next door and see your Mom, too."

I accepted his invite. I knew it would be a difficult transition, because I knew I wasn't in a good place.

I was just running again— in a different direction.

- When I enlisted in the Marines, *I was running from cocaine and my other addictions, as well as lack of purpose.*

   Marines looked impressive— I ran from being unimpressive.

- When I returned to Alabama, *I was running from heartache and alcohol and a nasty meth habit.*

   Consequently, I was still unimpressive. I acquired the dress blues, but I learned that— contrary to the popular saying— the clothes emphatically *do not* make the man. *The man is still the man.*

Dad concocted a plan and ran it by me one Sunday night when we were talking.

"I'll fly out to Vegas," he said. It was December 2001— the planes had been up and flying for a few months by then from (post-9-11 attacks), but security was still amped-up. "You load whatever you're bringing with you into a U-

Haul. Drive from Reno to Vegas. I'll meet you at a hotel near the airport, and we'll drive back together."

"That's a 7-hour drive. Why don't you just come to Reno?"

He explained his rationale: "Flights are cheaper to Vegas, because I can get a straight shot there. And, you're right, it's 7 hours. That's 7 hours closer to here. That first little leg will make it a bit shorter getting back to Birmingham and back to your Mom. I don't know how long I should be away..."

I low-key knew Dad liked playing cards. Meeting in Vegas would give him a day to play Blackjack, too.

"That makes sense," I replied. "Let's do it."

I went to work, locating a moving truck and packing my belongings.

Our plan should have worked well. It would have except for two big factors.

First, the LSV airport sits about 1 mile from the strip. Planes takeoff and land with a clear site line to the massive hotels and gaming casinos. It's a cheap, quick cab ride. Heck, it's walking distance if you don't mind a little desert heat.

Second, between the extremely short time we created the plan and the moment Dad landed in Vegas, I met Ronnie...

Whereas Liz was the quintessential suburban Mom— the kind of gal who enrolls her kids in all the sports, signs up to be school's "room Mom," and brings decorated cupcakes to class on birthdays— Ronnie was the pro-typical free spirit who was always down for anything at a moment's notice. This isn't to paint a poor portrait of her (my story is proof you shouldn't judge anyone's story by the chapter you dropped-in on). It's just where she was in life at that moment— just like me.

We were two peas in a pod, as the saying goes...

Set five lines of cocaine on the table, she'll snort two-and-a-half. Grab a case of beer, she'll split it. Ronnie knew one speed: *full throttle*.

I talked Ronnie into packing up her house and placing all of her belongings — what little she had— into my U-Haul.

"Where exactly are we going?" she asked.

I relayed what Dad told me...

My first clue that this was going to be a shit show— besides her capacity to keep up with me on the drugs and the alcohol— should have been her availability to nonchalantly load her things and just leave one city for another. She had no roots, no long-term relational connections, and no obligations (such as a job or anything else that anchors people to a real life).

The day before Dad's flight landed, Ronnie and I made the drive from Reno to Vegas. It's a winding road that takes you, basically, through the middle of nowhere. The difficulty of the drive, I learned, escalates based on the volume of alcohol you continue consuming as you roll your way down those roads.

We headed to the Luxor. It's the big pyramid-shaped casino with the Sphinx in front of it. It's close to the airport *and also* out of the "busier side" of the strip. It should have been an "easy in, easy out" option to meet Dad and make the drive back.

When I got there, Dad was playing Blackjack. Just like I envisioned.

I thought, "Hmm. We really haven't seen each other in person in a few years. We've talked a lot, but he probably won't recognize me with the long braids, colored bands in my hair, and earrings in both ears."

I looked nothing like my Marine Corps picture.

I sat beside him at the table and just watched him play. He looked my way a few times and never recognized me.

After a few hands, the dealer looked at me and asked, "You want in? Those seats are really for people who want to play…"

"Deal me in," I said.

Dad double-taked.

"That you, Rob?"

"Hah!"

We hugged, talked about my appearance, and went through the usual pleasantries about the flight, catching a cab, and getting settled into the hotel.

After a few minutes, Dad noticed Ronnie standing beside me.

"She with you?" he asked.

"Yeah. I thought Ronnie could come with us."

Dad remained calm and clear.

"No, she's not," he said.

"Oh, yeah, we've got plenty of space in the U-haul. She can help drive…"

Dad asked if she even had a license.

"I've *had* one," she interjected.

"Do you have a *valid* license *right now*?"

She looked away, puffed a cigarette, then looked back with puppy dog eyes.

Dad told me slowly, "She. Is. Not. Coming." Then, to her— "No disrespect, Ma'am. I just found out about you."

Dad wisely saw through it. Ronnie was in a bad place.

What he didn't know— or perhaps he knew only in part— was that *I was in an even worse place than her.*

When I worked as a civilian contractor, I made good money— about $1,700 each week. That seems like a great check, but I had three vehicles and a major substance abuse issue.

My version of the Malcom Luck during this season was that the more I made, the bigger the hole inside me got, and the more I spent trying to fill it with something flimsy and unsubstantial.

I was already struggling, but the breakup with Liz really sent me spiraling. I lost most of my stuff but kept my substance addictions.

The news about my Mom pushed me down even further, and I made my way all the way to the bottom of the funnel.

All the time I spent with Ronnie… well, turns out you CAN go lower than rock bottom. I was there.

I didn't have anywhere to go at that point except Birmingham, and Dad was already there. I had all my belongings, the few I had left, in the U-Haul. I didn't have much money, and I no longer had a job.

I agreed to send Ronnie back to Reno.

As the Malcom Luck would have it, Ronnie and I decided to go out with a bang. Thanks to the availability of cheap alcohol and free cocktails, we bounced from place to place and made the most of the time we had left.

The only vehicle we had access to was the U-Haul, so that's how we got around. Some people in Vegas take a cab or a limo; others drive fancy rentals. We drove a box truck for one night of pandemonium.

When I left Dad at the blackjack table, we agreed to meet at a specific time and place in the hotel lobby. We planned to drop Ronnie at the airport as we began the trek home.

I no-showed.

Thinking I might have changed my mind, after waiting 15 minutes or so, Dad looked across the parking lot.

"Well, the truck is here, so I know he's here..."

He marched to the front desk and asked for a key. Somehow, they agreed to not only provide him with my room number but to also give him access.

He walked through the door and found the two of us completely passed-out. It took 10-15 minutes to even get me to wake up.

He never yelled.

I could tell a cocktail of emotions coursed through him. Part disappointment, part anger, part anxious about starting the trip and getting back to Mom, he shuffled me.

"Where are the keys?" he asked. "We need to go. I'll go start the truck and make sure we have fuel in it while you get dressed and come down..."

"They're in my pants pocket," I said, pointing across the room.

Dad checked. Each pocket. Then each pocket again.

No keys.

"They're not here."

"Throw my pants to me," I said.

I checked. Nothing. Just an empty wallet.

I asked Ronnie, "Where are the keys?"

She didn't know. I had done all of the driving— I think.

We looked through each article of clothing, inside every drawer, and on the top of each surface in the hotel room.

Still.

No.

Keys.

We called U-Haul. Not even the local branch had a spare key. Not that it would have made sense for them to, but might as well check.

We finally rented a second U-Haul and backed it up to the first. We transferred all of my belongings. I paid a fee for not returning the U-Haul to the exact location, and an even bigger fee for losing the key. Not to mention the mileage and the jacked-up fuel charges for "returning" the vehicle on empty.

They also downgraded me when I re-rented. The first U-Haul was a 1999 model or so— pretty decent considering it was 2001. They replaced it with a piece of shit 1980 truck that should have been retired over a decade ago. The odometer didn't even work.

....

We dropped Ronnie at LSV. I'm still not sure what happened to her stuff, or if she even had anything other than the bags we set with her at the curb.

An hour outside of Vegas, Dad and I— now alone— bumped into yet another obstacle that demonstrated this would be everything but a normal cross-country move. Namely, we arrived at the Hoover Dam.

Under regular circumstances, this would have been a non-issue. However, the U.S. was walking through the post-9-11, hyper-sensitive-to-terrorist-threats era.

Plus, two years after the feds raised the Branch-Davidian compound outside of Waco (causing 76 deaths in a firestorm), Timothy McVey used a box truck to bomb the Federal Building in Oklahoma (ca. 4-19-1993 and 4-19-1995). No law enforcement agency allowed box trucks to go anywhere near federal properties— much less across the Hoover Dam where a bomb could not only destroy the dam but also take out a power grid and create the havoc an ensuing flood might cause.

"Can't drive that U-Haul through here," a guard said. "You're going to have to go around."

I don't blame him. Dad looked honest. Me— and the truck— looked shady as hell.

We had to go the long way around the dam, adding hours AND mountains to our journey. That piece of shit truck that could barely muddle its way across a flat road routinely overheated and smoked on the hills.

On the way up, we struggled to hit 9 miles per hour. On the way down, we zoomed as fast as we could. We needed the downhill run to gain momentum to make it halfway up the next climb.

Ugh.

I was worthless all day because of that overnight bender with Ronnie. Not to mention the subsequent reload of the U-Haul in a Vegas parking lot. The HVAC in our truck went out, to boot, and I simply drifted to sleep.

The ride *sucked* for me. I can't imagine what it was like for Dad.

Night settled in and it got super-dusky— like the artwork you might see at a "starving artist sale" at the civic center. Everything looked hazy— like a bad watercolor painting.

Dad told me— for miles— "We're almost out of gas. We gotta find something."

Fading in and out of consciousness, I had heard him...

There was nothing on those backroads we had to take when they boomeranged us around the Hoover dam for fear we would blow it up. Dad prayed we would find something, anything to gas up the truck.

I fell asleep again...

At some point I woke up to the sound of the truck rattling. Everything shook, as if riding in a mini-earthquake. Both windows were down, the whipping wind adding to the fury.

Our speed increased as we rolled down a mountain.

"95 miles per hour!" I said, peaking across the dash.

"Buckle up," Dad said. "We're out of gas. I've got this thing in neutral and we're coasting as far as it will go."

It felt as if we were on an airstrip in one of those small propeller planes. I grabbed my seatbelt, fastened it, and wondered if it would even matter if you crashed with a seatbelt in that jacked-up box truck.

"Look!" Dad exclaimed. "There's a light flickering at the bottom of the mountain." As the speed maxed-out he suggested, "That's probably a gas station!"

As we got closer and the building came into view, it became apparent he was right. It *was* a gas station. A tiny one. The kind with just one pump.

The building was less than 600 square feet. It was made completely of painted cinderblock.

Dad was right. It had a pump.

"It looks closed for the day," I said.

Dad coasted under the canopy and saddled up to the solitary pump, anyway.

Even though the rest of society was already fully-committed to the pay at the pump option (we discussed this earlier), which effectively enables you sometimes to fill up even when there's no worker present, this small place knew no such technology. They had the old school fueling stations, the kind where the numbers scroll like the Vegas slots.

"I don't seen anyone here," Dad said. "We might be out of luck for the night."

"What do you mean?"

"We don't have any gas. We may just need to sleep in the truck and wait until the morning when someone shows up."

Someone— inside— had to turn those pumps on in order to get fuel. Usually, due in part to guys who used to live like me, rushing off with a stolen tank of diesel in the silver Cutlass Supreme, most places now required you to pay in advance.

"Nah, I don't see anyone," Dad said, as he approached the glass door of the small store.

"I gotta take a piss," I said. "I'll be right back."

I started walking left, but quickly discovered that only led to a ledge— off the side of the hill. I backtracked and went right.

"Wrong way," I said, nodding to Dad as I looped back.

I went behind the building— that's where gas station restrooms used to be. I figured if it was locked, I could just pee against the side of the building or find a tree.

It took a while. First, I really had to go. Second, I got caught up thinking about the bullshit I had just put my Dad through...

- If I didn't bring Ronnie I wouldn't have gone on that drinking and drugging spree the night before.

- If I didn't go on that spree, I wouldn't have lost the keys.

- If I hadn't lost the keys, we would still be in the Cadillac of U-Hauls instead of the butt wipe of box trucks.

- If we were in the Cadillac we would be racing through these hills, and we wouldn't be running out of gas...

- If we weren't slugging through the hills, we wouldn't be at this gas station— we'd be miles ahead.

You probably know how this kind of mind-fuck works. Once you start thinking about one negative thing, it's on. You jump down rabbit holes you have no business visiting— and go to places in your head, asking questions you'll never find answers for.

That's where I went...

- If I hadn't started using cocaine & MDMA, I wouldn't have gotten my ass beat on the beach.

- If I hadn't gotten my ass beat on the beach, I wouldn't have stolen gas.

- If I wouldn't have stolen gas, I might have not gone into the Marines...

But, shit, that was a great experience....

- If I hadn't gone into the Marines, I wouldn't have visited the Bunny Ranch and the Mustang and met Liz and then met Ronnie and then...

- If I hadn't done all of that, I wouldn't have gotten on this box truck and be here now.

What.

The.

Fuck.

Was I just living one big loop?

Did nothing I did actually matter?

I started, somehow during this mental madness, blaming myself and all the drugs for my Mom's illness.

"Is Mom sick because of me?"

If so, I was responsible for everything my Dad was going through, too. And that meant...

"Shit, I gotta go check on Dad and the gas..."

I walked back around the building. Dad sat in the driver seat, the air blowing, the truck now cranked again and running smooth.

"You decide to just run it out and stay here the night?" I asked.

"No. We were already out. We rolled into this place on *nothing*."

"Oh, yeah," I recalled.

"C'mon. We're full."

"What? They're closed."

"A guy walked from behind the building and turned on the pump. I handed him my credit card and he put $50 bucks in— that topped it off."

(Remember, gas was a whole lot cheaper back then.)

I told Dad, "I was just back there. There's only one way around the building. There was no one there. I took a piss and didn't see anybody."

Dad sat there a moment.

"There is absolutely nothing around us," I clarified. "We are in the middle of nowhere."

He looked back into the store. It was still closed.

I looked over at the glass door. It appeared to still be locked.

"There's nobody anywhere around here," I observed. Then, "Where's the man who pumped the gas?"

We looked at each other.

"I believe that man was an angel," Dad said.

He was serious.

I think he was right.

....

We made it back to Birmingham a few days later. The truck never performed like a racehorse after that angel-encounter, but it did actually ride better.

I moved in next door to Mom and Dad, in the other side of the duplex, just like Dad offered. As cliche as it sounds, it was good to be home.

I didn't have a job, of course, so Dad asked one thing of me while I got all of that sorted: "Help me look after your Mom, a bit."

By then he was finished doing manual labor. Though he still worked in real estate, he had a few work crews doing all of the labor. He rode around, bid on jobs, bought houses, got the men going, and collected checks. His schedule was flexible enough to watch out for mother, but he still couldn't be with her 24/7.

You might think that seeing Dad's grace to me in Vegas, getting the boost from an angel, and navigating across the states with him might help me "man up" and take more responsibility for my decisions, but it didn't.

I lost Mom multiple times. She'd spring up from the couch and, not knowing where she was, just shoot off down the street walking....

A few times I received phone calls from strangers— we made sure she always had identification on her, as well as instructions as to what to do if she wandered.

Then there were times she made stuff up— as dementia sometimes causes people to do. She told people her husband was beating her and that she was being held hostage.

Once, the cops picked her up from a neighbor we didn't know. They wouldn't release her back to Dad because they didn't know she had Alzheimer's and she made a few accusations— all untrue— that warranted them keeping him away (if they were true, of course).

This all occurred on my watch.

I started working for my Dad— so that one of us could get back and forth to her. This could have been a win-win, but I wasn't ready. I squandered yet another opportunity to help my family and honor my parents.

And then, amidst it all, I called Ronnie.

"How the hell are you?" I asked.

"What do you think? I thought I was making that drive with you, and you dropped me like a hot potato there in Vegas."

"You wouldn't have wanted to make that ride," I replied.

I told her about the long way around the Hoover Dam, the engine barely scaling the Rockies on the way back, *and the angel story.*

"That sounds fucked," she suggested.

It probably did. The more I thought about it, I didn't know what to think about it myself.

Somewhere in that conversation, we decided Ronnie could catch a flight to Birmingham just as easy as she caught a flight back to Reno. Within a matter of days, I sent her enough money for a one-way flight to BHM International Airport.

You know where this goes. It's too predictable.

- Forget all the nonsense we thought about her helping me with Mom and the "Oh, great, someone will always be next door to her!" bullshit line we believed.

- Forget the crud about "we've got an awesome place to live— and with this accountability next door we'll get things right and stay clean."

- Forget all the good intentions and fulfilling our "uphill dreams" while living downhill habits and making sewage-level decisions.

Within just a few days, we used faster and more ferociously than I ever had. We were terrible for each other— and probably even worse for the stress level of my Mom and Dad and all they were legitimately juggling apart from us.

In a single day, Dad delivered a strong one-two punch + knockout sequence. It was a left hook, right jab, followed by an uppercut.

"You're not welcome here anymore," he said. "You can come visit anytime you'd like, but you can't live here anymore. I can't decide if you choose to be with Ronnie or not. That's your decision. Regardless, you can't stay here..."

Boom.

I knew right then that this wasn't about her finally joining me— something he was against from the moment he met her at the blackjack table in Vegas. This had nothing to do with her. This was about me and my bullshit.

Instant eviction was the left hook.

"There's another thing," he added. "You're fired."

"But I won't be able to find another place to live..."

"Yes, you can. You've been making enough to save money— and you haven't been paying rent."

"It's gone," I told him. "I've spent it..."

Immediate unemployment was the jab.

As I thought about what to do, all of the sudden feeling dizzy and light-headed and weak in the knees, Dad continued talking...

"You'll need to figure something out," he said. Then— "You need to give me the keys to the truck, because that's a work truck, and you no longer work for me…"

That was the uppercut, the knockout punch.

In a day, I lost my house, my job, and my transportation…

....

Not knowing what to do, I did what most addicts do. I just threw myself completely into another nonsensical adventure. Namely, Ronnie and I— newly homeless and jobless— went to Fort Walton Beach, Florida.

As I had done back in the day of the silver Cutlass Supreme, I sold enough cocaine, meth, and pills to fund the hotel while keeping enough to party. It worked like a charm until the two of us got into a fight. It wasn't a fistfight— it was just an argument. I was pissed enough to go to a strip club, though.

While at that club, I spent and tipped away every last bit of money we had to our name. It was all the money I had earned (probably from selling some of my stash), but still…

At some point in the middle of the night, I hitched my way back to the cheap, faded-paint job, smoke-stained motel we'd bunked at. She was high on pills, lost like a kite in a hurricane with no tether to reality.

"Where you been?" she asked.

I told her.

No sense in lying about it. When I left I had told her where I was headed, and that's exactly where I went. Might as well keep the truth consistent.

We exchanged a few words, and things got louder. Being the kind of place we were staying, no one could really tell it was us causing all the commotion.

At some point in the middle of it all, Ronnie told me, "I'll fuckin' show you..."

She walked into the bathroom, raised the plastic seat up from the toilet and then smashed her head against the porcelain.

Whack!

I saw it— I was standing just a few feet away from her.

"You head-butted the toilet?" I asked.

Thonk!

She smashed her face a second time.

"What are you doing?" I asked. "Stop that."

Smack!

As the blood began flowing, she looked at me and grinned an evilish type of sly smile. It's as if the drugs ripped the pain away, such that she could carry out the scheme deliberately, almost mechanically.

"I told you," she growled. "I'd get you."

She walked to the hotel phone. She punched 9-1-1.

"My boyfriend just beat me up... Yes, he's still here. We're in room number..."

I watched the entire episode play out in slow motion.

Moments later, the Okaloosa County Sheriff arrived. They knocked on the door, asked her a few questions, and took me to jail.

13. We Met an Angel but I Kept Running With the Devil (R)

All of the explaining and story-telling and even truth-declaring about the whole evening didn't help a bit. The more I told, the guiltier I looked.

The curve ball here is that *she called my Dad.*

"Lyn, this is Ronnie. Rob is in jail..."

I can't imagine what she might have said when he asked why— or if he finally stopped asking at some point.

He bailed me out, but the deal still stood. I remained fired and evicted.

I phoned a friend I knew from Gabriel's. His name was Patrice. He had an apartment not too far away from my parents' duplex. I moved into his spare room for a bit.

Patrice eventually introduced me to Shannon.

13. We Met an Angel but I Kept Running With the Devil (R)

14. I Can Stay Up All Week But Still Can't Show Up (S)

Shannon learns of Rob's odd habit. She reflects on men who helped her with no expectation of anything in return. The two relocate. She reminisces about traveling everywhere by foot.

Rob and I started hanging out on the daily.

He lived a few miles from Gabriel's— the bar / pool hall. I lived, according to him, "in the sticks." Though it's not really that far from everything else (and was close to my kids, my other relatives, their school, and my lack of job) the little town where I lived DOES seem like stepping into the outer banks…

"This is what Columbus probably felt like when he sailed to America," Rob said. "Am I gonna actually get somewhere, or are we going to just fall off the edge of the earth?"

Rob never fell off the earth coming to get me, and the routine was always predictable:

- 7:20 am— Load kids on the school bus at my Mom's

- 7:30 am— Kids gone for 8 hours, Rob rolls up in his black Mitsubishi Eclipse, 6-pack of tall boys in hand
- 7:31 am— Zoom off for the day, ripping & roaring, drinking & getting drunk for the rest of the day

Next day's agenda = rinse and repeat.

The details of each day varied slightly, but the core component remained steady. There was never a 24-hour period during which we didn't sell slightly more drugs that we used (to cover the cost of our own), guzzle a case *or more* of cheap beer (usually more), and partake of drunken stupor sex (often in the car but not always).

One day, Rob thumbed through my wad of money. I didn't really have a wallet— I just kept a it stashed in by bra, along with whatever drugs I had, and two small pocketknives for protection (you'd be surprised what security two tiny blades bring when you consistently tip-toe the ledge of absolute nonsense).

"You've still got a Texas license, Shan!"

Since the day of Marshall Mayhem, I'd been a resident of the great state of Texas. I knew I need to change-over back to Alabama, but I never made the time.

"We're not doing anything tomorrow," Rob observed. He was both right and wrong. All day, every day, we did nothing— nothing important—but it was *always* something. He continued, "Let's go tomorrow."

The next day, Rob honked the horn of the black Eclipse at exactly 7:30am, and we headed towards Tuscaloosa. The small town where I lived WAS technically closer to the State Trooper's office in T-town than back to Birmingham, so we headed down I-20.

Rob brought the everyday liquid-breakfast of tall boys. We drank all 6 over the next 30 or so miles.

Now, here's something you need to know about Rob: he's wired. Especially in those days. Even now, he exudes the energy of three people who are each three times his size. When he speaks, it's *always* with urgency, intensity, and conviction— regardless of whether he's talking about a home repair, one of our kids' needs, or something he learned on a coaching call.

But when he stops moving, he crashes. If he pauses, he "passes out." He's known for it.

We arrived at the Trooper's office early, so I could beat the line.

"I'm staying in the car," he said.

I walked inside, reeking of below-average beer, and grabbed my spot in line.

It didn't take more than two minutes for a female officer to approach me and ask, "Ma'am, have you been drinking?"

It was just barely past 8:00 am. They had just opened the doors. The government workers who man the desks hadn't even poured their morning coffee. But, yes, I had been drinking. A lot.

"No, Ma'am," I told her— I'd been around law enforcement enough to know that voicing a *Ma'am* or a *Sir* always diffuses the tension just a bit— "I just got here."

"I can smell it," she replied. Then— "Did you drive here?"

"I did not. My boyfriend brought me."

"Where is he?"

"Outside."

"Let's go see…"

She led me back through the double-glass front doors and into the parking lot.

"Our car is over there," I said, half leading her, half being led.

"Your boyfriend brought you? Where is he?"

Rob wasn't in the front seat. It looked like I lied.

"You *sure* your boyfriend brought you here?" she asked.

I was a bit nervous as to what I knew came next…

"Shit," I thought. "He's passed out in the back!"

As we neared the car I spotted the keys dangling in the ignition. We rarely took them out.

I glanced to the back….

Here's *another* thing you need to know about Rob and his "passing out." It almost always looked planned, because he always stripped down to his boxers, folded his pants, and then just stretched out wherever he was. Living room, bedroom, party— it didn't matter. Back of the car at the State Trooper's— no problem.

"Ma'am, why is your boyfriend laying here in his underwear? He's been drinking, too, hasn't he?"

I stammered.

As quick as I was on my feet, thinking of what to say to get out of virtually any trouble in which I found myself, I couldn't concoct the words to explain that "Yes, he's drunk, but he's a functional drunk. We both are. And it's not a problem for us, even if it is for you. He also strips down like this all the time, anyway, so drinking isn't a factor here."

The female officer, who also spotted the keys, walked around to the driver side and grabbed them.

"I'm not arresting either one of you," she declared, "but I'm not letting you drive drunk, either. You need to go find somebody sober to drive you out of here. I'll give the keys to them."

Rob slept through the entire exchange. It was obvious he wasn't going anywhere, so I looked around to identify my next step.

In the near distance, about two blocks away, I spotted an Express Oil— one of the "in and out" shops where they change your oil, replace your filter, and level-up all your fluids for about $15 in "15 minutes or less or it's free." That was the sales pitch back then, anyway.

Two bay doors were open, and another was in the process of being opened.

"Damsel in distress!" I called, approaching the first opening. "Damsel in distress!"

A youngish guy who looked like he'd either slept in his work clothes and just rolled out of bed OR stayed up in them all night from after work yesterday peeked outside.

"I got you," he said. "What's up?"

I explained the situation (mentioning nothing about a half-naked boyfriend asleep in the back of the car), offering, "I'll buy you a six pack to drive the car off the lot. I can handle it from there."

"Deal."

He walked back to the Trooper's office with me and greeted the officer.

"You're driving?"

"Yes, Ma'am."

He knew the drill, too— always include a *Ma'am* or a S*ir.* It goes a long way when dealing with the Law.

The officer tossed him Rob's keys, and we strode to the vehicle.

"Hmm. There's some dude in the backseat," he said, sliding in and adjusting Rob's super-short set up to accommodate his long legs.

"No problem," I replied. Then— "Let's go over to that gas station right there, and I can get you that 6 pack."

He parked near the front door.

"I'll meet you inside," I said, "Let me get some money."

I circled around to the driver side of the car, made sure he was back near the fridge wall, and then took off. Like they say, *no good deed goes unpunished.*

Rob got kicked out of his apartment, and I got kicked out of my Mom's. The reasons were simple:

• *Rob had been crashing at Patrice's, who was the only tenant on the actual lease.*

  After getting booted from his Dad's, Rob tossed him a few dollars whenever he could. The lack of consistent income combined with Patrice's jealousy of me and Rob (he had been one the guys I casually hooked up with in the past, and now that was obviously a thing of the past) cemented the deal.

  Rob was out.

- *Mom's place had always — according to her — been a temporary situation.*

She never anticipated me staying more than just a few days, and I never expected to. But, the days all blur when you're on one constant bender.

I was out, too.

We moved into the Mitsubishi. That's where we spent the bulk of our time, anyway.

That black car ended up being "free," by the way. With all of Rob's moving in and out of state, up and down the street, and consistently living at inconsistent (and borrowed) addresses, Mitsubishi lost track of him. He stopped paying, and they ceased looking for him.

He had money for drugs, beer, and gas — but not for a car. All addicts do that kind of thing.

You've seen it:

- Homeless man has nowhere to live and no job but somehow has an iPhone.

- Addict doesn't have money to pay a power bill but scrounges the money to post bail.

- Druggie can't get to work for a 10:00am retail job at the mall, but can make it up every morning at 7:20am for a life of self-defined, supposed "freedom."

Anyway, after Rob straightened up— which happened before I got clean— he set out making amends to the people he wronged during his addiction(s). It's the 9th step in AA and, though I think it was driven more from a sincere heart to set things in order rather than navigating his way through the big 12, he really got after it. He financed the car through Mitsubishi USA, so they were on his hit list.

"Mitsubishi doesn't have a record of it, anymore," he declared.

If you know Rob, you know he speaks "from his tippie-toes." He shouted his shock with sheer intensity.

"They said to just *keep the car*. I mean, I told them— I really intend to pay you. I owe you. I have THE CAR. But they just said not to worry about it. They're even sending me a letter..."

Sure enough, a letter from Mitsubishi arrived a few days later, thanking him for his call and verifying that they did indeed know about a black mid-90s model Eclipse with his exact VIN#, but they had no data on any money being owed for that car. They enclosed copy of the title.

That scenario— a different version of Malcom Luck— was still a few years off in the future, though. So, back to the story.

We needed a place to live.

Around Y2K, Target and Best Buy and Pier One and a few other up-and-coming retailers anchored a new shopping strip on 280, a jam-packed parking lot of a street that leads east from downtown Birmingham through the elite suburbs and off to the middle of nowhere. Suburban people have money, and merchants want more of it, so the already-overloaded road saw more and more retailers pop up.

Apartments— like Patrice's— dropped into every available nook that wasn't already filled with a house, occupied by a new store, or slated for a new megachurch complex. Turns out, the "Target parking lot" was 300 yards up the hill from Patrice's (where Rob got kicked-out), and it was always full of cars.

We kept our vehicle there.

Every few days we moved it around the lot, just a bit, so the rent-a-cop-$9-hour-gunless-security-guards never caught on that we lived out of it.

At night, we laid the seats back and pulled a stack of clothes OVER us, so the Eclipse would look empty if they came by and checked with the only weapon they actually carried, a matte-charcoal Magnum flashlight. (It was difficult to see through the deep black tint, anyway, and it's not like they invested too much energy checking. Not at that hourly rate, and not on the night shift.)

I started working two jobs, both at restaurants.

Buffalo Wild Wings employed me from 8:30am until about 4:30pm. Then, I changed into tan dress pants, put on a white button-up and tie, and walked 50 yards across the parking lot to Carrabba's Italian Grill. I ran tables until close. Yes, that's a direct run through the entire day, every day, from early in the morning until at least 10:00pm.

I didn't stop there, though.

We generally jumped a few blocks across to the other side of 280— most often, using our mobile home Eclipse as transportation— and partied at Hogan's bar as long as we could possibly stay awake.

Staying awake is easy when you drip a steady stream of uppers into your system. And you pretty much stay out of trouble with the Law when you do all of life in a 1/2 mile loop.

We showered at Patrice's.

Rob rigged a window we could use to get in and out. Besides, we both knew where Patrice kept a hidden key.

Sometimes, we snuck in during the day— to grab a quick rinse after he went to work. Other times, we waited until he was asleep in the evening— then we climbed through the window so we could sleep in the closet of the second bedroom (this only happened if we ran out of drugs and had to stop partying).

For the most part, there weren't any incidences.

Once Rob forgot to go to the restroom outside before we jumped inside for the evening. He miserably held it, laying in the closet, until Patrice left for the work the following morning.

Our stealthy squatting ended one Friday.

Patrice stayed out late the night before, and then he brought a random girl back to the apartment. She spent the night and slept in while he went to work. Since we slid through the window after his bedroom light went out, we had no way of knowing he wasn't home alone.

The next morning, we listened as he got up and worked his way through his standard morning routine.

- Shower
- Television on in the living room as he lingered in the kitchen for a few moments
- Television off

- Sound of keys being scooped from the kitchen bar counter

- Door open, door close, deadbolt

After that, I knew it was safe to exit the second bedroom closet and make my way to the hall bathroom. That's the one we always used.

But this time we didn't know a second person remained behind. The girl opened his bedroom door just as I opened the bathroom door.

"What the hell?!" she yelled.

It shocked the shit out of me, too.

We stammered our way through the explanation of it all, and then she called Patrice.

Patrice. Was. Pissed.

(But not so pissed that he stopping partying with us whenever the opportunity arose.)

He fixed the bedroom window and stopped the hide-a-key thing. That abruptly ended that arrangement.

....

Somewhere in the middle of all of this, my manager at Carrabba's pulled me aside. For the sake of the story, let's just call him Burt.

"I'm worried about you," Burt said. "Seems like you're always wired— like you're constantly going from one thing to the next and not getting enough rest."

He knew I used. That particular manager actually purchased drugs from me from time to time.

Most people in the service industry use *at some level.* If all the church people who frequent the litany of chain restaurants that litter the landscape in lush places like 280, taking their family to those places every Friday night and Sundays after worship, knew what really happened in the kitchen and behind the kitchen, they would immediately opt for more family dinners around the kitchen table.

The availability of quick cash, the long hours, and the lack of helicopter supervision make those spaces easy places for addicts to find employment. And, they make it easy for you to become an addict once employed.

That said, don't judge the person until you've walked the path or, at least, are willing to take the day-to-day journey with someone who wants out of the addiction. No one, self-included, ever sat in first grade and responded to the customary "What do you want to be when you grow up?" question with "I want to be a strung out loser who struggles to make ends meet and can't ever seem to get their shit together before the next crisis hits."

As strange as it sounds, most of us— despite the hurt we inflict on others— are doing the best we can, simply struggling to make it through another day. The bar for "our best" just happens to sit really low until we learn a better way.

Anyway, whereas numerous church people sat at my tables and knew I was sinking in something and never even acknowledged my name, Burt saw me. And he saw something was off.

"I want to help," he said. "Why don't you quit one of these jobs? You can't keep up the hours, rushing back and forth."

"We can't afford it," I replied.

"If you quit B-Dubs"— that's what everyone called it— "I'll cover a place for you and Rob to stay while you save enough to get on your feet. You can rest during the time you were working the other place."

He could tell I was thinking about it.

"No strings attached," he said.

I knew he meant it. He was one of the few men who always treated me with respect.

"Deal," I told him. "I need to turn in my notice and work out whatever days they want me to, but I'll quit at my next shift."

My manager believed in me and saw something inside just waiting to burst forth, but he didn't account for one thing— the extent of my addiction. Again, at the time the bar for my best was extremely low.

With less working hours, I didn't have as much cash flowing through my hands, but I didn't have to worry about housing— he provided a pay-by-the-week-extended-stay hotel for us. I could sleep in AND I could party more.

Rather than returning "home" to the extended stay after my shifts, I played human Frogger across 280 and meandered my way back to the bar. Rob was always waiting for me.

When *that* bar closed, we moved down the road to *another*, known to stay open most of the evening. After all, I could sleep in, because I no longer needed to arrive at B-Dubs by 8:30 am. Even though my manager gave me more hours, I never had to arrive at Carrabba's until around noon.

It wasn't long before I effectively ran the same schedule I had been, squeezing just a 90-minute nap in the morning before I had to start walking back down the hill to work. My manager, well-intended, didn't only provide me with a place to stay, he also provided me with more time to play.

Rob and I left the car parked, unless we *really* needed to use it. We didn't have money for gas, but we had plenty for drugs and everything else. And, with everything in walking distance, we expanded our living loop from a 1/2 mile circle to a mile or more.

....

In time, the distance we traveled on foot grew...

For instance, one evening, Kimberly had a middle school play— way down the highway "in the sticks," as Rob used to call it. I figured I could get off work early— my manager agreed to it— AND WALK there. Or, walk most of it.

It was 45 miles "as the crow flies." More, when you consider roads. And longer than you would expect, when you add after work-traffic. Plus, multiply it exponentially when you put all your cash into funding your addiction rather than fueling your automobile, giving a friend gas money, or even paying for a taxi.

Whenever Rob was with me, I walked.

Whenever I was alone, I tended to pull a half-walk-half-hitchhike-combo.

I figured I could walk-ride-walk-whatever to make it to my daughter's school play. So, late that afternoon— read: already nearing the time of the play— I left work.

I made it down 280 and hiked down to the Interstate. About 6 miles later, as I neared the Galleria exit, a white Progressive Insurance car— just like those you see in the commercials, the kind that say PROGRESSIVE in large navy letters that stretch the length of the vehicle— pulled over in front of me.

I broke into a trot as the driver leaned out his door and shouted, "Can I give you a ride?"

I had my money and a few drugs in my bra— along with my two knives. And he was in a marked vehicle.

I felt safe.

Plus, let's be honest, I never *really* worried too much about safety. I kidded myself about it, but I wasn't actually over-concerned.

"Where are you headed?" he asked.

As I neared the vehicle and could see his facial expression more clearly, it was obvious he was probably more afraid of me than I ever should have been of him.

I told him the name of the school and the exit I needed to hit to get there.

"I'm headed right by it. I can drop you at the school."

"Sir, you don't know how far that is off the exit. It's a big distance."

"No worries. I'll take you all the way."

"Just drop me at the exit."

As we rolled down the Interstate, he continued looking at the radio clock and voicing different versions of the same concern: "I don't think you have time to get there if I don't drive you."

And— "We're cutting it close as it is— and I really don't mind."

Then, as he pulled off the exit and stopped the car— "Look. It's about to begin."

I knew he was right.

I sat back in the seat and told him "Thank you."

He taxied me 10+ additional miles to the school. He looked like a family man who likely had a much better concept of a clock and a true awareness of "children's play" performance times.

"Thanks, again," I said, jumping out of the Progressive car as he pulled into the school parking lot.

"Yes, Ma'am. Have a good evening."

With that, he drove off, and I marched towards mom-duty...

....

The distance of that entire trek never concerned me. By then it was NOTHING for Rob and I to, on my day off, hoof it from the extended stay hotel all the way back to Gabriel's. One afternoon, on the way BACK I ran the math.

- It was about 1/2 mile from the hotel to Valleydale Road, assuming we cut through a shopping strip parking lot— which we always did.

- Valleydale winds 7 miles from 280 to Riverchase Parkway, at which point you can take a shortcut.

  (We always debated the shortcuts when we walked. If you took them, you were less likely to be able to hitch a ride. If you stayed on the main roads, it was a longer trip, but you upped the chances of not having to walk the entire way.)

- The shortcut is about 1.5 miles— and saves you about a 1/2 mile.

- You then jump on highway 31, which basically runs parallel to 280 at that point. You go another mile.

•   From there, it's just a few blocks to Gabriel's.

The total distance is 10 miles plus the parking lots to get from door-to-door. At twenty minutes a mile (an average walking pace), that's almost 3.5 hours one way.

I didn't have that math figured out the night I hiked to Kimberly's school play. I only ran the math after walking TO Gabriel's on an off day only to be denied entry, because Rob bailed on a huge tab the night before.

"Pay the tab in full and then you can come in. Until then, you're out."

We sold enough drugs— or something of the sort— to pay it within just a few days, but they wouldn't even let us in to ask a friend for a ride back that day.

(This was the flip-phone era, well before everyone carried mobile phones everywhere they went. Some people had them, and some didn't. People who had them managed their minutes meticulously, and then turned them off before the next month reset them. Sometimes, we had minutes— often, we didn't.)

On another day, when our tab was up-to-date, we strolled to open the door...

"It's locked," Rob said.

He knocked.

Then I tried— as if I might have some magical grip or twist he didn't have.

"It's still locked."

"Shan, I just told you. I just tried."

We looked around. No signs, no notice about special hours, nothing unusual...

Finally, we recognized a familiar face— not necessarily someone we knew personally but someone we had seen inside before.

"They're closed today. Problem with the plumbing or something," he said.

"Shit. We walked."

"I'll give you a ride, but I need some gas."

We forked over a few dollars of what would have been beer money for inside the joint. Not drinking for a few hours was worth not having to walk back.

....

Anyway, Kimberly's play...

"Be there for your kid," I told myself.

I meandered my way from the parking lot to the double metal doors of the school.

"Rob is right," I told myself. "We live in the fuckin' sticks."

I *finally* found the correct hall. It was like a scene just out of the movies.

I saw through the back doors of the gym-shift-into-auditorium, the sounds of claps and cheers in the background. I slid through the cracked doors and bumped into someone I thought to be a man.

I turned to apologize.

"Way to show up, Mom."

It was my 15-year old son. He looked larger than I remembered. He was no longer a little boy...

I turned towards the stage, ready to watch the show begin.

But I was too late. The play wasn't beginning, *it was ending*. I had missed it.

14. I Can Stay Up All Week But Still Can't Show Up (S)

Rob missed the play, too, but he had an excuse. He was on the road working in Mississippi at the time.

That's where our car was. That's why I hitchhiked.

....

We cobbled enough money together— between the drugs and the shifts and the walking and the partying and the odd jobs— to move out of the extended stay and into an apartment of our own. Patrice's complex was just a block from the Target parking lot where we used to sleep in the Eclipse, the same lot where I hovered from B-Dub's to Carrabba's then across 280 to the late night bars and parties and everything else we did in our spare time besides Gabriel's. We liked the place, so we signed a lease there.

We didn't stay there long, though.

As the months wore on, I wore down.

Finally, one day I didn't show up for work. That was unusual. I could stretch a normal day into 3-4 days by the time I took methamphetamines. I never missed work.

I knew how to manage my energy levels. I could reverse a drug crash with a cocaine high and keep myself going...

When I no-showed without calling in, and then I didn't answer their phone calls, they came looking for me. They *knew* something wasn't right.

Two co-workers came and knocked on the door.

No answer.

They tried the bedroom window.

Nothing.

They even tried calling and knocking *at the same time.*

No response.

I had been up for far too many days in a row and my body finally just stopped working. I didn't pass out. I didn't overdose. My body just quit.

I never knew about any of the calling and knocking and beating on my front door and bedroom window until a few days later when my manager— out of genuine concern— met with me and fired me.

Burt cried as he told me, "I'm sorry, Shannon. I've got to let you go."

I sincerely felt like I let him down. Even though he was only an employer and he was never anything more than that…

- He was the first human to show genuine concern for me without expecting anything in return.

- He had provided a way for me to scale back my hours— so I could work at a functional level rather than a frantic pace.

- He provided a place for me to live for two months— without wanting payback and expecting me to "put out."

I often tell people, "You have no idea of the impact you make on people. Ever. You might not see it in the moment, but it often leaves a massive ripple effect behind."

In reality, you need not be perfect to make an impact, either. Many of us— wrongly— set some artificial marker to denote when we feel we're worthy of making our mark on this world.

But Poe is the one who introduced me to cocaine AND he ALSO told me, "Enough! You're drinking too much. You can't even make it through the day."

And Burt, though he purchased drugs from me, offered me a lifeboat I didn't exactly use in the most honorable way.

Apart from BOTH of them intervening, though, I probably wouldn't be where I am today. That means I wouldn't have married Rob...

- which means we wouldn't have started EXIT Realty Birmingham

- which means we wouldn't have started coaching people and leading others at this level

- which ALSO means we wouldn't have written this book

- which means you and I wouldn't be having this conversation right now

- which means anyone you impact based on anything you pull from this content wouldn't have come to pass...

... and it rolls back to the imperfect men, Poe and Burt, who cared enough to step in when there was nothing to gain.

14. I Can Stay Up All Week But Still Can't Show Up (S)

15. The Absurd Belief Our Parents Will Always Be Here (R)

Rob sees another side of Lyn. Some church people give bad advice. Rob reflects on what faith actually looks like in the real world.

Many of us live with the mistaken notion that our parents will always be around. That is, we never dream of a time— a statistical likelihood— that the day will come when we'll bury not only one of them, but both of them. For sure, their death dates don't usually hit on the same day, but they do come…

Mom's death hit hard. Her diagnosis was— on the surface— one of the reasons I left Nevada and came back home.

Dad's death hit harder. That seems to be one of the consistent factors I see in the men I know.

- We all know we'll likely outlive our fathers.

- We know that, when it happens, we'll look back and take for granted the access to them we had and the wisdom they carried (because other men we know and trust who've lost their fathers have clearly shared this with us, AND by the time we hit our 40s or 50s we see the reality for ourselves).

- We experience the loss and find our worlds flipped over far more than we expected.

Dads matter.

Regardless of whatever bullshit-of-the-moment society spews about toxic masculinity, the supposed non-difference between men and women, and whatever other politically-correct-concept-of-the-moment you can think of, the presence (or absence) of an older man in a person's life makes a massive difference.

I saw it as a bystander while working at the rehab / re-entry program after I got clean. The men in The Program who had a father in their lives somewhere— even if he was a messed-up father with addictions of his own — actually gave those men a head-start in moving forward.

I know. That seems like it makes absolutely zero sense whatsoever. But, I saw it play out time and time again.

Moreover, I experienced it firsthand with Lyn, my father. Far from being a mess-up like some of the other dads I saw (who *still* made positive impacts)...

Lyn.

Was.

Awesome.

And, like all dads, he was gone well before I expected him to be.

....

I have great memories of Dad going back to the time I was a kid. Road trips. Vacations. Laughing around the dinner table.

The stuff that made a bigger mark and— just maybe, left a deeper hole— comes from the time I knew him as an adult. During that season I was still his son, because that never changes. But I also experienced him as a trusted advisor and peer.

After Mom received her dementia / Alzheimer's diagnosis, men I thought to be Godly men encouraged Dad, "Divorce her, Lyn. She's gone. Her mind isn't there. She doesn't know what's happening. It's just her body that's there."

For sure, there were reasons the average man might consider their words.

- "You don't make enough money to take care of her and do all of this medical stuff," they said. "It's time to just move on…"

- "She doesn't know you. She even told the cops things that aren't true."

- "It's just the spirit that matters— that's only her body."

They never saw the Lyn I saw…

… or, at least, the man I knew.

Some of my favorite times with my Dad were the early morning impromptu business meetings we had. By the time 3D was rolling, Dad and I invested in some projects together. He never limited his expertise to those— he offered me wisdom about everything.

I loved sitting down with him— as he might have done back in his land man days in Louisiana with his boss at the deer head office— and saying, "Hey, Dad, I'm trying to figure out this property deal here. Sit down and let me explain it— and then show me what you would do."

Or just talking, before the day hit full speed and everyone else began bouncing in and out of the office.

Lyn was a fixer. He knew what to do about everything.

Moreover, he didn't just fix the things that affected him— like family. Lyn was the confidant and trusted advisor for a lot of people. Even to some of the men who gave him that bad advice about Mom.

And, he had the stamina to suck it up, put his head down, and just grind out the work…

Well, he knew how to do that about everything except for one thing…

....

During one of those early-morning business meetings, Dad confessed to me, "I took a shower and broke down about all of it last night. I collapsed and laid there on the living room floor, arms stretched out, looking through the ceiling towards Heaven. I told God that— if You're actually real, I need You to do something here. This is so hard."

This was a stark contrast to the man whom I heard praying from a completely different location throughout that season I was tormented by those demons (I'll come to them later). And, rather than lessening the depth of his faith in my eyes, it enhanced it.

I thought about John the Baptist...

He was Jesus' slightly older cousin. Born to Elizabeth and Zechariah, much older relatives of Mary's who were well beyond the child-bearing years, his conception was miraculous. After Mary became pregnant and began to show, Joseph— it seems— sent her to stay with Elizabeth for a few months. It kept the pregnancy quiet, and it protected her.

The penalty for fornication back in those days was stoning. How would Joseph convince others that the Holy Spirit actually impregnated her?

Easy...

Just hide her for a few months. Once the baby arrives people don't tend to think about those things. They either enjoy the baby or move on to the next bit of gossip.

Anyway, John the Baptist— while in utero— recognized Jesus' presence while he was still in Mary's belly. When Mary walked in and greeted Elizabeth, Luke (one of Jesus' biographers) says John "leapt for joy" in his mother's womb (see Luke 1:41-44).

Thirty years later, Jesus approached John in the Jordan River to be baptized. John had baptized hundreds of converts by the time He arrived, most likely. Yet, based on the presence and power of the Spirit on Jesus, John totally recognized his now grown cousin (see John 1:33).

John initially objected to the baptism request.

"You should be baptizing me," he said— "I'm not even worthy to take the role of a servant and untie your shoes" (see Matthew 3:14).

Later, when his own crowds began leaving him to follow Jesus, John actually affirmed the transition as part of God's plan (see John 3:27-31). He encouraged them to go.

In other words, John knew *exactly* who Jesus was...

But then there was that time he found himself in prison. He knew he was most likely about to be executed for his faith (which turned out to be the case — Herod beheaded him for telling him to stop shagging his brother's wife).

John sent messengers from prison to Jesus with a profound question (see Luke 7:19f.): "Are you the One that was promised to come or should we look for another man who is yet to come?"

Think about that question...

Are you the One?

John knew He was—

- He sent his own disciples away, so they could follow Him.

- He baptized Him and saw the sky split open, then heard a voice from Heaven declare, "This is My beloved Son."

- He knew Him from before either of them were born.

Even the strongest heroes of faith get shaken. I figure that if a man who knew Jesus face-to-face for as long as John did could get rattled, we should almost expect it...

Jesus didn't belittle John's doubts. He took time to answer him. Moreover, he didn't answer by providing more *education* about Him, though; He pointed to a living *encounter*.

"Go tell my cousin what you see," Jesus reported to John's messengers. "The deaf hear, the lepers are cleansed and made whole, the lame walk, the blind see... the poor have good news proclaimed to them" (see Luke 7:22).

Turns out, God is better experienced than explained.

I wondered what God might have said to Dad as he laid sprawled out on the floor...

- *Yes, I'm real.*

  Rob isn't coked up, strung out on dope, and running wild. Your relationship with him actually is restored— and it keeps getting better.

- *Yes, I'm real.*

  Look at how your daughter, Abbey, loves people and exudes grace and joy just like your wife, PK.

- *Yes, I'm real.*

  Your grandson definitely didn't get his musical talent from you or even his Dad. The way he can strum a guitar is straight from Me and the halls of Heaven.

- *Yes, I'm real.*

  The Malcom Luck isn't just random happenstance— it's my guarantee that even the bleakest of situations turn beautiful in just the right time.

- *Yes, I'm real.*

  Look at all the crazy experiences you've been part of.

I don't know. I wasn't there. I don't know what God told Lyn.

Mom passed before Dad.

Watching her die proved far more difficult than I anticipated. Whereas some people just "go" suddenly, early onset Alzheimer's causes the person to slowly drift away. It's confusing for them until they no longer recognize the changes; it's excruciating for the family.

As difficult as it was for Dad, he handled with it the grace, too.

With Mom & Dad 1998

As Mom's condition worsened, she often got confused about simple things such as which shoe goes on which foot. It wasn't uncommon for her to walk into the living room with the right on the left and an un-matching mate from a different pair's left on the right.

Sometimes, she put her jacket on inside-out. This makes sense if you think about the way we sometimes take clothes off— we pull them such that they "come off" like that. When you put them back on, that's how they go. The next time you remove them, you pull it back to the correct way... such that it goes back on as it should. Every other time, it is what it's supposed to be if you don't fix it and keep turning it right side out.

Other times, she got dates and times and basic facts out of order.

"Don't argue with her," Dad told me. "In the bigger picture, this doesn't matter."

It wasn't like Dad was trying to take the easy way out— there's nothing "easy way out" about the disease. Rather, he wanted her to have a good day. It didn't matter if the story she was telling actually happened thirteen years ago instead of three, or if so-and-so was the President or not, or if we ate Italian last night instead of Mexican.

Sometimes the facts are important. Other times, they're not. Dad was wise and knew when— and what— things really mattered.

But when Mom died, I hated a God I didn't know.

....

Later, I tried to reconcile some of the faith stuff myself. I jumped way to the back of the New Testament, to Hebrews 11.

Church people refer to that passage as the "hall of fame of faith." I read and reread that passage a few times and decided that faith isn't "less faith" when it doesn't work out like you thought it would. In fact, it may be "more faith."

Read the passage and you'll notice a lot of exploits by great stalwarts of belief— people like Moses and the former slaves who crossed the Red Sea, the Israelites who shouted the walls of Jericho down, and Samson and David and other people who even "received back their dead" (Hebrews 11:35).

This all looks like unwavering certainty amidst chaos. That's generally where we stop reading.

But then there's the section of the chapter— the part I never heard a sermon about.

Verses 35b and following, still referencing the heroes of the faith, tell us that…

- Some were tortured.

- Some were stoned.

- Others were sawn in half.

- Others were destitute, penniless, wandering, hiding in caves and dens…

… and didn't receive what was promised.

Yet this, too, was great faith. And their propensity to keep pushing forward amidst the calamity landed them in the hall of fame. In fact, to emphasize how incredible these people were, the author of the text says "the world wasn't worthy of them" (Hebrews 11:38).

In the Rise Up Community, we teach a lot about mindset and accelerating towards your dreams. We tell people they shouldn't make excuses. We provide people with tools to move from where they are to where they're designed to be.

(This book is one of those tools, as are the resources in the back.)

I'll be honest.

It's easy to (eventually) tap out when things don't seem to be going right.

But I don't think a delayed dream is any "less-faith" and makes you "less-than" anymore than John's doubts and Dad's desperate cry to God made them less faithful. Again, sometimes that's MORE faith and more faithfulness — not less.

It's easy to claim a great victory like Daniel in the lion's den and— after the fact— declare, "Yes. I looked the beast in the face. This was great faith."

But what did they feel like in real time when it all happened?

And this is important, too...

- Great faith happens when your lion lunges at you, as well.

- Great faith is demonstrated when your walls of Jericho *don't* come down.

- Great faith is evidenced when your Red Sea *doesn't* part before the enemy gets to you.

You get the idea...

- The illness doesn't leave.

- The loved one dies.

- The accident happens.

- Restoration + reconciliation is withheld.

- Important things break.

- Breakthrough doesn't come.

Sometimes, great faith means trusting when there doesn't seem to be anything to trust, hoping that all things will be made beautiful in their time. Somehow. Some way. Even if you don't see it.

15. The Absurd Belief our Parents Will Always Be Here (R)

Application for Part 5 | Implementation > Information

Main idea: Many times we already know what to do; we just need to do it. Think progress, not perfection; think direction, not distance. We often overestimate what we can do in a moment but underestimate the power of significant moments strung together consistently.

John Maxwell once said, "We often try to marry uphill dreams to downhill habits."

In chapter 13 Rob talked about building a life, but the old habits made that life unsustainable (of course, this also relates to the "wherever you go, there you are" concept from Part 3).

Be honest about some of the habits you have that don't fit the life you want. And, note, they might not all be bad habits. Sometimes even "good" things can hinder us from the "great."

....

....

....

....

....

_____

_____

_____

_____

_____

_____

_____

In chapter 14, Shannon talked about walking through another rut.

"It's just a season," we often tell ourselves. "Things will change."

Stuff happens. Sickness, financial twists, recovery, and other issues occur. They can set us back.

At the same time, we need to be honest with ourselves if our current experience is "just a season" or if the season has extended itself into a way of life.

Have you let a season become "the entire year" or even a series of years?

_____

_____

_____

_____

_____

_____

_____

_____

_____

_____

_____

_____

In chapter 14 we also discussed judging others without understanding where they are and what they're walking through.

In what ways can you "judge" to help— with no expectation of something in return?

And are their ways you can help in "intangible" yet impactful ways, by implementing things like love, tenderness, and hope into your interactions instead of just chasing a goal?

How might this transform how you interact with strangers and waiters and people who serve you in the marketplace?

_____

_____

_____

_____

_____

_____

_____

_____

_____

_____

_____

_____

In chapter 15 we talked about the interplay of faith and doubt. They often co-exist.

Faith— even apart from all the answers— is an important component of a wholistic life.

Where are you on the "faith" issue?

_____

_____

_____

_____

_____

_____

_____

_____

Part 6 | Direction Determines Destination

We always end up where the road we're traveling goes. Success always leaves clues, as does "un-success." Continue moving consistently in the intended direction, and you'll— sooner or later— arrive.

16. A Supposed Sting-Op Gone Bad (S)

An officer makes a mistake, Rob makes a strange escape, and Shannon has more time to think things over

I hung on to the apartment for a few months, but with the job gone and with no prospects of work nearby (a ludicrous excuse, given the busy-ness of the street where we lived), I gave up. Rob rolled back into town with a fresh pile of cash, and we amped up the partying. By the time he returned, I was at least one month in the hole, anyway.

"Might as well just live it up and then let it go," I said. "Start over. We know how to get by on nothing."

Amidst this, I heard that Burt passed away. It hit harder than I thought.

That settled it...

"Level-up the partying another notch. What's the use of trying...?"

We found our way back to Patrice's one night— this time by invitation. There was a whole crew of us— the usuals.

At some point, the police came to bust up the party, something I believe Patrice actually intentionally orchestrated on his own.

You see, the circumstances were weird.

- One minute he was there, and things were fine.

- The next minute, he was gone. That's when the police showed up.

- But then he returned *right after they arrived*.

They walked straight to him, even though he wasn't there when they first knocked on the door.

"This is your place?" one of the officers said.

I couldn't tell if he was *asking* a question or *stating* a fact. To me, Patrice seemed in on the entire thing. For sure, that could just be *methampheta-paranoia* speaking, but the next tidbit leads me to think it's not.

The police walked us outside. They had a legit paddy wagon. *Paddy wagon* is just slang for "police van or truck used to transport people who've been arrested or prisoners." As opposed to the typical cop car that carries just 2 or 3 (but ideally only a single arrestee), these UPS-looking vehicles work like 10-12 passenger police machines.

They loaded us up. Four men. Four women.

Destination: Jefferson County Jail.

....

The apartment sits close to the Jefferson County / Shelby County line, which zigs and zags its way through that particular neighborhood. On some streets, you actually see the "Leaving Jefferson County" sign and then bump into a "Leaving Shelby County" sign a few blocks later, only to meet another "Leaving Jefferson County" and yet another "Leaving Shelby County" in a quick sequence. In that area of Birmingham, your neighbor might live in one county while you live in the next— and the kids down the street might enroll in a totally different school system.

The officer screwed it up.

The wrong jurisdiction came, and they weren't about to transport us 35+ miles from the JeffCo jail all the way through the backroads to Shelby County's jail. It takes almost an hour to make that drive on a good day. It was the middle of the night, and they had already taken us from the farthest edge where one jurisdiction blurs into the next, BACK to the center of the county...

... and no one from Shelby was willing to extradite at 3am.

(*Extradition* means one jurisdiction will hold you and hand you over to another if you're wanted there— provided the other comes to get you. For example, if someone is accused of murder in Alabama and is picked up in Georgia, then Georgia will extradite. That is, they'll detain the wanted person until Alabama comes to get them. Georgia won't hand-deliver the detainee, however.)

As a result of some shoddy policing (and perhaps the attorney who partied with our group and got stuffed in that paddy wagon), everybody except me received a "get out of jail" pass that night.

"You're free to go," they said. "Everyone except *you*."

I got pulled for a charge I never heard of— nor have I heard of it since. (And I've been around a lot of stuff and lots of people who've gotten apprehended for doing that stuff.)

"Why am I staying?" I asked. "What's the charge?"

"Promoting Prison Contraband."

I mean, I knew you could get that in an actual State prison— or even if you were booked into a jail and became an inmate— but we were never processed. As soon as we arrived, they started searching our stuff— wallets, pockets, and purses.

As I boarded the paddy, I had asked, "Want to search this purse?"

They waved me onboard.

"No. Let's just get this thing going…"

When they looked through everything at the jail— before they discovered the jurisdiction issue— they found a single Loritab (read: pain killer) in the bottom of my purse.

"It's probably been there for months," I protested. "I'm an addict— I would have taken it if I knew I had it…"

....

The funniest part of this fiasco is that they could have nailed me for more. While standing in line to do the booking drill— the fingerprints and pictures and paperwork— I remembered I had an eight ball of cocaine tucked in my bra.

(Most users agree it's called an *eight ball* because it's 1/8 of an ounce, about 3.5 grams. Others refer to the white stripe on the black eight ball of some billiard sets— and note that cocaine is most often snorted after being lined-out. The street value is about $100– $200, based on who sells it, how pure it is, and how bad you want it. It's a solid amount that packs an intense high— and is enough to be shared with another person if you're not greedy.)

"Shit," I whispered to Rob, standing there near the back of the line.

"What?"

I held out my hand.

"Look!"

"Hand it to me," he said. "I'll take care of it."

Rob noticed a random guy— an inmate— sweeping the floors. Prisons and jails *always* have the inmates do all the cooking and cleaning.

"Psss."

He got his attention.

Rob showed his hand, and tossed it towards the pile of trash on the floor.

The man winked, swept it into the dustpan, and scurried off.

Score for him. Win for us.

Everyone made their way back to a friend's home. It took a few hours to sort it all— because everyone had to call someone to come get them, and no one anyone knew had a paddy wagon to load everyone, and, well... seat belt laws, particularly when the Law looks over your shoulder.

Some of the seven paid a little bond.

Others sorted warrants (no extradition on those either, so they were able to pay a fine and go).

Anyone who needed it had cash from pushing drugs.

And then there was the attorney and the dentist who were part of the group. Many people (incorrectly) assume that most addicts look like strung out single moms and lifeless-looking dead beat dads. Or, they presume the only addicts who exist live in trailer parks or the inner city. My experience has been— and my stints in rehabs (as a patient and a professional)— that more addicts come *from the suburbs and the middle class-and-up* than the lower classes and the inner cities...

- They have more cash.
- They have automatic credibility when they tell you nothing is wrong.
- They have access to "clean" drugs.

What no one knew about the paddy wagon night is that *one* of the local jurisdictions actively worked on building a case on a few of us. We just weren't sure which one it was.

My thoughts...?

Something followed me back from the days of Marshal.

Anyway, everyone met backup and noticed I wasn't there.

"Where's Shan?" Rob asked.

It took a bit to put the pieces together— they had separated us during the booking and bonding and releasing processes. Rob and "Little Katy" (I'll explain her name in a moment) made their way back to the JeffCo jail to bond me out and take me back to the party.

....

A few days later, everyone ended up at the attorney's girlfriend's. He had money; she came from money. She lived in a massive rental townhouse not far from those county lines. We just moved the party from Patrice's to the paddy wagon to the attorney's Person of Interest after pausing for a bit.

The attorney's gal— let's call her Katie (not to be confused with Little Katy)— became our main drug source at that time. She had an open door policy, which worked well for me and Rob. We were so far behind on the apartment rent that we couldn't go back. They had no way to track us anyway, so we just stayed out-of-sight-out-of-mind.

"Ya'll party here," she offered. It was a big place (especially when you can sleep in a car, a closet, wherever). "You can sleep here— there. Whatever. Make yourself at home."

During that season, I wondered why I was still here...

I watched others do so many drugs they seized out and had to be taken to the hospital. I envied them. I'd built such a tolerance over the past three decades I couldn't do enough to seize out.

I truly wanted to use so much that I might overdose and die. I knew what it looked like— I saw enough death in the Mayhem days of Texas to script it and see it coming when someone in our group was about to have a seizure.

(I almost gave in to the thought of going back to Mark as a surefire way of dying. An easy out. I had given myself an expiration date of 35 years old— just like my Dad. At this point, I was 34.)

One morning, Katie called *for me.*

Me, Rob, and few others were asleep at the house, caught in the stupor from the previous few days of partying.

"Shannon!"

It started as a call, but escalated to a screaming shout.

"Shannon! *The police are here!*"

I'm not sure why she called for me. Probably because I never freaked out or lost it when crazy stuff happened. Due to my past experiences, I was always hyper-vigilant when nothing was happening but ultra-calm when it finally did. It's almost like I over-anticipated trouble but then easily adapted.

16. A Supposed Sting-Op Gone Bad (S)

This time it was the jump-out boys— the guys outfitted in all-black who ride in a blacked-out SUV. The kind who wear tactical gear with tear off patches and plug and play parts. The kind who ride in *vehicles* with plug and play parts.

"Come on," I said.

I walked through the front door, raised my hands, and assessed the situation. As I walked past their vehicle, I noticed manila folders— with each of our names— on the front seat.

"Sit down," I told Katie. "And be quiet. Don't say a thing— other than your name— even if they ask. Just your name."

She should have known that. Her boyfriend was an attorney.

"Do what I do," I said.

I dropped and sat criss-cross Indian style on the pavement.

"Just wait here. Stay calm."

I placed my hands behind my head and told her to do what I did.

She didn't. She stood and screamed and starting barking out answers to questions they weren't even asking.

The longer it went, the louder Katie got. And the louder Katie got, the more Rob— asleep (no pants, just boxers) began stirring.

At some point, Katie yelled the F-word and it was loud enough— and at the right frequency— to wake Rob up from his drunken, drug-induced slumber.

He looked out the second story window where he slept. The SWAT guys hadn't moved into the townhouse yet, because when Katie and I walked out — and they knew it was her place— they automatically assumed everyone was out.

Rob could see *exactly* what was happening.

He ran over and tapped "Little Katy," labeled as such because— even though they spelled their names differently, you can't distinguish the sound of *-ie* from *-y* and it's easier to just say "Little Katy" rather than "Katie with an -ie" or "Katy with a -y."

"Let's go," he said. "We gotta go, now."

"What?" she said, half awake herself.

Pulling on a pair of shorts and slipping into an old pair of wheat-colored work boots, he clarified, "The cops are outside. They've already arrested Shan and Katie. Let's go."

He led her to the back of the townhouse, went out a bedroom window onto a back deck, jumped to the adjoining neighbor's back deck, and began shimming down a wooden support.

"What are ya'll doing?" the neighbor asked, morning coffee in hand.

He had been on his part of the back deck throughout the entire ordeal and was oblivious to everything happening in the front yard. He had no idea...

"Just sliding down this little pole," Little Katy said.

"Oh, OK, then..."

The neighbor— we still don't know his name— hoisted his coffee in the air as if toasting them.

Rob and Little Katy ran through the woods behind the house and disappeared. "Regular" Katie and I got taken to jail.

Later, I learned we actually had a way out— if we'd taken the warning.

16. A Supposed Sting-Op Gone Bad (S)

Katie's boyfriend, the attorney, saw a string of black SUVs as he was leaving that morning. He pulled over to let them pass and then began following them to see where they were headed...

They lit him up.

Just before he pulled over, he called Katie's cell phone and warned her, "Get everyone and everything *out of the house right now!*"

She ignored him.

"Big Katie" (she wasn't big— just bigger than "Little Katy") immediately bonded out. Her attorney-boyfriend knew the system and got himself out, then did the honors for her.

I had no such luck.

···

Within a day or so, I had a hearing before the judge. Foolishly enough, Rob showed up for my court case.

As he approached the metal detectors, an officer asked him for his name. He lied and offered up a false one. Now, this is a big deal— even bigger than some drug charges. Depending on where you are and who you lie to, you can be charged with false reporting or even obstruction of justice. Some jurisdictions classify the offense as a misdemeanor; others mark it as an instant felony.

Rob didn't know about the file folders sitting on the front seat of the SUV at Katie's house. He had no idea they *already knew* exactly who he was...

That officer started chasing Rob down the hall...

Which led to another chasing with him...

Which resulted in a handful of officers chasing, tackling, and arresting him.

Rob phoned Lyn, his dad.

"It's Rob. I've been arrested..."

He knew his dad wouldn't likely be surprised at that.

"... I need you to NOT ask questions. I just need to know if you can help."

He knew Lyn would certainly have NUMEROUS questions, but Lyn agreed not to ask them right then. He consented to help, so long as they could talk at a future time— whenever Rob was ready.

Preliminaries out of the way, Rob continued, "Go to where my car is parked. Open the glove box and you'll find an envelope with a TON of cash. Bring the cash, and bail me out."

Whereas Rob called his dad, I called Mom.

In fairness to her, she never answered the call. *Technically*, she didn't know it was me— even if she might have guessed.

Whenever you answered a call from jail, you were greeted with an automatic recording. A robotic voice, in a distinct rhythm I can clearly hear in my head even now, said, "You have a call... from an inmate... in Shelby (pause) County (pause) Jail. (Longer pause). Will you accept the charges?" They never tell you *WHO* the inmate is— just that there is one.

Mom never accepted. I called repeatedly. No one ever picked up.

Rob was out within 24 hours.

I was there four more months.

16. A Supposed Sting-Op Gone Bad (S)

Rob always tried to beat the system.

Now, he does it in ethical ways. He creates better processes and systems for his workflow and for his clients. Back then, he just, well... "win at all costs."

He even tried to get the upper hand on things that don't matter.

An example...

Shelby County Jail permits one visit per day. Technically, it's not even a visit — it's a video call. Rather than the face-to-face interactions that require super-close surveillance (that's when a lot of contraband travels into the facilities as well as a lot of orders and other things make their way out), Shelby County built a new facility that allows visitors to sit in a room on one side of the campus— with a camera and screen— while the inmate sits safely locked in their assigned block on the other side of the campus— with a different camera and screen.

The live call, which happens in real time, works just like Zoom. The only difference is that it's always recorded, and it happens over the jail's cable network rather than the Internet.

I thought Rob was going to get me in trouble— or get inmate privileges revoked. He learned when the shift change happened and begin gaming the system.

He came to the jail in the mornings, sat at the visitor kiosk, then appeared on my screen— old school corded phone in hand. We could see each other and talk.

Later that same day, after shift change, I regularly heard my name called over the speaker...

The other females were pissed, jealous, and a mix of just about every other emotion. Whereas many of their families— and men— dropped them like hot potatoes, I routinely received second calls from a man who I wasn't even sure how to label.

"Hah! Can you believe it? They let me in again, Shan. Two times a day— every day this week!"

He was proud of himself each time he got through— even though he did cause some problems for me behind bars with all of these shenanigans.

At the same time, I was always happy to see him. There's not much to do in jail.

And, without those repeat offenses and all the sneakery, I'm not sure where my mind might have fully gone. At that point, I had told others in the jail that I was ready to die— at 35– just like my Dad. I was 34 when I got arrested, and I just assumed it was time to go out with a bang.

All that said, at the same time, I often wondered— and even wished— it might be my Mom. Just reaching out. Simply checking in.

It was *always* Rob.

Blake's 16th birthday was just a few weeks away. I wanted to let him and Kimberly know that I loved them, I missed them, and that I was alright. It's odd how you can hold contradictory things in tension— like wanting to see family and be with them and also wanting to die and just forget about it all.

I slept most of the first month I was in jail.

I detoxed, and my body (finally) got the rest it needed. With a roof over my head, food 3x a day, and no "coming and going" of extra roommates, the hard metal bunk with the 1 inch blue mat of a mattress was still a drastic step up from some of my past living arrangements.

16. A Supposed Sting-Op Gone Bad (S)

One day my Mom accepted a call.

She scolded me for the repeat calls: "I was letting it go to the answering machine," she said. "I didn't want the kids to know you were in jail."

It wasn't uncommon for them to *not* hear from— or see— me for *weeks* at a stretch. This was routine for them.

(I later learned that Mom and Lisa were always waiting for the news that my body had been found and that I was dead.)

After speaking briefly with my Mom, she put Blake on the phone. He didn't have much to say. I'm sure he was upset.

I missed Blake's 16th birthday in early April and thought I would miss Kimberly's 13th at the end of May. Those are both milestones— big birthdays.

Kimberly— often the one to diffuse heavy situations with humor— asked, "Are there any redheads in jail with you?"

"I haven't noticed. Why?"

She had a quick reply: "Because redheads don't look good in orange."

We laughed.

I was released a few weeks later, sometime around late April or early May, just in time for her 13th.

17. Gotta Get the Prison Out of the Prisoner (R)

Rob experiences a supernatural encounter. He reevaluates his choices, and he impatiently waits for something to happen.

I met Jesus in a strange way.

I grew up knowing about Him, but the thing that finally pushed me over the edge was when I was high one night— back when I had three demons who continued taunting and tormenting me. Amidst the mind-crunk that drugs always cause (heck, that's why addicts take them— for the temporary delusion) I saw into a completely difference space...

One night I overdosed and woke up in a hospital.

I heard a ventilator pump, back and forth. The apparatus moved up and down.

I heard a faint drip. I looked around and noticed I was attached to tubes and wires.

And then I saw my demons...

By then, the three of them had been with me *for years*.

17. Gotta Get the Prison Out of the Prisoner (R)

"You need to know this. I have demons," I told Shannon— multiple times, before they each showed up again that night. "They follow me and torment me."

"Everybody has their own demons," she replied. "I've got demons, you've got demons, that person over there has some demons…"

She went on and on about how everybody has baggage from their past AND how they also have things that keep tripping them up in the present.

"No," I clarified. "I actually have *REAL* demons. Three of them. They follow me around. I can actually describe them to you…"

I told her this the first time we met. We were at Gabriel's. My friend / roommate, Patrice, promised to introduce me to a girl he knew that he thought I might like. He had been genuinely concerned for both of us and rationalized that we would either help each other accelerate our death date by amplifying our versions of insanity OR, just maybe, two negatives might (as in math) actually merge and create a positive.

"This could be a horrible thing or a great thing," he told me. "You'll either save each other, or at least neither one of my friends will die alone."

That's the most bunk introduction to a face-to-face meeting I've ever heard. What's worse is that the night I was supposed to meet Shannon, I had some other random girl with me…

"She's coming to the bar tonight," Patrice said.

That should have been my clue. Stay away from other girls— at least for the evening.

Shan walked in, walked straight up to me, and told me she was coming home with me.

"Boom, boom," I thought.

But then, after speaking with her for a few minutes, I thought I needed to let her in on my little secret. The demons. All three of them.

She didn't get it. No one ever did.

But at least I tried…

....

The strangest part of that whole admission was that, even if she didn't believe me about those demons or remotely understand who they were, she got to meet them over the next few years.

"They're here," I often told her.

I could physically see them with my eyes. As real as it was when I saw (and heard!) my Dad praying for me with his friends (I'll come back to that in a moment), I could see and hear these demons.

- One of them looked like an extremely old lady.

- The second looked like a humongous wolf, about three times the size of a normal wolf.

   (Picture it, because most wolves are way smaller than you think. This wolf was way bigger than you're thinking.)

- The third looked like a dark cloud that constantly changed shapes. It morphed rhythmically and seemed to just… follow me.

I tried to discern the ONE THING that made them show up.

Was there a place I went, a thing I did, or even a drug I took that caused them to manifest?

It wasn't any of that...

Drug addiction, though often said to be from the "pit of hell," is a biological response to neurological and physiological processes happening in the body. For sure, the devil is probably behind most of it, but you can physically explain it. It makes sense.

The demons never made any sense at all. They just presented themselves at will and caused confusion and chaos.

- Sometimes, they woke me up in the middle of the night and began shaking me.

- Other times, they just moved into whatever physical space I was— a living room, a restaurant, an alley, or even a random building— and just showed me they were there before leaving.

- A few times they followed me for days at a time, appearing wherever I was, doing nothing except lingering.

Here they were, in the hospital...

I couldn't move. I tried, but nothing in my body worked— the command didn't make it from my head to whatever part of me I wanted to shift.

Was I paralyzed?

Or was this what it was like to be dead?

Whatever this situation was, there was no running from it— and no "eject" button, something you can mentally press to awaken yourself from a bad dream.

As the demons trounced around, I actually prayed and made a slew of empty promises to God, thinking of each possible thing I might have to offer. There wasn't much there...

17. Gotta Get the Prison Out of the Prisoner (R)

And then something strange happened...

There, I watched— *and audibly heard*— my Dad, my sister Abbey, Dad's friend Harvey, and two other men pray out loud for me. They stood in a circle, each of them praying fluidly and fast. It was as if they were in conversation together with another unseen person, Jesus Himself.

I didn't see Jesus in that... let's not even call it a vision... because days later I actually approached my father, after months of not talking to him because of shit I did and how I let him down, and Dad confirmed a few things...

- Those same people were, in fact, in a room together.

- They prayed the exact words I repeated to him.

- They did so at the same time I told him I saw them.

I really believe I saw through time and space and stepped into another realm. Trust me, I know that seems weird to read. It feels even weirder admitting it to myself and then writing it down on paper.

With the demons surrounding me, and with an open "portal" to see my Dad and the other folks praying for me, I began praying myself...

I begged God to let me live— just as if we were talking in the same way you and I might talk to one another.

"Rob," He said, "come to Me."

"I won't do drugs anymore if you let me live," I promised.

"Rob. *Just come* to Me."

God didn't want me to perform or promise or ponder what I thought He might want me to do. Rather, He just wanted me...

His voice felt strong. Yes, I could tangibly *feel* His words.

It was soothing at the same time— like a good strength in the best way possible, the kind of strength that protects and defends, the kind of strength that's both intense and tender at the same time.

As terrified as I was, I also sensed complete peace in His presence.

Turns out...

... and there's no way to say this other than to just state it— because I can't rationally put the pieces together in a way they make logical sense— I wasn't in a hospital at all. I had crawled into someone's attic, presumably going there to die.

I fought my demons that night, but I didn't wage war against them on my own.

....

After that encounter, I knew I needed to make some adjustments in my life. Serious adjustments.

Although I made promises to God before, none of them stuck. About a year later, I ended up in Shelby County Drug Court and joined Celebrate Recovery.

Celebrate Recovery was a 12-step group south of Birmingham that welcomed people like me. Whereas most church people turn and look at you when you walk through the doors of their buildings after a prolonged absence, this place was unique. When you walked through the doors of those meetings, everyone looked your way and embraced you— even if they knew you were struggling. They affirmed you decided— in that moment— you needed the group more than you needed to cave to your addiction. They made you feel welcome, and it was empowering.

I moved back in with Dad, too.

(We tried this before, but remember I invited a woman from my past to move in and that turned into a shitstorm of a different level altogether— especially when adding my *chaos* to her *crazy*.)

He had two rules for me when I moved in this second time.

- Rule #1 = Go to church. He didn't care where I went, as long as I found a community of faith somewhere.

- Rule #2 = Work a full time job.

That was it.

I'm not sure which rule was more important to my sobriety, to be honest. A lot of people act like "it's all Jesus."

They say things like, "You won't make it without Jesus."

Or, "It's all God. All glory to God!"

They're right.

Well, they're *half-right.*

I attended church with Matt & Abbey at Fullness. I joined a men's Bible study. I soon agreed to join the men for a retreat.

Pastor Bart knew my color might be called (a condition of drug court), meaning I would need to report for a drug test during the event.

"Alrighty, then… we'll make sure it happens," he said.

I don't know another way to explain the final piece of my conversion story other than to just tell you the way it happened— how I experienced it. A group of men surrounded me, praying for me. I knew that during that time we were fending those demons off for the final time. If they were *gone* before, now we were *fencing them out permanently.*

Then, suddenly— *WHOOOSHHH!!!*

A wave of *something* invisible knocked me back. It was a good something, *a supernatural holiness of delight and bliss and wonder all wrapped together.*

"This is what you've been looking for, Rob."

I knew that Voice. It was my Creator, my Redeemer...

It was the same Voice that said, "Come to Me. *Just come.*"

It was that now familiar Voice of God.

"Every high you sought, every single thing you pumped into your body in order to feel something was a search for a supernatural experience that's right here."

I laughed.

It wasn't a silly laugh— like the expression that's appropriate for a joke or one of those odd bets I later made with Ben. It was a laugh of deep, robust joy.

If I asked you to describe what God is like, you might use "Bible words" like *holy, just, righteous*... descriptions like that. Those words are accurate, indeed.

But the Scripture also tells us things like—

- In God's presence there is fullness of *joy*, as well as pleasures forevermore (Psalm 16:11).

- The prophet Nehemiah suggested the *joy* of the Lord is your strength (Nehemiah 8:10).

- When Jesus was born, the angels told the shepherds that they were bringing "good tidings of *great joy*" (Luke 2:10-11).

- Jesus prayed that our *joy* would be full (John 16:24), after saying that He taught us how to live so that our *joy* would overflow (John 15:11).

So, as it turns out, *joy* is a Bible word, too— it's just not one that we talk about all that often.

Like I just mentioned, you won't make it— I don't think— without Jesus. Or, if you do, you'll make it at a diminished level of what's truly possible, given the supernatural potential God has placed in you.

At the same time, I need to add this…

… the "other half" of being right about moving forward.

Part of survival is having something significant to do— every day. I don't think you'll make it without Jesus AND something significant to do. Both matter.

I meet guys all the time— even addicts— who are afraid of work. I tell you… *work is part of your God-ordained purpose.*

Way back in the Garden of Eden, before Adam and Eve ate the fruit (the Bible blames it all on Adam, by the way— see Romans 5:12), God gave them *the gift of work*. Moses— or whoever wrote the book of Genesis— describes how God created the two of them and then placed them in the garden to work it… to tend it… to add value to it and make it even better than they found it (see Genesis 2:15).

The Fall didn't happen until the following chapter. At that point, work became toil rather than sheer delight (Genesis 3:17). The work wasn't a curse or result of sin, though. It was always God's intent for us.

I tapped into that as I walked my road to recovery. God designed me to work...

- It's why I love taking a dilapidated house, genuinely enjoy the entire process of rebuilding it to reveal something beautiful, and then stepping back to affirm a job well done.

- It's why— as much as I hate spreadsheets and office work— I like hearing Shannon talk through the systems she creates to run our EXIT Realty Birmingham brokerage.

- It's why I enjoy coaching potential "empire builders" to learn the process of finding, fixing, and then flipping their first investment property— and then continue growing their business.

We were designed to work. In fact, I don't think you'll find yourself fulfilled in life until you identify work that matters and makes an impact.

That said, I found tremendous excitement in going to work every day with Dad. It hit different this time around. I wasn't using, I didn't have any ancillary relationships that were unhealthy, and I didn't have any money.

Oh, about the money situation.

As soon as I started working with Dad again, he told me, "Alright. I've been thinking. It's obvious that you've had a problem..."

"No kidding," I replied. "I've had a MASSIVE problem."

"*Massive* might be an understatement," he laughed. "Here's what I'm going to do— I'm going to hold the money for you. I'll keep up with it, but I'm going to make sure you don't have the temptation to run out and squander it."

Dad's plan seemed good for me. By now, I had a super-high level of trust in my Dad. I knew that, as much as I would like to cash a big check every

Friday and fill my pocket with a roll of Benjamins, that probably wasn't a great idea.

....

One Tuesday morning, we knocked off for lunch a little early.

"We need to go ahead and leave for lunch," Dad said. "We're going to the church to eat."

"What do you mean?"

He described Power Lunch to me: "Once a month the pastor at my church hosts a business leader luncheon. They'll have a quick cafeteria line. We'll grab our food, pay $5– that I'll deduct from your check— and then sit down at a table. After about 30 minutes, the pastor will stand up and talk."

"That doesn't sound like a good lunch to me," I said. "I don't want a church lunch."

"This isn't. Danny, my pastor, will talk about a leadership book he's been reading, or offer some insights from a video he's recently watched. This is for business people."

"I don't want to be singled out as the token addict at a little lunch."

"You won't be," Dad promised. "There will be 200 or more people there…"

Dad was right.

We arrived at the church— early— to a full parking lot. We walked in and there were all kinds of business leaders. Some wore suits. Others wore tan pants and golf shirts. A few, like me, wore yellow leather construction boots and clothes more suitable for doing demo or cutting grass.

They opened the line at 11:30am and people began grabbing their food and making their way to round, cloth-covered tables evenly spaced across the massive room. At some point, about 20 minutes into the meal, Danny walked to a short stage, prayed, and welcomed everyone.

"We're so honored to have you at Power Lunch," he said.

That's what they called it— *Power Lunch*.

The pastor asked a staff member to draw a name from the basket...

"That's the basket we dropped our registration in," I told Dad.

"Watch. Maybe you'll win something..."

The man handed the pastor one card at a time, and he started giving away SPAM and SPAM-related swag. He had normal-sized cans of SPAM and mega-sized cans of SPAM. He had SPAM hats and SPAM shirts. He had SPAM banners and other things I didn't even know SPAM made.

"That's one of his things," Dad whispered. "He always gives away SPAM."

I'm not sure why he decided on SPAM. Apparently, he gave away SPAM for years.

Everyone laughed. Everyone remembered it. Everyone wanted to win...

After the event ended— right on time, just as it had started right on time— Dad asked if I'd like to meet the pastor. It might have been the pastor's dress-casual outfit (slacks and collared shirt with the church logo embroidered on the top left chest pocket) or it might have been his easy going nature...

I don't know why, but I said, "Sure. Let's meet him."

Dad wove his way through the round tables and against the crowd, all the way to the front of the large room.

"Lyn," the pastor said. "Is this your son, Rob?"

Oh, shit...

"Has he already heard so much about me that he's already formed an opinion?" I thought. Then, "Well, if he has, it's probably well-deserved..."

"Yes, sir!" I replied, offering the same intensity I might give my Sarge back in my bootcamp days— even during that time he tricked us into celebrating Christmas.

"I've heard *so much* about you," he offered.

Shit, shit, shit... again.

"Well..."

(I didn't know what else to say.)

"I'm so happy to meet you," he said. Before I could get my next words together in my mind, he added, "Your dad says you've been through a recovery program and that you might like to help others who are facing the same challenges you've overcome..."

I liked the way he said it. He didn't look at my past only. He affirmed it, but he acknowledged I was walking towards my potential.

"Yes. We've talked about that," I replied. "I'm just not sure how I would even get started doing that..."

"I've got a guy you need to meet," he said. "I'll get you his number. He started a church downtown. Our church helped support them financially, and I've been mentoring him. I'll get you his number..."

"It's a church?"

"It is. But people continued knocking on the front doors of the building needing help getting out of an addiction— they meet in a renovated warehouse downtown. About a year ago, some people in the Governor's office called and asked if they would consider taking prisoners on early release into that program even. They did. He's doing all of that. Maybe you guys should meet."

"Shit," I thought. To be honest, I almost said it out loud. I didn't— I just confirmed, "Yes, those are my people. I would love to meet him."

"Let me reach out to him, and I'll tell him you'll be calling. After I get permission, I'll pass on his cell phone number to you…"

⋯⋯⋯

Dad tried to get me to wait for Pastor Danny to make the connection, but I couldn't…

"This is my shot!" I thought.

Now, to be fair to the story, the guy Danny was talking about later told me that Danny actually called him right after we met. In fact, he was in the room that day during the Power Lunch— but none of us knew.

He apparently told Danny, "Sure, pass my number along. I'll be happy to meet with him."

But, again, I didn't wait.

"I need off tomorrow," I told my Dad.

He agreed to let me have the time off, as long as I understood his "no work, no pay" policy. In my mind, it didn't matter.

- For one, he wasn't letting me hold any cash anyway.

- For two, as much as I loved renovating houses, I knew the next chapter needed to include some way of giving back and helping other people like me.

The next morning I rode downtown to the warehouse. The name of the church was painted across the top of the building, right across the brick.

"Nice," I thought, rolling up to the covered drive-thru area.

They had large planters and some concrete patio furniture out there in the shaded overhang. I noticed a few places where smokers had extinguished their cigarettes on concrete planters, and I spotted a few ashes and cigarette butts.

Don't get me wrong; the place was clean. But people with a past— and people walking with their own stuff— actually notice that sort of thing. Those small imperfections revealed that people like me were welcome.

I knocked on the door and waited.

No answer.

I looked around and saw another door. I walked to it and read the sign: *ring doorbell*.

I rang.

Waited.

Nothing.

I sat on a concrete bench situated against the round concrete table and just… sat.

"Maybe somebody will come," I thought.

They didn't.

I lit a cigarette and then another and then another and then smoked through almost an entire pack as I waited a full day outside that warehouse-church. As the rush hour traffic began making its way out from the city, I figured today might not be the day.

"Every day's not a good day," I thought. "Maybe I should just get the number from the pastor."

But then I wondered if the guy at this warehouse-thing would even agree to give away his number...

I thought about it most of the evening, and created Plan B.

"I need off another day," I told Dad. "I'm going back downtown..."

"What if he's not there, again?" he replied. Then— "Why don't you just wait for Danny to get his number?"

"I don't know. It seems important..."

I rolled back downtown.

I knocked on the first door, rang the bell at the second, and then walked back to the table and chairs. I lit my cigarette and waited.

I had enough circumstantial evidence by now to know this guy wasn't going to be offended by anything in my past, much less a little bit of tobacco in my present.

After a few Newports I looked at my watch.

"Three friggin' hours," I said. "Maybe Dad was right."

But right about then a guy driving a grey Ford sports car— some coupe-type of thing they made around 2000 to compete with my black Mitsubishi Eclipse — pulled up next to my car. He fumbled around a few minutes in the vehicle, obviously getting his shit together.

As he stepped out of the car, big box of crap in hand, I asked him, "Are you Andrew?"

He half-ignored me and half-looked at me with this we-see-people-like-you-around-here-all-the-time gaze that I couldn't quite read. He walked towards the front door, not saying much of anything.

Raising the key from his right hand, he opened the front door.

"Give me just a second to turn off the alarm," he said. "I'll be right back."

I watched him through the glass storefront— all the way from the front door to the other side of the lobby. He punched a few buttons on a keypad and then came back, just like he said.

"What can I do for you?" he asked.

"Are you Andrew?"

"No. I'm Rodney."

"Can you put me in touch with Andrew?"

I explained the entire story. The stuff about the Power Lunch and Danny (he knew Danny), the stuff about the prisoners and the addicts (he knew about that, too, but assured me that they all lived at undisclosed locations near that warehouse-church building), and that I wanted to get in touch with Andrew "because Danny said."

I told him pointe blank— "I'm called to work with addicts. I want a job here."

Rodney quickly replied— as if he had heard it hundreds of times before— "We're not hiring."

"Well, is Andrew here?"

"No."

"Can you give me his number?"

"No."

(He wasn't much for words, I thought).

"What about if I give you my number, and you pass it to him?"

With that, Rodney lightened up.

"Tell you what," he said. "I'll call him right now, and tell him about you. Then we can see…"

"Right here? You serious?"

"Sure."

Rodney flipped open his cell phone. He speed-dialed Andrew and held the phone to his ear…

"Hey, I've got a guy here at the warehouse who…"

He filled in the blanks, telling this mysterious "Andrew" everything I told him.

Then, after a few moments, he looked my way: "He's at his house— he has an office there. You want to go there?"

"Right now?" I asked.

"Yeah. He said he could meet you…"

"Sure. How far away…"

"About a mile from here."

"Abso-freakin'-lutely," I answered. I almost didn't say freakin', but caught myself mid-word since I'd learned I was talking to the worship pastor.

I drove to Andrew's house and told him a bunch of my story. None of it rattled him. In fact, after a while, I got the feeling some of it was small potatoes in comparison to some of the stories of the guys they served.

I didn't land a job that day, but I did learn that— for sure— I wanted to work in recovery. I wanted to serve people.

And, I realized there were people out there who weren't just spewing information and holding meetings, they were helping people build a completely new life and live in ways they hadn't yet imagined.

"Even if you're not hiring right now," I said, "I want to help..."

He had a quick answer— "If you really mean that," he replied, "I'll take you up on it. We're about to move 40 men into that warehouse. I need to add a few showers. With your skillset, you should be able to do it."

"I took off two days to try and meet you. I left my Dad in a bind, I think," I explained, "but I can do it this weekend."

"Get me a supply list," he said, "and I'll have everything ready to go..."

As I left his home that day, he promised, "Now that I know you want to do this, I'll call you if something opens up."

....

That Friday night and all day Saturday, I worked on the showers. I transformed an old bathroom they didn't need into a stand-up, walk-in while a few men built bunks.

I packed my things to leave and began driving off when I received a call on my cell. It was Andrew...

"What are you up to?" he asked.

"What do you mean?"

"Like right now. What are you doing *right now*?"

I looked at the clock radio on the dash of my black Eclipse. It was 9:15pm on a Saturday evening.

"Nothing. Just headed home, actually. We finished the showers..."

"You want to jump in my car and ride to Walmart with me?"

"Walmart?"

"Yeah," he said. He clarified— "I'm going to grab a bunch of food for the houses. I've got a list. If you want to go and help push a buggy, we'll load up. We can talk while we get the food, and then we can run by all of the houses to deliver it..."

He didn't push it all. It was obvious he was doing this with or without me.

But, what else was I going to do? I mean, I used to go on all-night benders that didn't even begin until 11:00pm. Here was a pastor that was headed to Walmart to grab food for a bunch of men in a recovery program...

"Yeah, I'll go." Then— "This is still early for me. I used to not even start until a few hours later than now..."

I rode with him to Walmart. We had a specific list of items to gather, so we hit the aisles super-quick. We collected food for the men in The Program. We grabbed donuts for people attending church the following morning. We loaded up with supplies to take to the homeless people in the park before church.

Then we bounced from house-to-house-to-house, visiting five properties in succession. At each one, we walked through the front door with a few bags, only to be greeted by men who returned to help us carry the remaining items.

I shook hands with most of the men, swapped names, and even shared a few pieces of my story...

"These are my people," I thought. "They're exactly where I was..."

The following week, I started working full time with Andrew. In hindsight, I think he basically "created" a job for me, something that didn't exist. He swears it wasn't that, because another guy who was working for him moved to something different. I don't know...

I worked with that rehab program for the next few years— until the day I got shot on the side of that same warehouse where I waited those two days.

If you believe in being at the right place(s) at the right time(s)— which happened over and over in my life, once I finally tuned in to see it...

... you know *exactly* what I mean.

17. Gotta Get the Prison Out of the Prisoner (R)

18. A Soft, Safe Place to Land (S)

Shannon learns how persistent Rob can be. Lyn gets creative about the roommate situation. Shannon gets exposed.

Jails are flooded with ministry teams.

I opposed all of these non-mandatory activities and adamantly confessed, "I don't want any part— I'm not participating."

Remember, I had *somewhat* of a church background, but I tossed all that out the window when the people who were supposed to protect me stole my innocence. None of that, along with the rest of the abuse and all the "lies" about God loving me and having a supposed wonderful plan for my life, landed well.

One day, the ministry teams (yet again) begged me to attend. "Come on. We'd love to have you."

I thought to myself, "I really want to be left alone…"

To *spitefully* show them how I felt, I walked downstairs, snatched the free Bible they offered every inmate, and stomped right back upstairs to my bunk.

I shoved it under the pillow. I made sure they knew that I certainly didn't want to be bothered, that I didn't want whatever it was they were sharing.

"She OK?" I overheard someone ask as I exited the meeting hall.

"God lost track of my soul a long, long time ago," I muttered to myself.

As I thought about God losing me *and me losing me* and me just wandering, I began humming the lyrics to a song.

A few years earlier I heard a song by Jonny Lang, a blues-ish type of singer known for rifting his faith AND his rough past throughout his lyrics. His confession was raw…

Wander This World

The tar in the street starts to melt from the heat
And the sweats runnin' down from my hair
I walked 20 miles and I'm dragging my feet
And I'll walk 20 more 'cause I don't care

And I'll wander this world, wander this world
Wander this world, wander this world all alone

I'm like a ghost some people can't see
Others drive by and stare
A shadow that drifts on the side of the road
It's like I'm not even there

And I'll wander this world, wander this world
Wander this world, wander this world all alone

Well I've never been part of the game
The life that I live is my own
All that I know is that I was born

18. A Soft, Safe Place to Land (S)

To wander this world all alone, all alone

Well some people are born with their lives all laid out
And all their success is assured
Some people work hard all their lives for nothin'
They take it and don't say a word
They don't say a word

Sometimes it's like I don't even exist
Even God has lost track of my soul
Why else would He leave me out here like this
To wander this world all alone

"That's me," I said. "That's how I actually feel— and that's precisely where I've been..."

I found the song and played it. I listened on repeat, letting the words bounce around inside and echo throughout my soul. I replayed it there in the jail.

"God lost track of my soul," I thought. "Just like the song says in the final lines. Maybe that's why I'm out here on my own, wandering..."

At some point, I decided to crack open the Bible.

Not knowing where to begin, but hearing somewhere in the past that all the stories in the Bible don't have to be read in order because the contents are *not* placed in the exact order they were penned, I decided to just open it up and see where it hit.

"Psalms," I said. "Those are song lyrics, too. Easy enough."

Now, it might have been the Holy Spirit that dropped the Bible open at those exact pages— I believe that CAN and DOES happen. Or, it might have been the fact that Psalms is in the exact middle of the text. Cut the pages in half, and 99 times out of 100 you'll land in a Psalm.

I think it might have been a little of both.

I made my way through to Psalm 116.

David (the author of most of the Psalms) wrote, "I love the Lord, for He heard my voice; He heard my cry for mercy" (Psalm 116:1).

He continued, "The cords of death entangled me, the anguish of the grave came over me; I was overcome by distress and sorrow. Then I called on the name of the Lord: *Lord, save me*" (Psalm 116:3-4).

He said, "When I was brought low, He saved me" (116:6).

As I read and re-read those words, my heart softened a little.

"It looks like David thought God lost track of him, too— until he was certain He didn't," I told myself. "Maybe I can relate to this…"

No, it wasn't a dramatic "jailhouse conversion," the kind you hear about where an angel walks in the room or someone sees an apparition, but I felt something shift inside.

I had nothing else to do in jail except soak in the words of Scripture— aside from talking to Rob via video conference.

Within a few days, I told myself, "Alright. This is my situation. If I don't go to the Lord, I'm probably going to be a statistic that either moves onto prison for their rest of her life OR— maybe worse— gets out, relapses, and dies a rough death."

I decided, "I'm in. I'm open to seeing what God can do."

....

I'm not sure how he did it— he has a story— but Rob eventually got me out of jail. It took him about 4 months, and my Mom made the trip with him to get me.

"How did this happen?" I asked.

"Well, Shan, I called the bail bondsman every single day. She kept telling me *NO!* and I kept telling her that I'd keep calling her back until she said *YES!* So, I think she finally gave in."

A bail bondsman provides bail bonds for people who get charged with crimes and don't have the entire amount of bail to put before the court. Bail is basically a financial guarantee that you'll show up for your hearing.

The higher your flight risk, the greater the crime, and the less likely you are to appear at your hearing, the more the price goes up. If you show up, you get the money— or other collateral you post, such as a house or vehicle— back. If you don't show, you forfeit.

People who can't afford the entire amount can go to a bail bondsman. The bondsman receives a fee (which is based on a state-approved schedule) in exchange for them putting up the collateral on your behalf. They're often the "poor man's way out."

You still have to show, or they may send a bounty hunter out looking for you — so they can get their collateral back.

The whole jail-thing is a nasty business. But, Rob worked and worked until he found a bail bondsman— or, in this case, bail bondswoman— who would help.

"How long have you been working on this?" I asked.

"Months…" he said. "I called her twice a day on some days— right after talking to you. She knows my voice by now. She would even greet me by name as soon as I started talking."

"Didn't you have to pay money for this?"

I knew he didn't have any. He used all of his money when Lyn posted bail for him a few months in the rear view mirror.

"Well, let's not talk about that. I handled it," he chuckled.

My hunch is that Rob sold enough drugs while pestering the bondswoman to meet the financial need by the time she agreed to post bond.

The one thing Rob could not do— and I'm not sure why, probably because he had a record with active cases— was sign me out. He convinced my mother to do it, the only condition being that I could *NOT* return to her place to live under any circumstance— *not even for the night*.

I'm not sure what surprised me more— the fact that Rob pulled if off, or that my Mom agreed to come and put her name on the line for me.

Rob had my living arrangements figured out, too.

As we drove off he told me, "Lyn said you can stay at the house."

"Where are you staying?"

"At Lyn's." Then, after a moment, he started laughing— "He's letting us share a room. But he took these twin beds and cut the legs down on one so that they're uneven."

"What?"

He laughed louder— "He wants to make sure the beds can't slide together, so we can't be in the same bed."

"Rob," I replied, "Neither one of us are big people. We can fit in the same twin bed without a problem."

"I know," he said, "I tried to explain that people have sex in cars and in bathrooms and in closets and just about everywhere else you can smash two bodies together, so if we were trying to do that we could just do that OR just use one of the beds at a time. Just let him take the win."

When we arrived, Lyn exuded grace. He *always* embodied grace to me.

"I only have two rules," he said. "They're the same two rules I've had for Rob the past few months..."

I learned that Rob had been staying with Lyn for a while by that point. He had been working with Lyn as well.

And Rob had gotten clean. Really clean.

Lyn helped with that by making sure he stayed busy and he didn't have extra cash laying around. Rob worked with him renovating houses— some to flip, others to just rehab as contract work.

As his boss, Lyn tallied EVERYTHING Rob spent. It wasn't uncommon for the two of them to roll into McDonald's or Wendy's for lunch and Lyn to pull out a little notebook...

"Let's see. Your combo meal was $5.75. The boots we got you this morning were $59 plus tax..."

By the time payday came, Rob had very little cash left.

As the two of them described the "program" they worked to me, it dawned on me that Rob probably didn't bail me out with drug money, he bailed me with money that's deducted on Lyn's ledger somewhere.

"The rules," I said. "What are my two rules?"

"Rule number 1," Lyn replied, "is you must go to church. You can go with me or you can go with Matt & Abbey or you can go anywhere else you choose. If you stay here, you go somewhere, though."

I told him a little bit about my Jonny Lang and Psalms experience and then asked about rule number 2.

"You've gotta find a job." He clarified— "A full time job. I don't care where it is, either, but you need to keep busy doing something productive."

The only caveat, he explained, was that he couldn't be responsible for taking me to and from work. I had to figure that out myself. I *needed* to figure that out myself.

Thankfully, Lyn lived just off the 280 version of Hoover, Highway 31. It was— is— just as full of layers and layers of stores and shops and restaurants and other businesses. I saw opportunity everywhere. Especially after living in a concrete room for a few months.

Within the day I found employment at Johnny Ray's, a local barbecue joint. It was less than 1.5 miles door to door— an easy trek when you're used to powering back and forth to Gabriel's for 10 miles one way. Plus, now I was over 4 months sober.

Lyn stood by his word. He made sure that I got myself to work.

"It breaks my heart," he often told his friends, "watching her walk out the door in the rain. But I think she needs to keep at it. She needs to see she can do it."

And I did…

Rob did his thing, too.

The uneven beds didn't always stay where they should— nor did it even matter. (Another story for a different time and place.) But, we both continued moving forward.

Lyn didn't do it perfectly. No one does. But he was incredible. He found that balance that seems so hard to locate. He gave each of us just enough of a platform to step up and climb higher without doing all of the work for us.

Too often, I think people see addicts and do nothing— "You deserve what you get. You got yourself into this mess. You figure out how to climb out on your own."

Or they go to the opposite extreme and do *absolutely everything* for the addict. That's almost worse, because they never figure out a new kind of self-sufficiency that's honest and healthy.

....

Matt & Abbey (Rob's brother-in-law and his sister) attended Fullness Christian Fellowship every Sunday. Before I got out of jail, Rob attended his dad's church a few times— a big Baptist megachurch that defies all the stereotypes you might have about church people and all the things they do. When I moved into Lyn's, we started going with Matt & Abbey.

The best way to describe Fullness is this: "charismatic with a seatbelt on."

As opposed to their Baptist counterparts— like the kind people at Lyn's church (and these are just the stereotypes)— charismatics believe that God still heals people, that He still actively speaks to us about the details of our daily lives, and that He is always near. The people at Fullness didn't run around the aisles, they didn't make everyone pray in tongues, and they didn't do some of the things that make many people uncomfortable in the caricature Pentecostal settings. They simply believed God was— is— real and that He hasn't changed since Bible times.

- If He healed the blind man or the paralytic or the woman with the flow of blood... He might heal you or me.

- If He spoke to Moses and Daniel and the disciples and all the other people… He might speak to us.

- If he provided financial breakthrough for Isaac, mended familial relationships for Joseph, or even redeemed the murderous past of Paul… He might open the same doors for us.

After hearing about Rob's encounter at the men's retreat, and after experiencing Matt & Abbey's grace, I wanted to go.

....

"I've got a meeting with Pastor Bart. Will you come with me?" Rob asked.

I'd been out of jail for about 8 months at the time. We'd attended the church for about that long, as well.

It wasn't odd to me that Rob invited me to the meeting. He met with the men in the church a lot— and even interacted with Pastor Bart regularly.

I thought Rob invited me for moral support. After all, we walked through a LOT together. But, everything felt wonky as soon as we settled into Pastor Bart's office.

You see, I sat down on one end of the couch, and Rob sat as far as he possibly could away on the other side. That wasn't typical behavior— normally we scooched in side-by-side.

I thought, "Shit. What's going on…?"

It didn't take long for the answer to come…

"Pastor Bart, I'm really trying to change my ways and live as a Christian man — like God would want me to. So, well... I've got to quit sleeping with Shannon, because she's married to somebody else."

I'd never seen Bart speechless until that moment. The air seemed to suck out of the room.

I felt Smurf-size, three apples tall.

The entire church— and it wasn't a huge church— knew Rob and I were "boyfriend and girlfriend." Nobody really knew about the busted up parties, sneaking in and out of Patrice's apartment to use the bathroom and get showers, and all the other shenanigans of the past. I mean, they knew we lived hard and fast, but they just knew a few of the things that slipped out every now and then. No one knew about Mark and the Mayhem of Marshall.

It's not like we felt as if we needed to hide anything from any of those people at all. They were all incredibly accepting. It's just, well...

I dunno.

Gulp.

I hadn't even thought about it myself. I was still technically, legally, really married.

Rob just tossed me under the bus. Then, he backed it up and ran me over again for safe measure.

Fuck.

Is it even OK to think the word *fuck* in Pastor Bart's office?

Within the hour my phone began ringing. This time it was a cell phone— we'd moved up to that point.

"You can't be living with Rob under Lyn's roof! You gotta figure out what you're doing here."

None of them were judgy. I know it's hard to tell that tone while you're scanning this on paper, but they were all lovingly tender. It's just, well, again… this was news to them. No one knew.

I wanted to tell them, "Oh, no, it's fine— Lyn has it figured out. He sawed the legs off one of the beds!"

But, as Rob just confessed to Pastor Bart, where there's a will there's always a way. And when it comes to sex, there's almost always a will.

Then I wanted to say, "It's been five years— at least— since I've even seen the guy. And the last time I saw him I was pretty certain he was going to let me die until, somehow, I didn't… and he just vanished."

And then there was the truth I wanted to say that "I tried to divorce him— twice— after that. One time he ripped up the papers and walked off; the next time he actually blacked my eye by punching me in the face. Now he's in either prison or jail— I don't know which— and that's a really safe place for me for him to be… so can we just let it sit and everyone stop giving a shit?"

No one meant any harm by calling out the living situation. Yet, at the same time, unless you've walked that same path, it's almost impossible to describe the degree of bravery it takes to walk away…

Sometimes you just want to leave "good enough" alone. But, to truly move forward— from where you are to where you're designed and destined to be — you can't.

19. Inside, Outside, Upside-Down (S)

Shannon gets new roommates, finishes drug court, and works at a rehabilitation center before hitting what seems to be a dead end.

It didn't take long for me to agree I needed a new roommate situation. Lyn became a father-figure to me (and would, in even greater ways, in years to come), and Rob was a close friend with benefits.

But I realized I DID tend to prop myself up with a man AND two gals from the church called at just the right time.

"We've got a three bedroom apartment," they said, "and we've been praying about a roommate. We feel like we should offer this to you."

I wasn't sure what to say.

The women from Fullness were some of the best, purest anywhere. In fact, they ARE part of the reason I feel confident sharing every part of my story today.

Back then, I was introduced to the word *prophecy*...

A lot of people think of prophecy only as "fore-telling" future events— in the Nostradamus sense of the word. Others consider it to be "forth-telling," that is, revealing secrets.

The New Testament talks about *both*.

Paul told the Christians in Corinth that prophecy (read: forth-telling) "reveals secrets" and "lays them bare" (see 1 Corinthians 14:25).

And, Paul confesses that he wishes that everyone in the church would do this (1 Corinthians 14:5).

Whereas we often think, "Oh, if someone knew what was really going on inside me, they would shun me, shame me, and shew me to the side"— because, let's be honest with each other, we've seen that happen too much for our own good, Paul reminds us— in the same passage— that the intent of prophecy is to "build people up" and breathe life into them (1 Corinthians 14:3). He didn't envision a breed of this sort of "truth-telling" that would suck the life out of people and debilitate them from walking in their purpose and potential.

In that fashion, God showed the ladies at Fullness truths about me that they NEVER would have known apart from Him revealing it to them. People often ask WHY God might do that. I think it's because He wants us to know, "Hey, I see you. I'm for you. I DO have a plan for you." And, whereas we might internally *think* we've heard Him tell us those things, when He goes out of His way to express it through another human we feel the impact of His best thoughts towards us on an entirely different level.

Plus, He never intended for us to figure out life on our own. He designed us for connection.

I decided the invite from these ladies was worth a conversation. I mean, I DID wonder what two single, innocent young ladies might think about someone with my past, but...

… well, you never know.

Fast forward: I moved in. They became an incredible support system for me.

Years later, they did admit that despite their sense that God led them to offer me the room, they were anxious about the prospect of me visiting their home before moving in.

"We hid our wallets," they laughed. "I can't believe we actually *thought* that might be a problem…"

They weren't wrong for worrying. Addiction is difficult to kick. Old habits die hard.

While living with them, I amassed enough small bills from my tips at Johnny Ray's to purchase a well-worn car. Then, I saved enough to make the leap to living on my own. That's when I moved two doors down from my Mom's apartment, so I could get close to my kids.

With a little over 2 years of sobriety, a new place, and transportation, I got hired at Bradford— a well-known (and highly reputable) drug & alcohol rehab. I was (finally) out of drug court, which is what made this transition possible.

....

Oh, about drug court…

Let's rewind a bit.

A few decades ago, the legal system rolled out a program called TASC. It's an acronym for Tactics Against Street Crime. Promoted as a clever way to build-in accountability for addicts and offered as a promise of a better life than prison, the program raises grant awards for various municipalities while simultaneously keeping the people the program is designed to serve hand-cuffed from moving forward.

Let me explain.

Participants bond out of jail time and maintain periodic check-ins with a judge. Each time they attend a court date, they receive a future court date. Court fees are added to each of these, of course.

Participants ALSO receive a "color." They're required to phone in each morning to see if it's "their color" that day. Seemingly, the colors rotate randomly. If your color hits, you're required to report— that day— for a drug test at the designated testing facility. You pay for the test, of course, and if you light up the panel they hold you. A condition of your bond is that you stay clean.

Most of the judges are great. They sincerely want to help the participants move forward.

However, the fees and costs can be debilitating. Plus, the fact you *might* have to leave on any random day and spend a half-day reporting for a drug test before getting back to work makes it extremely difficult to find consistent employment.

Rob worked with his Dad until he found a job working at a re-entry and residential rehab that totally understood and offered him flexibility. I waited tables, so I could slide in just before lunch (if my color got called) until I was able to finish my "real world" drug court sentence.

Our pack of previously arrested peeps were assigned the color "peach." Not surprising, peach popped every other day for 15 months— even on Christmas. I lived with the gals from the church the entire time I did this and truly was the "quiet" roommate who kept to herself.

- Go pee.

- Go to work.

- Come home.

- Shut my bedroom door.

- Sleep, realizing I might be able to sleep in a little bit tomorrow since my color came up today.

- Wake up.

- Check and see if my color was called, because… well… you never know and if it does get called you gotta go pee (and pay) again.

- Rinse & repeat the following day, knowing peach would hit tomorrow if it didn't hit today.

I graduated the drug court program and then moved "back to the sticks," as Rob called it. That's when I began working at Bradford, thinking it would be a great way to give back and help others who were facing the same demons I had defeated.

....

The only problem…

Well, there's yet ANOTHER story in the Bible about a person who actually has a demon. The demon gets expelled, so it goes wandering about, looking for somewhere else— or *someone* else— to occupy.

In time, the demon returns to the person from whom it was evicted and observes, "Hmm. This place has been cleared out. Nothing has been put back in my space" (see Matthew 12:45).

The demon leaves, goes and finds seven MORE spirits— "more evil than itself," the story goes— and then takes everything to a new level of devildom altogether.

Some Bible scholars say the entire story refers to Mary Magdalene, a "woman of the street" trounced and tormented by seven demons before Jesus finally freed her. She, recall, was one of the ladies who discovered the empty tomb.

In full disclosure, I eventually discovered this "empty tomb" and resurrection life for myself, but I wasn't quite there. I was between the "one demon leaves me" stage and then "brings back 7 more" stage because I didn't "fill the newly cleaned house with something more awesome."

Here's how it happened.

I worked most Monday through Friday nights at Bradford. As the staff person on call, I talked to addicts during most of my working hours. By now I had disassociated myself from being one.

Like many addicts with a significant stint of clean time behind them, I rationalized, "*I'm on the other side of this.* I'm doing really good."

I don't recall the details of how and why, but my little brother came to live with me. With me living on one side of my Mom's (with Blake) and my sister living on the other (with Kimberly), it seemed like the family was getting back together.

My brother behaved just like that demon, though. I'm not saying he IS a demon, and I'm not suggesting he was demon-possessed. What I AM saying is that shortly after he arrived, he invited a litany of cousins and other assorted people from his dad's side of the family to move into my apartment with me.

My once clean place became cluttered.

I hooked up with one of the cousins. Most of them had rap sheets the length of those long receipts they give you at CVS and Walgreens.

That man moved his entire family into the apartment as well. This included, but wasn't limited to, his mom, his two brothers, and a girlfriend.

You read the last line right. *Girlfriend.*

I had a knack for finding men— husbands and long-term boyfriends alike— who always had a side hustle going. It just seemed *normal* in that culture.

Put the pieces together—

- I decided to help my little brother.

- Little brother "helped" cousins.

- I hooked up with one of the cousins.

- The "hook up" brought his own family, a few friends, and a female.

Am I a dumbass?

I wondered…

Allen, my new whatever-you-call-it, was bipolar. And he was an addict. And, well…

You know where this road goes, don't you?

Before spelling it out, I do want to say this: because of my past as compared to where we are now, people amidst their struggle often ask for advice. I'm always happy to offer it, as well as sit and just listen.

I always tell people, though, "Look at the road you are on, and note where that road goes."

Here's what I mean: Rob and I live near downtown Birmingham in a historic neighborhood known as Norwood. If I want to go see my son Blake— which

19. Inside, Outside, Upside-Down (S)

I've resolved to do for a week at a time, twice a year, outside of holidays— I must drive north. (I love the long drive, by the way, because I relish the alone time to just think and *be*.)

If I head south, I'll never end up at Blake's, where I can visit him and his wife and see my granddaughter. The road to Blake's is north.

If I take a wrong turn and go south, I have two options.

- Option 1 = intentionally stop, reverse course, and move in the right direction
- Option 2 = continue moving in the wrong direction and miss the visit

This is important: all of the wishing, the positive thinking, and the prayer in the world will not help me reach Blake and his family if I head in the wrong direction and continue without changing my course. To reach him, I must move in the correct trajectory.

This is an easy lesson to apply to driving. But, we forget the same principle is equally true in life. The road always goes where the road goes.

Let me state it again with slightly different language: the road you are on always goes where the road you are on goes.

I was clean. For almost three years. I had a car, I had setup a home near my kids, and I secured a great job.

The road I moved to— by inviting that man into my life— *was a different road than the one I would have told you I actually wanted to be on*. And all the prayer and positive thinking and positive energy and everything else doesn't magically make the destination of any given road somehow change.

To arrive at the destination you want, you must find the road that gets there and stay on it. If you're on the wrong road— or moving in the wrong direction — you must make a shift.

Allen beat me up.

I discovered I was on the wrong road.

(I knew it before I admitted it. This episode made it painfully obvious.)

I called Rob. Though we weren't together as a couple, he always had my back.

"I need help," I told him.

He was running a work crew from The Program where he now worked on staff. Since guys couldn't find employment until they had identification, and since most addicts and former prisoners don't have an up-to-date ID, Rob had the idea for the rehab to start a renovation business— that he ran— so they could employ those guys in the interval.

"Shan needs our help!" he exclaimed, as soon as my call came.

The staff and his crew all knew who I was.

Within a few hours, he had paused the remodel job they were in the middle of and had the crew at my apartment.

Charles, a former drug dealer who looked like an NFL tight end and had— in his wayward days— been known to kick in doors to go collect his money, channeled his former self and walked through the doors of the apartment without even knocking.

"Where you at boy? You come on out and fight a man like a man…"

He started looking through closets. Charles would have folded Allen like a paper doll if he found him.

"Nobody's here but me, Charles. He's gone."

"Well, OK. OK." Then— "You OK? Let's get you loaded up and out of here…"

19. Inside, Outside, Upside-Down (S)

Rob and the boys moved me 30 miles away, south of town. It was a new place where no one should have been able to find me.

I got away from Allen by moving away from my kids and family (again) into an apartment in Alabaster— a 30-minute drive south of Birmingham.

I could rationalize the move: "I'm getting away from him, and this is closer to the Bradford Health Services office in Shelby County."

But you remember what I told you about domestic violence, abused women, and how many times it takes to actually leave…

And you know that most abusers know *exactly* what to say to make you think they've really changed *this* time— no matter how many times *this* time happened before— so that you agree to take them back…

"Alright. You can come back," I told Allen over the cell phone. "I'll come get you. Just tell me where you are."

I actually drove and picked him up.

Turns out, I was just another "newly clean house" with nothing in it. So, like the demon who whistles for his seven friends, Allen— within just a few weeks— brought his mother, his brother, and his brother's friends.

One night, he gave me a shot of something and spiked it. I don't even know what was in it. I had already relapsed (while still working at the rehab, mind you), but this hit different.

I passed out. For a few days.

I missed work, and Bradford called. My phone rang and rang and rang until Allen finally answered it.

Probably in a drug-driven, drunk stupor himself, he answered, "Hello…"

"Yes, I'm looking for Shannon. She missed work, and I was checking to make sure she's OK. It's not like her…"

(I never missed work. Not even when I bumped from B-Dub's to Carrabba's and then froggered across the street to party before going back to the mobile home Mitsubishi in the Target parking lot did I miss work.)

"She can't come to the phone right now. She's, like…"

Allen said something outrageous. I'm still not sure— even today— what he said.

(In fairness to him, it could have been his intoxication speaking or it could have been the bipolarity. No one knows.)

What I do know is that Bradford called right back, and he sent the call straight to voice mail.

I listened to it when I came to and realized I screwed up again…

- The medical insurance company.
- The hospital in Texas.
- The rehab.

Three great career-type jobs all flushed because of drugs, and I never even took the drug test.

I pulled myself together and called my supervisor.

"I'm so sorry," I told her— there was nothing else to say.

I didn't make excuses (typical addict behavior), and I didn't create a secondary story to deny what happened (even more typical addict behavior). I just owned it (atypical— evidence I was moving in the right direction).

"I'm sorry, too," she replied. Then— "I'll get you a place in the rehab, so you can work this thing out. I'll make sure you get treatment. We can make a place for you here."

I couldn't do it, though. I couldn't go be a resident in a place I had been filling up with patients. I couldn't flip from counselor to client.

"It took me *less than three months to lose three years of progress*," I whispered to myself. That's how long it had been since I moved into the apartment in Alabaster, 90 days. "I am a failure."

I looked across the living room.

Allen sat there, smoking a cigarette. He acted oblivious to everything happening around me.

He was bipolar, and he was an addict. He probably *was* oblivious.

I looked his way.

I was angry— and grew angrier by the moment. His mental health condition. His *laissez faire* attitude about how he handled my job. The fact he brought everyone else into my home after I took him back...

Mostly, I suppose I was angry at myself.

I threw something at him. I don't even remember what it was. I just remember hurling it as hard as I could.

Predictably, he retaliated with a punch. Then another. Then a slam. Then who knows what...

I blacked out, and then I came back to, and then I wound up in the nearby medical center. One broken nose. Two bruised ribs. And he stole my car and took my cell phone.

Here's what stands out to me the most about that day, though: *The men in the ER were pissed that a man beat me.*

In my world, men always cheated on women. They slept with them when they wanted— and begged or even raped them to get sex. And they hit them. Those were normal, expected behaviors.

No. No woman likes being on the receiving end of those activities, but we all acknowledged that's the way things were. For us, anyway.

The men and women in the Emergency Room disagreed. They were angry at a man *they didn't even know* because he treated a woman *they didn't even know* in a way men should never treat a woman.

"Who did this to you?" they asked.

I wouldn't tell. I figured if I ratted Allen out, they would tell the cops, and the cops would put him back in prison. It's bizarre that I wanted to protect him.

A female nurse came into the room, and the men left.

"Hey, do you want to talk about it? He's probably threatened to harm someone you love if you ever say anything…"

She knew the script.

"That's exactly what they do," I told her. "Abusers don't threaten to hurt you after they've already hurt you; they promise to hurt the people who mean the most to you."

"I know, honey. I'm so sorry…"

Somehow, I knew she knew— probably because she *really knew*.

The entire team embodied the same grace as the women at Fullness. It showed me that anyone can be called and live-out a God-ordained purpose, regardless of where they work full time. Preachers can be called, and high school principals can be called, and plumbers can be called, and health practitioners *for sure* can be called…

"We're ready to discharge you, but we're not going to let you leave until you agree to tell us who did this and file a police report or at least go to a safe house."

I didn't think about the fact that they couldn't legally hold me to either standard. I was free to walk out the door anytime I chose— from the moment I arrived.

I spent one night in a safe house.

To be clear, this was the first time I ever sought medical attention. Until the hospital staff, police, safe house representatives, and others questioned me and demonstrated genuine concern, *I never realized that beating women was frowned upon.*

The next day I called Rob and relayed everything that happened. "I can't do this shit anymore," I confessed. "I'm too old, my body doesn't heal as fast, and I'm just tired…"

The re-entry / rehab where he worked had been helping a new women's shelter. Tajuan had lived as hard— or harder— than I had. She found her way out of human trafficking. A few years clean and sober, she decided to become the life boat and help others find freedom.

She didn't have a way to start-up, but the guys where Rob worked believed in her and offered her free office space and the use of a house. The first women they rescued lived in the Jenkins' house— the guy Rob worked with. This was the same house where the two of them first met after Rob waited two days at the warehouse-church to try and meet him.

When the women's program, known as the Wellhouse, had enough ladies to fill a home, they relocated down the street to another property Andrew and his team provided. Today that organization has rescued hundreds of women. At that time, they had been open for just a few weeks and had welcomed about five into a new life of freedom.

Rob walked down the hall and checked with her.

"Yeah, of course," Tajuan said. "Let's help her."

Someone went and stole my car back for me, and Rob came and filled the tank with gas. He followed me to the offices...

Originally, I thought I was going into that program, but he spoke with Andrew. He talked with Tajuan and the other leaders of the women's ministry. The ladies had recently moved into the new house. The Jenkins now had an empty room.

They decided I could just do the medical screens and tests they always provided for the ladies and then stay at his home— in the guest bedroom— with his wife and six kids.

In less than two months, life would upend itself again when Rob got shot.

19. Inside, Outside, Upside-Down (S)

Application for Part 6 | Direction Determines Destination

Main idea: We always end up where the road we're traveling goes. Success always leaves clues, as does "un-success." Continue moving consistently in the intended direction, and you'll— sooner or later— arrive.

In chapter 16, the gang got off on a technicality. Predictably, they got caught just a few weeks later.

If you were there, you might have said something like, "I knew it! Of course this happened."

Make it personal, though.

Where have you seen your own behaviors eventually catch up with you?

_____

_____

_____

_____

_____

_____

_____

_____
_____
_____
_____
_____

Sometimes it takes bad behaviors a while to "catch up." In like fashion, we also must remember that it often takes good behaviors a while to "catch up" before we see the evidence of them— if you're doing the right things, don't quit too soon!

What are some of the actions you need to continue?

_____
_____
_____
_____
_____
_____
_____
_____
_____
_____

Rob said that we're designed to work and create (chapter 17). Part of living life at your full capacity is discovering why you're here— your purpose.

What are you designed to do?

_____

_____

_____

_____

_____

_____

_____

_____

We've seen several instances of "right place at the right time" in this book (i.e., Lyn meeting the contractor in chapter 2 and starting a wallpaper business, Rob meeting the pastor at Power Lunch who knew a person to introduce him to, etc.).

How much of life is hard work? How much of it is happenstance? Or do they just work together and you trust the process as you walk the right path?

_____

_____

_____

_____

_____

_____

_____

_____

_____

Get clear about the road you're on (see chapter 19).

The "road" is comprised of the daily actions you do.

Where does your current road go?

Do you need to make adjustments?

_____

_____

_____

_____

_____

_____

_____

_____

_____

_____

_____

_____

_____

At the end of chapter 18, Shannon talked about leaving "good enough" alone. She was trying to hide an unresolved part of her past.

It's almost impossible to step forward if you're clinging to the pains of the past— especially if you're hiding them.

What do you need to resolve, so you can go "all in" and move forward?

_____

_____

_____

_____

_____

_____

_____

_____

Part 7 | Arrived & Always Arriving

Fulfilling your purpose has no finish line. We live in a constant tension of "we've come so far" (we should celebrate) and still having further we want to go (we must guard against complacency). Enjoy the progress, live a life of balance, and overcome the gaps you continue to notice between where you are and where you want to be.

20. Three Dogs & a Little More Malcom Luck (R)

Rob needs a new business plan. He learns some circumstances are clearly out of his control. He sees what it means to sign a contract.

The year I got married Ben and I started renovating houses under the moniker 3D Properties. We didn't have a name for the business and knew we needed to call it something...

"What about naming it after those three dogs we've got?" Ben asked.

"Good enough."

That was it. *Three dogs* became *3D*. It wasn't about *Design* or *Develop* or *Decorative* or any of the words— like even *Decorum*— that make sense for a company focusing on home renovation. It was just complete nonsense.

That kind of nonsense carried over into some of our business decisions, too. I mean, we didn't intentionally try to be non-sensical, it's just that, well... we really didn't have any idea what we were doing.

"We'll just figure it out," I often said.

Or, to say it another way— "Sew the parachute together after you jump out of the airplane."

One of our favorite sayings actually was "If it doesn't fit, smash it!"

I can hear Ben's voice now: "Ram it!"

He lived in our house a few of the months during our first year of marriage. That wasn't the greatest marital decision, but you've got to remember that Shan and I didn't need a lot of space. We lived in a car, spent multiple nights in an actual closet, bunked on random couches, slept at rehabs, rested in abandoned buildings, and routinely experienced a litany of roommates coming and going such that you never knew who might be there for the night. Old habits like that don't just stop because you get married.

One day, Shan walked through the kitchen to get her first cup of morning coffee. The sun was just coming up.

"You been up all night?" she asked.

"Is it *already* the next day? Yeah, I guess so…"

"What are you doing?"

"Babe, I just bought our next house on this auction site!"

"What?"

"Ben and I purchased this house on auction dot com."

"Have you actually *seen this house* you bought?" she asked.

"No, but how bad could it be…?" I replied. Then, I boasted, "It's only $9,500."

This was in 2011. Back then you could by houses *cheap*.

This was before we started learning from other legitimate renovators and discovered that we needed to consider the roof, the wiring, the foundation, and so many other issues...

"You ought to check into your $9,500 house," she suggested. "You might have just bought $9,500 of bullshit and problems."

At the time, I didn't realize it was generally a *horrible* idea to purchase a home site-unseen. And, I didn't know I could simply identify a real estate agent, develop a professional relationship, and work with them long-term on all of my deals. They could do some of the legwork for me.

(I tell you all of this, because where we are now is definitely *not* where we began. We did it; you can do it, too.)

Ben and I learned how to find houses, fix them, fill them, and then flip a bundle of them to investors. This worked well until— overnight— it didn't.

As dishonest as we had been about the tarps and sign-stealing, we were the complete opposite about our craftsmanship and the houses we sold.

"We're creating a place where someone is going to house their family," we often reminded each other. "Their wife and kids are going to stay here. Absolutely no skimping."

We never skipped any steps, we never skated around the permit process, and we never shortcut any of the finishes. We stayed within the budget parameters and completed the homes at the right spec, but we did it well. Extremely well.

Other groups weren't so sincere, and that had a major impact on our business model. You see, the problem you face when you don't hold the homes and act as the landlord but, instead, offload them to investment groups is that other renovators in the area inevitably hear about the same groups. Not only do you find yourself competing for the business (on some level), but the others can sour the experience for your investors... fast.

Another crew doing what Ben and I did— let's just call them 2B, for 2 Boneheads)— started flipping bad real estate. Whereas Ben and I created a file on each property...

- A pic of the mailbox or address

- A copy of the original acquisition contract— when we purchased the property

- A file of all receipts for the renovation process

- A folder full of pictures— before & after— in the same format for each home

- A copy of the original renovation permit, a copy of the completed permit with all signatures, and a copy of the certificate of occupancy

- A copy of the signed tenant agreement

... the 2 Boneheads created a similar file system with one notable exception to ours— they never did *any* renovations.

They snapped a photo of the address signage, and then copied photos from other homes that had *already* been renovated.

Some of the houses they packaged and sold to the investment group had trees laying across damaged roofs— with water continuing to accumulate inside and add to the needed renovations. Others had broken windows and unattached siding. Some had no power or water. Most of them weren't habitable.

They were paid the same margins for their houses as we received for our pristine homes. The only difference was, well... we actually did the work on ours.

Everything collapsed because of the property flow:

- We bought one property at a time and renovated it, before filling it with a tenant.

- We sold the properties in groups of 10 to an acquisition group— like the one the man from Utah led.

- The acquisition group generally took several bundles of 25 or 30 to Vegas and sold the bigger batches to other investment groups.

"People fly in from all over the world," I heard. "They sit in a theatre-style room and review the pictures on the screen. Then they bid based on the pictures from those files."

We weren't even the middle man. We were the first in a string of 3 or 4 transactions that might lead up the line until major investors purchased homes— which they believed to be overhauled and occupied.

The shit shot out of the canon when the investors no longer knew which photographs they could trust. Eventually, one of the bigwigs somewhere in the chain found out they were buying empty houses that were still in the original condition— some which could have easily just be demolished.

We knew nothing about all of this, of course, until we discovered 3D was in the minority— the vast majority were like the 2 Boneheads, simply gaming the system. They bought houses for about $15,000 and sold them for $50,000.

A few of those guys went to prison.

Distrustful of the entire process, the entire system just evaporated. After all, when you're buying hundreds at a time, it's not worth your time and energy to look for two unknown guys in one random city who happen to be doing it the right way. We were the needle in the haystack.

The movie *The Big Short*— the true-story film in which Christian Bale plays Michael Burry and realized a massive number of subprime home loans were about to default and collapse the market— refers to this specific time in history in which 3D began. The economy collapsed because of junk bonds and junk mortgages... and the junk houses simply added to our small piece of the pie.

Overnight it ended.

"It's the Malcom luck," I sighed, half-overwhelmed and half-laughing.

....

The end of the acquisition pipeline meant nothing to the dishonest developers, but it crushed the honest teams like ours.

We initially had a great rhythm.

- Purchase a house at $15-20K

- Renovate it fast by infusing another $15-$20K in, including the costs of paying our contract labor

- Fill it with a tenant, by having a steady advertising flow and a constant incoming application process of potential occupants

- Flip it to the initial acquisition company for a $10-$15K profit per house

We generally had 20-30 homes in our pipeline, each of them in one of three stages:

- Month 1 = Stage 1 / Acquire, permit, and demo

- Month 2 = Stage 2 / Renovate and get final certificate of occupancy

- Month 3 = Stage 3 / Occupy and sell

The 90-day process worked well— as long as it worked. Plus, local investors (once we got thru the initial 69 who turned us down) were happy giving us 90 day loans at a guaranteed 10% return. That meant if they provided us the up to $40K for the purchase and renovation, we would return an additional $4K to them when we closed just three months later.

We moved fast.

All of the sudden, though, we hit a dead end.

"Let's see...." Ben said, looking at the whiteboard.

I scanned the wall and quickly tabulated, "Eighteen... we have 18 outstanding houses in the pipeline— plus the outstanding contracts on everything we planned to acquire in the next two weeks."

It was the weekend of Thanksgiving

when it fell apart.

"What the hell are we going to do with the 8 that are ready to sell and the 10 that are almost ready?" Ben asked.

I looked back at the list.

"People have always asked us why we don't hold these properties more often," I observed. "Our business model has been to sell everything we get— and it's been easy. We haven't had to manage tenants."

"Are you suggesting we should learn how to do that, now?" Ben asked.

I laughed, "We might not have a choice."

....

We tabled the conversation until we could loop Shannon in.

With a spreadsheet stretched across the kitchen table, I said, "Here's where we are…"

I described the flow of what we *thought* would sell, what we needed to finish before we could do anything else, and all the ambiguities I could think of.

"The big question mark across all of this," Ben stated, "is deciding what we do *fast*. We've got to really make some decisions *now*."

"Do you want to be landlords?" Shannon asked.

Neither of us did. We didn't know how to do it. Since that night we'd learned the mechanics, for sure— in terms of both regular tenant relationships and short term / AirBNB-types of offers. Back then, we knew *less* about rentals than we initially understood about selling to acquisition companies, though.

Shannon looked at both of us.

"Why don't you just start selling them yourself?" she asked.

"Maybe that's what we need to do," I replied. "We could change the asset class— from low income and Section 8 tenants" [read: government assistance].

"You mean that we should make them even nicer?" Ben clarified. "That we should level them up and go for an $80,000 or $90,000 home or more...?"

"Yeah, maybe even acquire bigger homes and sell at $125,000 or $200,000 or even more..."

"We could do *less* properties with *bigger* profit margins..."

"Do you have a realtor?" Shannon asked.

(This happened while she ran the office at the community medical clinic— about 5 years before she moved into real estate and about 6 years before we ever considered launching EXIT Realty Birmingham.)

"We would need to find one," I said. "We need someone who is really willing to work a constant flow with us. Instead of packaging 10 to sell to a single investor, we'll be doing up to 10 different transactions a month."

"This is going to be s hard transition," Ben added, "but we've learned how to do harder things before. And, this will move us to the place where we aren't allowing the whims of massive hedge funds to determine our financial outlook."

As he spoke those words, I thought about the entrepreneurial journey. It's strange to me that so many people in our society think nothing of attending a 4-year college (and paying $40,000 or more to do it, often going in debt and then struggling to payback those student loans) for the chance to go work for an employer.

"That's true security," the thought-line goes.

Think about the logic of that. I'm certainly not against college. But you pay all of this money to go (or you repay all of this money after you went), and you only receive the opportunity to then apply to work for "the man."

A college degree does not guarantee you a job. And having a job does not guarantee you'll be employed forty years from now when you reach retirement age— much less four years or four months or even four days from now.

Yet most people have been so conditioned to fall for the "go work for someone else" and "let them determine your financial security" narrative that they not only fail to question it, they see anything else as utter nonsense.

"Let's create a plan that— as best we can— allows us to control our future," I suggested.

Everyone agreed.

....

With the new plan in head, I had to approach our lenders about our ideas. Remember, we had worked through 69 of them to find the first backer (before identifying others). They had all signed on for a $15-20K house plus $15-20K in renovations AND a 10% return in 90 days.

We could clear our board of the existing homes by selling what was ready and finishing what wasn't. That was the easy part.

To work our way into the "retail flip" space, we needed two things:

- A whole lot more money (i.e., a $100K house plus $50K in renovations), AND

- A little bit more time.

We could still make it lucrative for them. In fact, we learned it works best when it's extremely profitable for your lenders— because they buy into the process and really get behind you.

However you view it, though, the new terms would be different than the previous plan.

I called John first. He was the guy who went to see the first— and only house— before using the "construction toilet" and soon thereafter agreed to fund up to ten houses at a time.

"The first time I drafted a deal with him on paper," I told Ben, "I suggested we needed enough money available to buy 10 houses at once AND renovate them. I told him we probably wouldn't draw it all in a single swoop— because you move them into a pipeline. We just need to know it's available, so we can purchase quickly when a good deal presents itself."

Ben asked, "How do you think we need to pitch it now?"

"I don't know…."

As I thought about the past few days I added, "I do think we need to tell him what happened with the acquisition companies we were selling to, because our entire strategy is changing. There aren't going to be any of those low ticket houses going forward."

"Agreed."

The two of us on the same page, I relayed the news to John and confessed, "We might be late on this next closing. That means we may be late getting the repayment and the 10% back to you. Can you help us a bit?"

Turns out, John didn't give a shit.

"It's OK if you're a little late," he replied. "Stuff that's out of your control happens. It happens to me all the time..."

He explained how the sandwich shop where we met him wasn't actually the place he planned to keep the joint. He signed a contract and hired a bunch of day laborers to work on the space behind that shop.

Once they got into it, they discovered all of these structural issues and a lack of water access and all of this other stuff that made it tough sledding.

"You were in the restaurant you were in," he said, "because the other location didn't work. And that meant I had two leases going. I planned to renovate the one place while running out the final three months of the previous. The new place didn't work, and I needed to keep the income going while I battled through it. Shit happens."

He was kind about the entire thing. And he understood. He had walked the same terrain in a slightly different way.

But he wasn't budging.

"Look at your contract. The money is due on whatever date is in the contract. There's a fee if you're late. I'm not bending..."

Looking back, his inflexibility actually helped solidify our decision to move forward with the new plan. If he would have given us even an inch, as the saying goes, we might have continued wiggling around where we are. We might have gone a mile off course.

We couldn't do that, though. We had to move forward.

Don't get me wrong, I was pissed. I actually punched the ceiling of my truck when I got back in after leaving the meeting. We made him a bunch of money at levels banks *couldn't* pay.

But I understood. His money is what made it possible for us to make money.

I probably wouldn't have flexed, either, if things were the other way around. That's how you can always tell if you're on solid footing.

Just ask yourself, "What if this happened the other way?"

Generally, you'll have a clear answer. You always know *exactly* what you would prefer if the rolls reversed.

At the time, we only had one outstanding property with John. Just before the "middleman" investors stopped buying, we serendipitously sold all of his. I'm not sure why I took the meeting so hard other than fear of the unknown.

We listed the house and sold it. Our repayment to John was a little late, so we owed some money. By the time the numbers on the HUD statement tabulated, we lost money on the deal.

But it was only $2,500.

Of the numerous houses we sold through the hedge fund strategy— and there were too many to count— we only lost money on that one.

....

We created a new set of terms with John and continued stepping forward. The houses got bigger, the renovations grew more complex, and the gains increased.

As we learned new things, we always paid outstanding loans on the agreed terms of those deals. When it made sense, we adjusted future deals. In time, I showed him how certain changes to future loan structures would benefit both parties in a greater way— offering us more flexibility and a faster draw and increasing this bottom line.

I learned that, yes, "business is business." You adamantly must honor what you've said you will do for people.

At the same time, "people are people." When you honor your word and show them that you're not just in it for you— a big adjustment for a former addict— they genuinely want to help. Most people want to succeed, and they don't mind helping you in the process— as long as it's a win-win.

Today, I have over 2 million dollars out with John— a big jump from, maybe, $150,000 to $200,000 at a time.

I also have other investors working with me, as well. Oddly enough, one of them met Ben and me for lunch to tell us how to find and fix houses back when we were first learning to get ready for the hedge funds and acquisition companies. Whereas we faked our way through the first few months, he was always legit.

I still joke with him about foxing him out of perfectly good properties by tossing those blue tarps across the roofs.

"Hah, those are the good ole days!" he says.

(I don't advocate such behavior as a way to start a new business, by the way. Remember, exchange your place with theirs in your mind. If things were the other way around, think about how you would see it...)

21. "For Better or Worse" Often Means Worse (S)

Shannon recalls key dates and times. She reflects on the lessons learned in starting a brokerage. She remembers an overlooked phrase in the marriage vows.

Anytime someone asks how long I've been sober— this time— I run the math back to our wedding.

First, "How long have I been married to Rob…?"

We got married on October 1, 2011.

I back it up from there.

- I called Rob from the safe house in April.

- I stayed with the Jenkins for about 8 weeks.

- Rob got shot on June 6.

- Rob proposed in August.

- We married 2 months later.

- *How long have I been sober?*

About 6 months longer than we've been married, and about 4 months longer than since Rob got shot.

The shooting is an odd story— Rob supplied the details.

I remember how a few of us found out.

My older sister and Kimberly were at home (Kimberly lived with her), watching the news when the news van popped up outside the re-entry program where it happened, tossed a reporter in front of a camera, and rolled to the live coverage. They frantically began trying to call my phone.

I never answered it because Andrew's ex-wife (I lived at their house at the time) also called me, loaded up their 6 kids, picked me up from work, and drove me to the downtown hospital where Rob was.

....

The funny thing about husband-wife relationships is that marriage isn't dating and dating isn't friendship and friendship isn't marriage and yet they all fit together.

I'll see if I can explain it...

Most people— even the people who know us well— don't believe that Rob and I dated less than 6 months before we got married. And most of that wasn't even dating. We went from... something... to engaged... to married two months later.

"But you two were always together," people observe.

That's true.

Rob showed up for me multiple times— and rescued me from dangerous situations, even. But, it wasn't— hasn't always been— easy.

And "not always easy" means I bailed on the marriage less than a year in...

Despite Lyn's self-congratulatory moment of presenting us with two twin beds of differing elevation, the two of us were intimate before the wedding night. Heck, Rob exposed me to Pastor Bart. Plus, we had all the time in the black Eclipse, Patrice's closet, and everywhere else we went together for years.

All of that seemed to *stop* after the wedding night, though.

About 9 months after we got married, Rob told me, "I've got an STD." Then — "This is from you."

I knew it couldn't be me, though. The ministry that took me in after the ER doctors *required* I go to a safe place always took incoming women for a medical check-up. They tested everyone for STDs, among other things.

"You're completely clean," the doc said, holding the report in hand.

I was surprised.

She could see it in my expression.

"Here, take a look," the doc offered, showing me the report. She smiled, adding, "You've got a clean start here. And, there's nothing you need to worry about medically at all."

Rob and I knew about each person's past. I mean, we never sat down and offered a list of names and places and dates and times— that would have been impossible. What we did know, though, is that we both lived hard and we vowed to lean in to each other even harder than that.

"It's not me," I told him.

We got into a big fight that morning.

Yet this fight went different than all the others. Whereas I punched and swung and hit and threw fists at him, Rob never retaliated. He never bowed up like that— never has. He just took the hits.

Don't misunderstand. He can raise his voice— and yell from the bottom of his tippy-toes (just like he talks most of the time). Even though I continued expecting him to physically come back at me (and may have even baited it), he never did.

It was late in the summer when I finally grabbed the keys to our green minivan, found his debit card, loaded up anything we had in the fridge, and took off towards the beach. An old high school friend's Mom lived there and always had an open door for me.

I expected a repeat of everything I'd seen in my past from other men—

- Clothes and other belongings randomly tossed in the yard like a farmer might scatter seed across a field

- Name-calling ("You're a bitch and a whore!", cursing ("Fuck you!"), and blaming ("This is all your fault— I knew you would pull this shit!")

- Lots of gossip to get their side of the story out first, framing it so no one sympathizes with you once you finally get the nerve to share what happened from your own perspective

He never did *any* of that. Frankly, when he didn't I wasn't sure what to do. It was like something, somewhere hit one giant *pause* button and all I could do was... wait.

....

Rob only told a handful of people— maybe 4 or 5– what occurred. His dad knew and Ben knew (who had moved into our house the first year were married, likely adding to some of our tension) and one or two others knew.

And the pastor— Pastor Bart knew.

After a few weeks, the ladies from the church began calling. Not because he told them to. Rather, they just hadn't seen *me* like they used to.

Rob left a few voice messages, as well. None of them were what I expected — from past experience— either. I could tell that, for him, this was a dark time that impacted him greatly. He wasn't sure what to do...

But he loved me, he said.

Was I going to not go back to the one person who was different for fear he might be a replay of the same insane stuff I saw before?

I finally agreed to have a conversation with Rob. Looking back, it's somewhat odd to me that it seemed to require so much to come back and talk with my husband. I provided the validity of the "average of 7 times leaving to finally leave" stat before with unhealthy men and rarely had a hard time taking them back— much less having a conversation. It's almost like, once you've seen unhealthy and dishonorable men for so long you don't actually know what to do when a healthy and honorable man walks into your life and accepts you.

I turned into our driveway and watched him walk down from the front porch. It's almost— like the father in the story of the prodigal son— he had been waiting, looking into the distance, anticipating the moment I would return.

I expected another fist fight— like the kind I knew…

He slowly approach the vehicle, opened the door, and hugged me. He held me for a moment.

"Are you okay?" he asked.

He was gentle…

Tender.

Calm.

He was concerned about me— not about what I "put him through."

He grabbed my hand, walked me inside our home, and led me to the couch. We sat down.

He looked me in the eye, and he told me how he felt.

The way he handled the entire situation— not just the way he maneuvered the few hours from the time I arrived back until we finished talking that evening, but the way he handled every bit of it from the second I left until I came back— transformed everything.

My mother and sister and kids already adored Rob, but his treatment of me during this chapter made them all pro-Rob even more.

....

Let me say something about our kids...

The kids were raised with two different paradigms— even though they grew up, for the most part, next door to each other.

Kimberly lived with Lisa, my sister, and Blake stayed at my Mom's. Though they rode the same bus, attended the same school, and lived within 25 feet of each other in those small apartments, their worldviews differ dramatically.

Kimberly threw herself into everything she possibly could. She attended every prom, each homecoming, signed up for all the extracurriculars, and had dozens of friends. My sister spoiled her in the best way possible— if there is a good way to do that.

Blake was raised by my Mom. She's quiet. They left each other alone for the most part.

As a result, Blake is content sitting in a room and being silent— just like Mom. Kimberly— like Rob— fills the space and every quiet second— with words and energy. Blake is an introvert; Kimberly is an extrovert.

Knowing my story, people often ask, "How is it that you have such solid relationships with both of them today?"

I don't take it for granted. I was absent for many— if not most— of the pivotal moments in their lives.

The simple (and honest) answer is *grace.*

The more complex (and equally honest) answer is I finally showed up one day and *kept showing up.* And then showed up again. And continued showing up. And showed up more.

I believe kids are predisposed to love their parents, just as parents are predisposed to love their kids. It's different, for sure. But, there's something about that God-given connection that just "works" when you finally decide to show up and be present.

The kids still face challenges I can directly trace to my decisions for sure.

- Blake blocked much of his childhood years from his conscious memory. He's seen some of his counselors in the Navy and even they haven't been able to unlock some of his memories.

- Kimberly still checks my location on her phone, multiple times a day, even as a young woman of thirty.

"Why are you there?" Kimberly sometimes texts.

She might notice that I'm in one of the old areas of my past, somewhere I actively sought trouble. In those days, she really didn't know if I was dead or alive.

Whenever I think, "Oh, this really isn't healthy for her to keep tabs on me like this," my heart softens and I recognize that there's no need for her to worry when she can just check and see.

"I'm showing a house" is usually the quick reply.

I read a stat which suggests the average person checks their smartphone 80 times or more per day. That's once every 12 minutes. Mom is probably "above average" and checks my location constantly— at least that often.

I remind myself that trauma impacts everyone connected to the relationship. It's easy for them to assume "the wrong story" and play an incorrect narrative in their heads based on past reality.

In this case, I remind myself that I created that story. Grace must flow in both directions.

Healing impacts everyone connected to the relationship, as well. When you make decisions that are genuinely good, it creates a ripple effect that touches others in ways you may not fully understand— just like Poe calling out my addiction and my manager at Carrabba's offering me a place to stay nudged me forward towards the life I now live.

My kids were marked by all of that.

Mom retired from UAB Medical West a few years ago. Rob and I gave her a house for Christmas closer to us. We bought the home next door to her and became neighbors. Then, in 2022 we moved her in with us...

After I came back home to Rob, one of my former roommates— one of the two gals from the church that I lived with— told me about a job opening at the clinic where she worked as a nurse practitioner.

"You've got this background in medical insurance AND in billing AND you've worked with people who struggle with addiction..." she said.

Located in one of the most drug-heavy neighborhoods in the city— by design— the neighborhood clinic was looking for someone to run the billing and admin.

I agreed to interview for the job.

"I've only been clean for just over a year. I relapsed after three years," I told the doctor who founded the clinic.

I decided honesty was best. If I laid it all out there and they *still* wanted me, great. If not, then it wasn't meant to be.

"I appreciate the honesty," he said. "My nurse practitioner highly recommends you, and you know medical coding, and you're obviously trustworthy..."

Was I?

I wondered...

He hired me on the spot.

I worked there over five years.

Towards the end of my run, Rob began teasing, "Hey, I've been flipping these houses. Why don't you get your real estate license and help me out?"

I couldn't envision myself doing it, but— if you know him you know exactly what I'm talking about— Rob eventually wore me down (just like he did with that bail bondswoman years earlier)!

"I'll do it under one condition," I told him.

"Sure. Anything."

"I can't do this while I'm working full time at the clinic..."

They were walking through a federal qualification process. The feds were moving from the old ICD-9 code system to ICD-10. The new system not only meant I had to learn something different than what I had been doing, it also required learning something quite a bit more complex.

"If I'm going to work at the clinic long-term, I'll go all in with this new system," I said. "But I don't think I can work the job full time, learn the new processes, implement them, AND study for the real estate exam at the same time."

"What are you saying, Shan?"

"If I'm going to go into real estate, that needs to be my full time job from the moment I start studying for the exam— not the moment I get my license and can start selling."

"That's fine," Rob said. "Ben and I have all these investors in a queue buying 8-10 a month. Let's go all in!"

It was October when I finally quit the clinic.

I originally gave them an open-ended notice that basically said, "Hey, I'm off-boarding here…"

Stuck in the middle of helping them get federally qualified AND doing the day-to-day medical and dental billing, I didn't feel like I could leave them hanging. Rob (wisely) reminded me they probably wouldn't proactively look for someone else unless they had a deadline.

I gave them two weeks' notice and then began studying for my exam. By February 2017, I was a licensed real estate agent.

....

I originally planned to focus only on Rob's deals and assist him. I thought I could locate houses, list them, and help with some of the books.

One day that changed, though.

Someone on the other end of the phone explained, "My grandfather died and left me $30,000 cash."

"That's a sizable down payment," I replied. "What's your budget?"

"$30,000."

"Oh, you want to use it *all* on the purchase price *only*," I clarified.

"Yes," the man said. "I'm looking for a small home for my kids, so they can have their own rooms when they come visit me every other weekend."

I pondered the man's situation...

"It's not a big commission at all," I thought, "but I'm licensed. I've got time. I'm going to help this guy solve the problem."

I made an appointment to meet him at a house. I arrived early and was waiting for him when he pulled up. He looked super-confused.

"You alright?" I asked, getting out of my car.

"I'm surprised you actually showed," he said. Then— "You're the fourth agent I called. The others all told me I wasn't worth their time."

"Really?"

"Yeah. Some even no-showed me and didn't tell me they decided that until after I made the appointment and drove to the house and called to find out where they were..."

"I'm so sorry," I told him. "We're not all like that."

I remembered how it felt to believe you weren't worthy of someone's time— that your volleyball or softball or other thing wasn't worth their attention. I remembered how deflated Blake looked when I walked into the auditorium that night, having missed Kimberly's play.

That first place we saw didn't work out, but I made it my mission to locate a home that worked for this man's family. It took about 3 months, and I stacked 500 or more miles on my car. In the end, we found an almost-new manufactured double-wide that looked like a house sitting on an entire acre of land.

$26,000.

That's what he paid.

$4,000 *under* budget.

Brandon— that's his name— not only showed me that I could use real estate to help people not only find "property" but also a treasured "place" to share moments with their loved ones, but he also became my biggest referral source.

Every few weeks I received a call: "Brandon said you could help."

Some of the people needed smaller, more cost-efficient houses. Others had much larger budgets.

A few years later, Brandon called again.

"I need your help," he said.

"Sure thing. What can I do for you this time?"

"Things have changed over the past 7 years or so. I need you to do two things."

"Name them…"

"First, I need you to write a contract for me so I can sell the house you sold me to my daughter and future son-in-law. They're going to get married and take it over."

"Wow! Where are you going?"

"That's the second thing. I need you to help me find another house. I have a bigger budget this time— $300,000."

We learned that real estate really can become a platform to serve people in profoundly personal ways— about one of the elements that matters the most to them, where they live and spend time with the people they love the most.

(We've also seen that we not only have the opportunity to serve buyers and sellers, but we can also help people create a career doing something rewarding. This provides us with a platform to coach them about life even as we mentor them in business. Some agents stay long-term; others move to something they enjoy more than property. Whatever the case, we seek to serve them well and breathe life into them while they're on the team. This part is jumping ahead in the story just a bit...)

....

People often ask, "How did you start EXIT Realty Birmingham?"

The first year I worked in real estate— with the approach of just helping people rather than chasing profits— I quickly became a Rising Star in the company I worked with (Rising Star is an industry acknowledgment). I was there for about 18 months.

I originally pursued my real estate license to help our family— to purchase and resale 3D's flips. But then I met Brandon and a few others. I felt a peace and a sense of purpose— deep satisfaction— after each of those deals.

Another opportunity opened with another brand where I could work closely with an experienced agent who also helped 3D purchase and resale. This agent also had a proven track record of selling high dollar homes in the Mountain Brook area (one of the wealthiest zip codes in the U.S.).

"He's been working with Rob and Ben, too," I thought.

That was a deal-*maker* for me. Face it, if anyone could work at Rob's pace and handle some of the highest-end transactions, I wanted to learn everything I could from them. Plus, I knew we would get along great.

I stayed with the second company and quickly became a Top Producer there (another industry award). They asked me to serve on their Leadership Committee.

I still remember certain milestones...

"Three deals going at once," I thought. "This is just like juggling!"

Though managing multiple transactions seems second nature now, it was new at that point. I found myself both overwhelmed AND excited.

But, as is the case with any new skill, the more you practice, the better you get. And the better you get, the more you can enjoy each moment.

Think about it like this: no pianist sits at the keyboard to play *Moonlight Sonata* or *any* of Beethoven's symphonies without first practicing...

In fact, they probably "chopstick" their way through the first few lessons...

Then they practice more.

And keep practicing.

At some moment, the practice transforms into actual playing— their fingers begin moving effortlessly across the keys.

I got better at real estate the more I leaned into it. And the more I leaned into it, the more I *loved* it and the people it impacted.

As I built my real estate business, I created spreadsheets and designed systems to help keep track of deals I was involved with— as well as which stage of the transaction each were in. This enabled me to better "juggle" those three...

And then five.

Then seven.

Then more.

During the pandemic of 2020, real estate agents were deemed "essential" workers. This enabled us to continue buying and selling homes.

Because we were unable to travel, I put my head down and leaned into the work as much as possible, serving as many people as I could. Remarkably, the year of Covid-19 was my best year in real estate.

This was also the year I realized I was walking in my purpose.

I look at it like this: God provided me a massive platform to serve others where they are at one of the most pivotal moments in their lives— right when they're making major decisions that impact their families. I help them navigate tough-to-understand transactions, I look out for their best interests, and I work with them to find sacred space where they will build a life and make memories.

And I'm good at it— really good at it. Working this business provided me with a sense of pride and accomplishment I hadn't ever felt about myself.

In time, I wondered if I might have more to offer. I demonstrated to myself that I could handle 12-13 deals at a time, effortlessly keeping everything and everyone moving forward towards the closing table. I began praying about my next step.

Really, I prayed.

During that season the regional owners of EXIT Realty Alabama-Mississippi called me.

"We see your name and keep hearing about you," they said. "We'd like to meet in person."

I was busy— even if I was good at managing all of the "moving parts," it still required time and effort. I turned the meeting down. To be clear, I turned it down *multiple times.*

One day I thought about it differently. After all, I had been praying just *before* they reached out.

"We ought to just take the meeting," I told Rob. "They keep calling. I was praying about this before. This could be an answer to that prayer that I keep pushing away."

I thought about a story in Acts 12…

The leaders of Jerusalem imprisoned Peter for preaching. So, a group of friends in the church gathered to pray for his release.

That night, an angel walked into the prison, and woke him up. The chains fell from his wrists, and the angel led him out.

The prison doors opened themselves, before the angel vanished.

Peter went to the Upper Room— the place they had the Last Supper, a spot they normally gathered to pray— and knocked on the door.

Even as people prayed for his release AND it occurred, they answered the door and supposed it was just a ghost (Acts 12:15).

Think about that a moment…

How often do we repeatedly ask God for something only to push His provision away or second-guess His solution— even numerous times?

We met, and they told us they thought we would be a good fit for the EXIT culture.

"We'll talk and pray about it," we said.

My prayer wasn't so much a petition but a bargain. Yes, I bargained with God.

"If this is from You, I need an office space…"

I didn't want just *any* office, though, I envisioned a *specific* place. Rob and I regularly drove past a building in our neighborhood that looked perfect. We tried to buy it before, but could never get it under contract. In the past, the owner insisted he wouldn't sell.

"I'm going to call him again— one more time," I told Rob. Then— "That's the deal I offered God. If he takes it, I'll know."

The next morning I phoned the owner: "I know you've said *no* multiple times. I'm going to ask *just once more* if you'd be willing to sell it."

I told him why we wanted it…

This time was different. I didn't receive a *no*— or a *yes*.

"I'll call you tomorrow," he promised. "Let me give it some thought tonight."

I believe sharing our vision with him opened his heart to the concept. Too often, we lead with ideas, but we don't tell people the inspiration behind it all. We tell them *what* we want, but we don't explain *why*. Understanding the reason behind something sometimes makes a monumental difference.

In this case, it certainly did.

I told Rob, "He said he would think about it. And, I've been thinking. I believe this is the price we can afford to pay for it if he agrees to sell…"

The number was a fair number. It wasn't high or low. Just honest.

True to his word, the owner called the following day.

"I'll sell it," he reported, "at this price…"

His number matched mine.

I started to ask God for *another* sign, but— upon hearing this— Rob blatantly said, "Quit negotiating with God! I think He just answered you— on two things, the not-for-sale building AND the price."

We signed a franchise agreement with EXIT Realty a few days later.

....

To open for business, I needed a qualifying broker.

There's a significant difference between brokers and agents.

- Agents can list, buy, and sell real estate. They can write and review legally binding contracts.

- Brokers are a "level-up" from agents in responsibility. They can do everything agents do. In addition, they can receive money into escrow accounts, make financial transfers, and hire agents to work on their behalf. They also agree to supervise all the real estate activity under the brokerage.

You can't run an independent office or franchise without a qualifying broker.

I knew someone with their broker license— she worked with me at the second company. Karen and I were friends, so I thought this would be a win-win for her to make the move with us.

We met for lunch, and I shared my heart about what we wanted to build.

"I'll pray about it tonight and let you know tomorrow," she said.

She sounded like the owner of the office building. Like him the following morning, true to her word, she *also* called.

"I'm in!"

"I'm so glad," I replied.

She confessed, half-laughing— "I was in yesterday, but I wanted to let you sweat a little bit."

We chuckled and then got to work. She was a major blessing to me.

About a year in, I felt like God told me it was time to stand on my own.

"Quit propping on other people. Pull yourself together. Do what I've called you to do," I felt Him say.

I knew what I was supposed to do.

I studied and got my broker license. I didn't talk about it, so no one knew this was my goal or that I planned to make that move. I thought I should have the credentials, though, just in case...

As I prayerfully made the move to step into the qualifying broker role for EXIT Realty Birmingham, I felt terrified.

Change is always scary, but Karen taught me so many things I needed to know. She held my hand through this transition before moving on and opening a successful brokerage of her own.

Starting and running a real estate brokerage wasn't— *isn't*— easy. Being responsible for every license in the office often feels weighty. We have to train our agents to be the best, which requires meeting them where they are, so we can lead them forward to where they're destined to be.

When we started EXIT Realty Birmingham, neither Rob nor I had run a real estate brokerage. There was a lot we clearly didn't know about the business. Plus, the "we didn't even know what we didn't know" reality soon set in. We made budgeting mistakes, we overspent on marketing, and we mis-hired at times.

But, when you walk in your purpose incredible things happen.

- Our office experienced tremendous growth.

- We topped 50 agents on the roster.

- I worked with friends who helped me create systems and training modules to resource our agents.

- We learned dreams often require more effort than we originally imagine, yet pursuing them is always worth it. Especially when you do it with the right people.

Even though some agents— and even friends— move to a next chapter of life that leads them away, we're always grateful for the role they play in our story. They each help us grow, stretch us to learn, and empower us to succeed.

One of my dearest friends still helps me on the daily. She stepped into a role as my right hand man (woman).

I honestly don't know how we could do what we do without her. She has given me the time and space to continue developing processes for every aspect of real estate sales.

With her 18+ years in the business, as well as her heart of being the "team Mom," we have been able to create content that not only helps new agents learn the basics of real estate sales, but also create content for experienced agents who want to grow their businesses and rise up to a new level.

On every front I've got her back, and she has mine. Friendships like this are pure gold when you're used to fending for yourself for your whole life.

She makes me better...

Every.

Single.

Day.

Her name is Ebonie Brown.

When you get married, the minister always says something like, "Repeat after me," and you do....

Amidst the repeating vows you say something like "For better or worse."

The pastor says it.

Then you say it.

Then, they say it again.

And the person you marry says it.

Though it's not back-to-back, that line appears four times in the ceremony. Most of us don't think about it when it does, because none of us walk the aisle hoping for the "for worse" part of the vows (no more than we grow up hoping to develop an addiction, spend months at a time in jail, and lose friends to overdoses). We (wrongly) assume we'll face nothing but bliss and the "for better."

When you join your life with someone else, though, you get both. You get the better— and you get all of "the worse," too.

And you don't just get the "worse" moments of now, you pick up all the baggage of their past and agree to carry it with you, unpacking the hurtful parts and healing them as you go.

Better.

Worse.

Good baggage and bad baggage alike. Everything in between.

Obstacles and opportunities.

Turns out, *they do the same for you.*

22. Should Have Said "They Eventually Become One" (R)

Rob recalls the darkest season. He gets good advice from Lyn, and he realizes something isn't what it seemed

---

I didn't do a good job asking Shannon to marry me.

Or, to say it another way, the proposal *sucked*.

After I got shot, I stayed at my sister's for a few days. Shannon came and visited. She might have even crashed there a bit herself.

Dad wasn't sure about taking me back in just yet. I don't blame him. Heck, on top of running a business and taking care of a wife with Alzheimer's, he had just bailed me out of jail. Aside from the stuff you know about, there were other busts, DUIs, falsified domestic charges with Ronnie, and all the "non-legal" times he got me out of jams.

Oh...

There was even a time Lyn pulled a .357 on a bounty hunter who was looking for me at his place...

Was I actually there?

That's a story for another time.

Whereas I was out of the slammer within a matter of hours, Shannon was stuck. She had an additional charge, and the judge wasn't budging. Not at first, anyway. It took months of phone calls to finally spring her.

I needed a place to go…

Matt and Abbey (my brother-in-law and my sister) prayed about the whole situation. They had been praying for years, as well as probably listening to my Dad's rationale for why he helped in some ways and why he stood firm at other times.

"You can stay at our place," they offered.

With 3 young kids in the house, as well as the fact that I was a known-addict who had pending cases, this was a big deal. *Huge*, even.

Matt's parents and friends pushed against it.

"This could get DHR involved in your life," people said.

They were right. With the stack of files they had on me, Shannon, and the others we ran with, no one would have been surprised had that happened. It never did, but Matt's position was clear.

"This is family," he said.

Whereas everyone expected him to say, "Hey, you're fresh out of jail. You're not even clean, yet. You're actually in drug court," he never did.

What stood out to me the most about his position was that he barely knew me. I met him at Abbey's wedding, but that was about it. I never flew home for the holidays when I was in the Marines or even after I got out and worked as a contractor. All he knew was that I was the coked-up, methed-out, jacked-around older brother of his wife and the uncle to his sons that— at that time— I barely knew.

Every other day my "color" came up.

"Peach," I mumbled, hanging up the phone. "Again. It's like every other day..."

"Let's do it," Matt always said. "Keep moving forward."

Matt helped me find rides, gave me rides, and stepped up in big ways. He stood up for me and believed in me at a time when I didn't know if anyone would. I knew, based on circumstances and past behaviors, no one should. He did, though. Matt is the guy who eventually baptized me.

....

I was living and working at The Program when Shannon relapsed and needed a safe place to stay. That's when the the director opened his family's home to her for as long as she needed.

"I think I'm going to move down to Florida and just start over," she told me.

She brought it up during one of our conversations about everything that scrolled through my head as I was being shot. I had told her about how so many things flash before you when you think you're about to die— how you think about people you need to forgive and people from whom you need forgiveness, about bridges you need to rebuild and scores you need to settle in a gracious way by verbally wiping some slates clean, and about relationships you promise to enhance if given the chance.

"I haven't told you *about you*," I confessed. "I haven't known how to…"

Don't get me wrong. I knew Shannon had feelings for me. She knew I had feelings for her.

Everyone in the office at The Program always told us, "You guys need to just get married…"

"It won't work," we always said. "We tried it. It doesn't work."

Everyone was convinced that the reason it doesn't work— or that it didn't before— was because we each carried so much past clutter with us. Whereas some people have baggage, we each had a dumpster full of junk.

Furthermore, most people don't recognize that we all "live out" of our past pains. If we don't heal them, we continue not only repeating the same harmful patterns, we inflict those hurts on others.

"You guys date all the time, anyway," co-workers observed.

Then, another— "Yeah, but you go to the Home Depot on all of your dates."

They were right. Neither one of us would have called them dates, but what makes it a date?

22. Should Have Said "They Eventually Become One" (R)

If you consistently find yourself taking someone out to both lunch and dinner (and paying for it) and navigating your day such that you can spend every free moment with them (gladly), you're in a relationship. You're most likely dating.

Young adults today jump through every conceivable mental hoop they can to NOT be dating but still have the benefits of connection with a special person.

- They snapchat and "slide up" into each others' DMs— to avoid a phone call.

- They "talk to" or "hang out with" someone else and go out of their way to do so, but they won't call it anymore than that, for fear they'll find themselves the victim of unrequited love.

- They commit to the other without ever actually committing and verbalizing that commitment. "We'll just see where it goes," they say.

I call bullshit on all of that, because that's kinda what I did...

Shannon always knew she could call me— and did— even if she was in a relationship with someone else. Likewise, I leaned on her.

But I never told her how I felt...

As she told me about her plans to move to Florida, even detailing how the Mom of a high school friend had a place she could stay until she figured out where she wanted to be, I finally told her: "I think we're supposed to be married. I want to marry you."

It wasn't so much a proposal as it was a statement of fact. I wanted her, and that's why she could always get me for whatever, whenever. My love for her was— is— unconditional.

She was pissed.

"Why are you just now telling me this!?"

What I envisioned as a tender moment of connection caused disconnection. I waited too long to tell her how I felt.

....

When I got shot, I was living at the rehab program, overseeing a massive apartment complex that housed about 60 men. The staff members told me to take whatever time I needed to recover, and they would cover things. They were planning to move to an even bigger facility and already had the wheels in motion for that. Everything would be different when they relocated, so this was a good time all around to be talking about a change.

I had planned to transition out of that position for about 6 months and focus on real estate for the next chapter of life. Everyone on staff knew, and I had an open-ended timeline of when the shift may occur. The hospital-to-Abbey-to-Dad-to-whatever seemed like a good time to make that transition.

With my living situation up in the air, as well as my relationship with Shannon now squarely in "no man's land," I began looking at houses. Ben and I already had the little Fulton house— we just didn't know what to do with it (this was before we met John the investor or the acquisition manager from Utah).

"I'm thinking about buying a house," I told Dad.

"You don't have to rush into anything," he said. "Focus on getting better."

"Well…"

I showed him a house I found— just a few miles from the program.

"That looks like it needs some work," Dad observed.

"It does. But I like the location…"

At the time, the program was slated to acquire a massive, empty hospital downtown. They raised over half a million dollars and began making plans to move in. Doors continued opening, and I figured I could live across the street and just volunteer to lead small groups or recovery meetings or something.

The program never moved there.

The director gave all the designated donations for that property back after a rep from the city showed up at the office where I got shot and affirmed he would push the zoning through… *for a price.* Yes, he wanted a bribe. Even though the property *already* had the correct zoning, and even though the top city officials had been in the conversations from the very beginning, in the end they were just holding out for money.

There's a line in a song that says, "You can always trust the devil or a politician… to be the devil or a politician."

This seemed *exactly* like that.

Anyway…

Someone on the other side of town ended up giving The Program property— no shenanigans involved whatsoever.

Anyway, I showed Dad the house. We drove to see it…

"How much is this?"

"$4,000."

As you might imagine, at that price-point it needed a complete overhaul. The only thing that didn't need to be addressed was the land and the foundation. Every other part of that structure needed something.

I bought the house…

A few days later, I learned Shannon decided to stay back. She changed her plans *because of me*.

"Surely that means something," I thought.

I decided to be funny and nostalgic all in one...

We were going out one night and I asked her to run by Home Depot with me.

"It won't take long," I said. "Just an in-and-out trip."

"There is no such thing as an *in-and-out* to Home Depot with you," she answered.

She was right. I knew the nearby Home Depot like the back of my hand, to use a worn out phrase. I knew exactly what was on every row, who worked which shift, and the most likely times for new inventory to arrive.

22. Should Have Said "They Eventually Become One" (R)

That doesn't mean I didn't still linger around the tool aisle or just mosey through the appliances, dreaming about the home I might build for myself and the homes I might— one day— create for others.

"I'll be fast," I said. "Come with me."

She agreed, but said she would wait in the car while I went in...

We arrived, and I still hadn't convinced her to go inside with me. I needed an excuse to get her in the store.

Finally, I just *begged* her.

She huffed. Puffed. Breathed deep, and sighed...

"Alright. Whatever. I'm coming."

We walked through the automatic doors and took a left bank shot towards the nuts and bolt aisle...

I wish there was a better story here, but by now you know... we just tell it like it is. You get what you get; you don't pitch a fit.

She walked past me, asking, "Alright. What are you looking for."

As she continued striding forward, I got down on one knee— as if stooping to reach for one of the low-lying box of nails.

"I can't read what size these nails are," I told her.

When she looked back, I asked her, ring in hand, "Will you marry me?"

It wasn't the best proposal, but she agreed. A few months later, we married.

That first season of marriage, I did so many things wrong…

- I listened to business associates rather than leaning into the wisdom of my wife (which seems laughable, now, given her real estate mind and her success over the past few years).

- I invited a friend to live with us (I know, dumb).

- I turned our home into an office AND a construction zone.

Let's focus on that final point for a moment…

By using our house as the office, that meant there was never a moment when home-life separated from work. Contractors constantly came by, and employees routinely walked in and out of the front door without knocking. We had no sacred space to call our own.

By moving my wife into an unfinished house (the only part of the property that was complete when we moved in after the wedding was the bedroom), I effectively placed her in the middle of a work zone. Not only did I fill every free moment with more work (on our home), but she never had any peace. In the morning, she had to walk through a living room that was stripped down to the studs, and then a dining room that held nothing but tools, just to make coffee in a half-complete (but functional) kitchen.

It added undue stress to what should have been a time of celebration.

One day the Pharisees asked Jesus if it was permissible for a man to divorce his wife (see Matthew 19:3f.).

He evaluated the question and told them, "You're hard-hearted."

He then elaborated that, "From the beginning, God designed that a man should leave his father and mother, be joined to his wife, and the two shall become one flesh."

He quoted Genesis 2:24 in that response. In His mind, the bigger question wasn't if a man should be able to divorce his wife (in that culture, men were the only ones who could initiate divorce— that's why the religious leaders framed the question like this), *the bigger issue was the reality that the two shall become one.*

Or, to say it another way, they should work towards *convergence and oneness* rather than fighting for divergence and separateness.

Furthermore, I think the way Jesus says this— "they *shall* become one"— is more honest than how we usually think marriage works.

- He portrays oneness as a future hope, *as an ongoing effort*.

- He doesn't say they are one; *He suggests they shall be one*.

The day Shannon left marks one of the darkest seasons of my life. We argued that morning, she took the van and a debit card, and vanished.

I told my Dad who coached me not to tell a bunch of other people...

"You need to prepare your heart now to receive your wife when she comes back home," he told me.

"You don't get it," I replied. "She's gone. That was it."

"Stand firm," he said. "Find just a few men you can share your thoughts with, men who will be confidants and hold this in confidence. It will be easier for her to return if you close the circle and *protect her* through this."

That really stood out to me. The strongest don't throw stones; they protect and defend— even when they feel wounded.

I remember the day she came back. I thought she was just returning to talk. I hugged her, we walked inside the house, and we sat there.

Two days later she left again. The first time she left she parked our van at a nearby parking lot. She didn't want me to think she stole it— an accusation that makes complete sense in light of her past experiences.

When she came back, she borrowed a vehicle. It needed to be returned.

As she drove off, I wondered...

Is this it?

Will she *really* come back again?

Then she moved back and kept a "go bag" packed and ready. It sat there in the corner of the bedroom for two years or more.

One day, I walked in and noticed her bag was gone. The visible reminder that she *might leave again* in the future disappeared.

Was she gone for good?

I froze.

I panicked.

And then I called for her…

"Shan?!"

She came to me…

Ahh, she was still here.

"Where's your bag?" I asked.

"I unpacked it," she answered.

"I don't need it anymore," she said. "I'm here for good."

She *is* still here.

The two *become* one…

It's a process. You intertwine your stories and weave your dreams together. You take each other's heart breaks and joys alike. Together, you create something exquisitely better.

It's still imperfect, mind you, because you're still you. They're still them. Yet, in all of its imperfection (because we are each imperfect), the covenant remains one of the most beautiful experiences we can encounter and give ourselves to.

That's where we find ourselves now…

We're committed to being one— and we are.

Yet there's so much more to explore— and we will.

We're in process.

A lot is in process.

And that is the best place to be.

22. Should Have Said "They Eventually Become One" (R)

22. Should Have Said "They Eventually Become One" (R)

Application for Part 7 | Arrived & Always Arriving

Main idea: Fulfilling your purpose has no finish line. We live in a constant tension of "we've come so far" (we should celebrate) and still having further we want to go (we must guard against complacency). Enjoy the progress, live a life of balance, and overcome the gaps you continue to notice between where you are and where you want to be.

In chapter 20 Rob and 3D faced economic uncertainty. Progress is often filled with setbacks and obstacles— it's rarely just a straight line up.

There are "peak moments," as well as "pit moments."

This is one of the reasons we need people with us. Sometimes, they're up while we're down (and can encourage us). Other times, we're up while they're down (and we can elevate them).

What are some of your peak and pit moments?

How does having the right people with you empower you to keep making progress?

_____

_____

_____

_____

_____

_____

_____

_____

_____

_____

The road always goes where the road goes...

This is a theme we've seen throughout the book.

Think back to the *Wizard of Oz*. Dorothy makes it to the "wizard," because that's where the yellow brick road goes. Along the way, she encounters friends (the Lion, the Scarecrow, and Tin Man), as well as foes. She meets obstacles, too.

But she continues towards her goal despite her fears.

What is your yellow brick road?

Will it get you to your intended destination?

What are some of the obstacles you can plan for now?

_____

_____

_____

_____

_____

Shannon talked about prayer (see chapter 21).

What are your hopes and prayers?

Will you notice the answer if it comes?

And will you act upon it or continue bargaining?

What does it mean that we're not only in process, but our closest relationships are also in process?

How can you take two imperfect people— such as in marriage— and create something beautiful, a sacred union that elevates both people and leverages the unique gifts and calling of each?

Where you are isn't who you are.

Where you are isn't where you must remain.

Where you are is where you must begin, though.

Separate your identity from your circumstances and continue moving forward through whatever location in which you find yourself.

What action steps can you take now to insure you find your identity in the valuations which truly matter? (And don't base it on accolades, achievements, applause, or other externals.)

Resources & Next Steps

Recommended Books + Online Resources

Rise Up can encourage, equip, and empower you to move from where you are to where you're designed to be in three lanes:

1. **Personal Development** = mindset training to overcome the obstacles and move from where you are to where you're designed to be

2. **Profitable Projects** = learn how to build your own renovation empire, create a legacy, and leave wealth for your family by flipping real estate with Rob's resources

3. **Professional Development** = create a career with the EXIT Realty Birmingham team or access Shannon's training system and implement them wherever you are

PERSONAL DEVELOPMENT
MINDSET, OVERCOMING OBSTACLES

PROFITABLE PROJECTS
RENOVATING & "FLIPPING" + SHORT-TERM RENTALS

PROFESSIONAL DEVELOPMENT
REAL ESTATE AGENTS + AGENCIES

Choose your next step at RiseUpOnline.info/store or scan the QR.

Join Rob & Shannon's weekly conversation

The Rise Up! podcast— available on the website or your favorite podcast provider.

ARISE FROM THE ASHES &
ACCELERATE TO ABUNDANCE—
IN ALL AREAS OF LIFE

RISE UP! PODCAST

Stream from our site or your favorite podcast provider

Free Bonus Access

Access the free bonus resources for this book at RiseUpOnline.info/7

WALK WITH US!
FREE BONUS ACCESS!

7 MIND-SHIFT LESSONS

RiseUpOnline.info/7

Renovation Courses & Coaching

Join the Rise Up Renovation Empire and learn Rob's 5-part framework to find, fund, fix, flaunt, and flip houses.

Available as a course, as a community, and as a coaching experience.

Details at RiseUpOnline.info/RURE (case-sensitive) or via the QR.

Careers & Systems

Learn Shannon's processes and build a purpose-driven and passion-fueled career in real estate.

About the Authors

Rob and Shannon know what it's like to hit rock bottom and actually think that you're better off dead. They come from two different backgrounds, showing that pain can hit anyone, anywhere.

Jailed, addicted, homeless, penniless, estranged from family— yet still able to move forward— their stories show just how far we can drift from the life we were created to enjoy.

Today, after years of struggle, they use their real estate brokerage and house renovation business to teach others the mindset and habits that helped them overcome the obstacles and step towards the opportunities they now enjoy.

Shannon was a Rising Star and a Top Producer in multiple companies before opening EXIT Realty Birmingham with Rob (where she leads as the Qualifying Broker).

Rob has flipped over 300 houses in Birmingham and surrounding areas, and has been part of 1,000+ transactions. He's only lost money on two of them.

Better than winning at work, though, is the reality that they're also winning at life at the same time. They have two adult kids, as well as a granddaughter.

Their hope for you is to:

1. **Envision the impossible for your life**— because God wants to do "immeasurably more than we can ask, think, or imagine— according to the power that's already at work in us" (Ephesians 3:19-20).

2. **Release the past**— God has already forgotten the mistakes of yesterday and He isn't holding today's or tomorrow's failures against you (see Romans 4:7-8).

3. **Live a better story**— walk into the life designed for you from before time began (see Ephesians 2:8-10).

Whether you are looking for easy-to-understand lessons in their mindset courses and workshops, want to start a career in real estate (or just learn better systems and processes for the career you already have), or desire to build a "renovation empire" of your own, they're here to help you move forward from where you are to where you're designed to be.

Platform Your Message

If part of your purpose is to share a positive message that encourages, equips, and empowers others to walk in their purpose, we want to help.

Go to AmplifyOnline.info/RISE (case-sensitive) or scan the QR code for a special message from Rob & Shannon about making your impact.

AMPLIFY

GET PAID FOR WHAT YOU KNOW

Made in the USA
Columbia, SC
16 March 2025

55213231R00248